GREAT

AMERICANS

IN THEIR

OWN WORDS

GREAT AMERICANS

IN THEIR

OWN WORDS

EXTRACTS BY 20 HEROIC MEN AND WOMEN

MALLARD
PRESS

An Imprint of BDD Promotional Book Company, Inc.
666 Fifth Avenue, New York, N.Y. 10103

This edition first published in the United States of America in 1990 by
The Mallard Press

By arrangement with The Octopus Group Limited

'Mallard Press and its accompanying design and logo are trademarks of BDD
Promotional Book Company, Inc.'

Copyright © 1990 Arrangement by The Octopus Group Limited

ISBN 0 792 45359 X

Printed in Great Britain

Contents

Benjamin Franklin

1706–1790

Benjamin Franklin was a successful printer, an enthusiastic scientist, and an inspiring thinker who became a leading supporter of the Colonies against Britain, one of the men who drafted the Declaration of Independence. This early extract from his unfinished Autobiography *traces his career as Pennsylvania's representative at the Albany Congress where he proposed a 'Plan of Union'.*

IN 1754, WAR with France being again apprehended, a congress of commissioners from the different colonies was, by an order of the Lords of Trade, to be assembled at Albany, there to confer with the chiefs of the Six Nations concerning the means of defending both their country and ours. Governor Hamilton, having receiv'd this order, acquainted the House with it, requesting they would furnish proper presents for the Indians, to be given on this occasion; and naming the speaker (Mr Norris) and myself to join Mr Thomas Penn and Mr Secretary Peters as commissioners to act for Pennsylvania. The House approv'd the nomination, and provided the goods for the present, and tho' they did not much like treating out of the provinces; and we met the other commissioners at Albany about the middle of June.

In our way thither, I projected and drew a plan for the union of all the colonies under one government, so far as might be necessary for defense, and other important general purposes. As we pass'd thro' New York, I had there shown my project to Mr James Alexander and Mr Kennedy, two gentlemen of great knowledge in public affairs, and, being fortified by their approbation, I ventur'd to lay it before the Congress. It then appeared that several of the commissioners had form'd plans of the same kind. A previous question was first taken, whether a union should be established, which pass'd in the affirmative unanimously. A committee was then appointed, one member from each colony, to consider the several plans and report. Mine happen'd to be preferr'd, and, with a few amendments, was accordingly reported.

By this plan the general government was to be administered by a president-general, appointed and supported by the crown, and a grand council was to be chosen by the representatives of the people of the several colonies, met in their respective assemblies. The debates upon it in Congress went on daily, hand in hand with the Indian business. Many objections and difficulties were started, but at length they were all overcome, and the plan was unanimously agreed to, and copies ordered to be transmitted to the Board of Trade and to the assemblies of the several provinces. Its fate was singular: the assemblies did not adopt it, as they all thought there was too much *prerogative* in it, and in England it was judg'd to have too much of the *democratic*. The Board of Trade therefore did not approve of it, nor recommend it for the approbation of his majesty; but another scheme was form'd, supposed to answer the same purpose better, whereby the governors of the provinces, with some members of their respective councils, were to meet and order the raising of troops, building of forts, etc., and to draw on the treasury of Great Britain for the expense, which was afterwards to be refunded by an act of Parliament laying a tax on America. My plan, with my reasons in support of it, is to be found among my political papers that are printed.

Being the winter following in Boston, I had much conversation with

Governor Shirley upon both the plans. Part of what passed between us on the occasion may also be seen among those papers. The different and contrary reasons of dislike to my plan makes me suspect that it was really the true medium; and I am still of opinion it would have been happy for both sides the water if it had been adopted. The colonies so united, would have been sufficiently strong to have defended themselves; there would then have been no need of troops from England; of course, the subsequent pretence for taxing America, and the bloody contest it occasioned, would have been avoided. But such mistakes are not new: history is full of errors of states and princes.

> 'Look round the habitable world, how few
> Know their own good, or, knowing it, pursue!'.

Those who govern, having much business on their hands, do not generally like to take the trouble of considering and carrying into execution new projects. The best public measures are therefore seldom *adopted from previous wisdom, but forc'd by the occasion.*

The Governor of Pennsylvania, in sending it down to the Assembly, express'd his approbation of the plan, 'as appearing to him to be drawn up with great clearness and strength of judgement, and therefore recommended it as well worthy of their closest and most serious attention'. The House, however, by the management of a certain member, took it up when I happen'd to be absent, which I thought not very fair, and reprobated it without paying any attention to it at all, to my no small mortification.

In my journey to Boston this year, I met at New York with our new governor, Mr Morris, just arriv'd there from England, with whom I had been before intimately acquainted. He brought a commission to supersede Mr Hamilton, who, tir'd with the disputes his proprietary instructions subjected him to, had resign'd. Mr Morris ask'd me if I thought he must expect as uncomfortable an administration. I said, 'No; you may, on the contrary, have a very comfortable one, if you will only take care not to enter into any dispute with the Assembly'. 'My dear friend', says he, pleasantly, 'how can you advise my avoiding disputes? You know I love disputing; it is one of my greatest pleasures; however, to show the regard I have for your counsel, I promise you I will, if possible, avoid them'. He had some reason for loving to dispute, being eloquent, an acute sophister, and, therefore, generally successful in argumentative conversation. He had been brought up to it from a boy, his father, as I have heard, accustoming his children to dispute with one another for diversion, while sitting at table after dinner; but I think the practice was not wise; for, in the course of my observation, these disputing, contradicting and confuting people are generally unfortunate in their affairs. They get victory sometimes, but they never get good will, which would be of more use to them. We parted, he going to Philadelphia, and I to Boston.

In returning, I met at New York with the votes of the Assembly, by which it appear'd that, notwithstanding his promise to me, he and the House were already in high contention; and it was a continual battle between them as long as he retain'd the government. I had my share of it; for, as soon as I got back to my seat in the Assembly, I was put on every committee for answering his speeches and messages, and by the committees always desired to make the drafts. Our answers, as well as his messages, were often tart, and sometimes indecently abusive; and, as he knew I wrote for the Assembly, one might have imagined that, when we met, we could hardly avoid cutting throats; but he was so good-natur'd a man that no personal difference between him and me was occasion'd by the contest, and we often din'd together.

One afternoon, in the height of this public quarrel, we met in the street. 'Franklin', says he, 'you must go home with me and spend the evening; I am to have some company that you will like'; and taking me by the arm, he led me to his house. In gay conversation over our wine, after supper, he told us, jokingly, that he much admir'd the idea of Sancho Panza, who, when it was proposed to give him a government, requested it might be a government of *blacks*, as then, if he could not agree with his people, he might sell them. One of his friends, who sat next to me, says, 'Franklin, why do you continue to side with these damn'd Quakers? Had not you better sell them? The proprietor would give you a good price'. 'The governor', says I, 'has not yet *blacked* them enough'. He, indeed, had labored hard to blacken the Assembly in all his messages, but they wip'd off his coloring as fast as he laid it on, and plac'd it, in return, thick upon his own face; so that, finding he was likely to be negrofied himself, he, as well as Mr Hamilton, grew tir'd of the contest, and quitted the government.

These public quarrels were all at bottom owing to the proprietaries, our hereditary governors, who, when any expense was to be incurred for the defense of their province, with incredible meanness instructed their deputies to pass no act for levying the necessary taxes, unless their vast estates were in the same act expressly excused; and they had even taken bonds of these deputies to observe such instructions. The Assemblies for three years held out against this injustice, tho' constrained to bend at last. At length Captain Denny, who was Governor Morris's successor, ventured to disobey those instructions; how that was brought about I shall show hereafter.

But I am got forward too fast with my story: there are still some transactions to be mention'd that happened during the administration of Governor Morris.

War being in a manner commenced with France, the government of Massachusetts Bay projected an attack upon Crown Point, and sent Mr Quincy to Pennsylvania, and Mr Pownall, afterward Governor Pownall, to New York, to solicit assistance. As I was in the Assembly, knew its temper, and was Mr Quincy's countryman, he appli'd to me for my influence and assistance. I dictated his address to them, which was well receiv'd. They voted an aid of ten thousand pounds, to be laid out in provisions. But the governor refusing his assent to their bill (which included this with other sums granted for the use of the crown), unless a clause were inserted exempting the proprietary estate from bearing any part of the tax that would be necessary, the Assembly, tho' very desirous of making their grant to New England effectual, were at a loss how to accomplish it. Mr Quincy labored hard with the governor to obtain his assent, but he was obstinate.

I then suggested a method of doing the business without the governor, by orders on the trustees of the Loan Office, which by law, the Assembly had the right of drawing. There was, indeed, little or no money at that time in the office, and therefore I propos'd that the orders should be payable in a year, and to bear an interest of five per cent. With these orders I suppos'd the provisions might easily be purchas'd. The Assembly, with very little hesitation, adopted the proposal. The orders were immediately printed, and I was one of the committee directed to sign and dispose of them. The fund for paying them was the interest of all the paper currency then extant in the province upon loan, together with the revenue arising from the excise, which being known to be more than sufficient, they obtain'd instant credit, and were not only receiv'd in payment for the provisions, but many money'd people, who had cash lying by them, vested it in those orders, which they found advantageous, as they bore interest while upon hand, and might on any occasion be used as money; so that they were eagerly all bought up, and in a few weeks none of them were to be seen. Thus this important affair was by my means compleated. Mr Quincy return'd thanks to the Assembly in a handsome memorial, went home highly pleas'd with the success of his embassy, and ever after bore for me the most cordial and affectionate friendship.

The British government, not chusing to permit the union of the colonies as propos'd at Albany, and to trust that union with their defense, lest they should thereby grow too military, and feel their own strength, suspicions and jealousies at this time being entertain'd of them, sent over General Braddock with two regiments of regular English troops for that purpose. He landed at Alexandria, in Virginia, and thence march'd to Frederictown, in Maryland, where he halted for carriages. Our Assembly apprehending, from some information, that he had conceived violent prejudices against them, as averse to the service, wish'd me to wait upon him, not as from them, but as postmaster-general, under the guise of proposing to settle with him the mode of conducting with most celerity and certainty the despatches between him and the governors of the several provinces, with whom he must necessarily have continual correspondence, and of which they propos'd to pay the expense. My son accompanied me on this journey.

We found the general at Frederictown, waiting impatiently for the return of those he had sent thro' the back parts of Maryland and Virginia to collect waggons. I stayed with him for several days, din'd with him daily, and had full opportunity of removing all his prejudices, by the information of what the Assembly had before his arrival actually done, and were still willing to do, to facilitate his operations. When I was about to depart, the returns of waggons to be obtained were brought in, by which it appeared that they amounted only to twenty-five, and not all of those were in serviceable condition. The general and all the officers were surpris'd, declar'd the expedition was then at an end, being impossible; and exclaim'd against the ministers for ignorantly landing them in a country destitute of the means of conveying their stores, baggage, etc, not less than one hundred and fifty waggons being necessary.

I happen'd to say I thought it was pity they had not been landed rather in Pennsylvania, as in that country almost every farmer had his waggon. The general eagerly laid hold of my words, and said, 'Then you sir, who are a man of interest there, can probably procure them for us; and I beg you will undertake it'. I ask'd what terms were to be offer'd the owners of the waggons; and I was desir'd to put on paper the terms that appeared to me necessary. This I did, and they were agreed to, and a commission and instructions accordingly prepar'd immediately. What those terms were will appear in the advertisement I publish'd as soon as I arriv'd at Lancaster, which being, from the great and sudden effect it produc'd, a piece of some curiosity, I shall insert it at length, as follows:

ADVERTISEMENT

'LANCASTER, *APRIL 26, 1755*'.

'Whereas, one hundred and fifty waggons, with four horses to each waggon, and fifteen hundred saddle or pack horses, are wanted for the service of his majesty's forces now about to rendezvous at Will's Creek, and his excellency General Braddock having been pleased to empower me to contract for the hire of the same, I hereby give notice that I shall attend for that purpose at Lancaster from this day to next Wednesday evening, and at York from next Thursday morning till Friday evening, where I shall be ready to agree for waggons and teams, or single horses, on the following terms, viz: 1. That there shall be paid for each waggon, with four good horses and a driver, fifteen shillings per diem; and for each able horse with a pack-saddle, or other saddle and furniture, two shillings per diem; and for each able horse without a saddle, eighteen pence per diem. 2. That the pay commence from the time of their joining the forces at Will's Creek, which must be on or before the 20th of May ensuing, and that a reasonable allowance be paid over and above for the time necessary for their travelling to Will's Creek and home again after their discharge. 3. Each waggon and team, and every saddle or pack horse, is to be valued by indifferent persons chosen between me and the owner; and in case of the loss of any waggon, team, or other horse in the service, the price according to such valuation is to be allowed and paid. 4. Seven days' pay is to be advanced and paid in hand by me to the owner of each waggon and team, or horse, at the time of contracting, if required, and the remainder to be paid by General Braddock, or by the paymaster of the army, at the time of their discharge, or from time to time, as it shall be demanded. 5. No drivers of waggons, or persons taking care of the hired horses, are on any account to be called upon to do the duty of soldiers, or be otherwise employed than in conducting or taking care of their carriages or horses. 6. All oats, Indian corn, or other forage that waggons or horses bring to the camp, more than is necessary for the subsistence of the horses, is to be taken for the use of the army, and a reasonable price paid for the same.

'Note.—My son, William Franklin, is empowered to enter into like contracts with any person in Cumberland county.

B. FRANKLIN'.

'*To the inhabitants of the Counties of Lancaster, York, and Cumberland.*

FRIENDS AND COUNTRYMEN,

'Being occasionally at the camp at Frederic a few days since, I found the general and officers extremely exasperated on account of their not being supplied with horses and carriages, which had been expected from this province, as most able to furnish them; but, through the dissensions between our governor and Assembly, money had not been provided, nor any steps taken for that purpose.

'It was proposed to send an armed force immediately into these counties, to seize as many of the best carriages and horses as should be wanted, and compel as many persons into the service as would be necessary to drive and take care of them.

'I apprehended that the progress of British soldiers through these counties on such an occasion, especially considering the temper they are in, and their resentment against us, would be attended with many and great inconveniences to the inhabitants, and therefore more willingly took the trouble of trying first what might be done by fair and equitable means. The people of these back counties have lately complained to the Assembly that a sufficient currency was wanting; you have an opportunity of receiving and dividing among you a very considerable sum; for, if the service of this expedition should continue, as it is more than probable it will, for one hundred and twenty days, the hire of these waggons and horses will amount to upward of thirty thousand pounds, which will be paid you in silver and gold of the king's money.

'The service will be light and easy, for the army will scarce march above twelve miles per day, and the waggons and baggage-horses, as they carry those things that are absolutely necessary to the welfare of the army, must march with the army, and no faster; and are, for the army's sake, always placed where they can be most secure, whether in a march or in a camp.

'If you are really, as I believe you are, good and loyal subjects to his majesty, you may now do a most acceptable service, and make it easy to yourselves; for three or four of such as can not separately spare from the business of their plantations a waggon and four horses and a driver, may do it together, one furnishing the waggon, another one or two horses, and another the driver, and divide the pay proportionately between you; but if you do not this service to your king and country voluntarily, when such good pay and reasonable terms are offered to you, your loyalty will be strongly suspected. The king's business must be done; so many brave troops, come so far for your defense, must not stand idle through your backwardness to do what may be reasonably expected from you; waggons and horses must be had; violent measures will probably be used, and you will be left to seek for a recompense where you can find it, and your case, perhaps, be little pitied or regarded.

'I have no particular interest in this affair, as, except the satisfaction of endeavoring to do good, I shall have only my labor for my pains. If this method of obtaining the waggons and horses is not likely to succeed, I am obliged to send word to the general in fourteen days; and I suppose Sir John St Clair, the hussar, with a body of soldiers, will immediately enter the province for the purpose, which I shall be sorry to hear, because I am very sincerely and truly your friend and well-wisher,

B. FRANKLIN.'

I received of the general about eight hundred pounds, to be disbursed in advance-money to the waggon owners, etc.; but that sum being insufficient, I advanc'd upward of two hundred pounds more, and in two weeks the one hundred and fifty waggons, with two hundred and fifty-nine carrying horses, were on their march for the camp. The advertisement promised payment according to the valuation, in case any waggon or horse should be lost. The owners, however, alleging they did not know General Braddock, or what dependence might be had on his promise, insisted on my bond for the performance, which I accordingly gave them.

While I was at the camp, supping one evening with the officers of Colonel Dunbar's regiment, he represented to me his concern for the subalterns, who, he said, were generally not in affluence, and could ill afford, in this dear country, to lay in the stores that might be necessary in so long a march, thro' a wilderness, where nothing was to be purchas'd. I commiserated their case, and resolved to endeavor procuring them some relief. I said nothing, however, to him of my intention, but wrote the next morning to the committee of the Assembly, who had the disposition of some public money, warmly recommending the case of these officers to their consideration, and proposing that a present should be sent them of necessaries and refreshments. My son, who had some experience of a camp life, and of its wants, drew up a list for me, which I enclos'd in my letter. The committee approv'd, and used such diligence that, conducted by my son, the store arrived at the camp as soon as the waggons. They consisted of twenty parcels each containing

6 lbs loaf sugar.	1 Gloucester cheese.
6 lbs good Muscovado do.	1 kegg containing 20 lbs good butter.
1 lb good green tea.	2 doz. old Madeira wine.
1 lb good bohea do.	2 gallons Jamaica spirits.
6 lbs good ground coffee.	1 bottle flour of mustard.
6 lbs chocolate.	2 well-cur'd hams.
1–2 cwt best white biscuit.	1–2 dozen dry'd tongues.
1–2 lb pepper.	6 lbs rice.
1 quart best white wine vinegar.	6 lbs raisins.

These twenty parcels, well pack'd, were placed on as many horses, each parcel, with the horse, being intended as a present for one officer. They were very thankfully receiv'd, and the kindness acknowledg'd by letters to me from the colonels of both regiments, in the most grateful terms. The general, too, was highly satisfied with my conduct in procuring him waggons, etc., and readily paid my account of disbursements, thanking me repeatedly, and requesting my farther assistance in sending provisions after him. I undertook this also, and was busily employ'd in it till we heard of his defeat, advancing for the service of my own money, upwards of one thousand pounds sterling, of which I sent him an account. It came to his hands, luckily for me, a few days before the battle, and he return'd me immediately an order on the paymaster for the round sum of one thousand pounds, leaving the remainder to the next account. I consider this payment as good luck, having never been able to obtain that remainder, of which more hereafter.

This general was, I think, a brave man, and might probably have made a figure as a good officer in some European war. But he had too much self-confidence, too high an opinion of the validity of regular troops, and too mean a one of both Americans and Indians. George Croghan, our Indian interpreter, join'd him on his march with one hundred of those people who might have been of great use to his army as guides, scouts, etc., if he had treated them kindly; but he slighted and neglected them, and they gradually left him.

In conversation with him one day, he was giving me some account of his intended progress. 'After taking Fort Duquesne', says he, 'I am to proceed to Niagara; and, having taken that, to Frontenac, if the season will allow time; and I suppose it will, for Duqesne can hardly detain me above three or four days; and then I see nothing that can obstruct my march to Niagara'. Having before revolv'd in my mind the long line his army must make in their march by a very narrow road, to be cut for them thro' the woods and bushes, and also what I had read of a former defeat of fifteen hundred French, who invaded the Iroquois country, I had conceiv'd some doubts and fears for the event of the campaign. But I ventur'd only to say, 'To be sure, sir, if you arrive well before Duquesne, with these fine troops, so well provided with artillery, that place not yet compleatly fortified, and as we hear with no very strong garrison, can probably make but a short resistance. The only danger I apprehend of obstruction to your march is from ambuscades of Indians, who, by constant practice, are dexterous in laying and executing them; and the slender line, near four miles long, which your army must make, may expose it to be attack'd by surprise in its flanks, and to be cut like a thread into several pieces, which, from their distance, can not come up in time to support each other'.

He smil'd at my ignorance, and reply'd, 'These savages may, indeed, be a formidable enemy to your raw American militia, but upon the king's regular and disciplin'd troops, sir, it is impossible they should make any impression'. I was conscious of an impropriety in my disputing with a military man in matters of his profession, and said no more. The enemy, however, did not take the advantage of his army which I apprehended its line of march expos'd it to, but let it advance without interruption till within nine miles of the place; and then, when more in a body (for it had just passed a river, where the front had halted till all were come over), and in a more open part of the woods than any it had pass'd, attack'd its advanced guard by a heavy fire from behind trees and bushes, which was the first intelligence the general had of an enemy's being near him. This guard being disordered, the general hurried the troops up to their assistance, which was done in great confusion, thro' waggons, baggage, and cattle; and presently the fire came upon their flank; the officers, being on horseback, were more easily distinguished, pick'd out as marks, and fell very fast; and the soldiers were crowded together in a huddle, having or hearing no orders, and standing to be shot at till two-thirds of them were killed; and then, being seize'd with a panick, the whole fled with precipitation.

The waggoners took each a horse out of his team and scamper'd; their example was immediately followed by others; so that all the waggons, provisions, artillery, and stores were left to the enemy. The general, being wounded, was brought off with difficulty; his secretary, Mr Shirley, was killed by his side; and out of eighty-six officers, sixty-three were killed or wounded, and seven hundred and fourteen men killed out of eleven hundred. These eleven hundred had been picked men from the whole army; the rest had been left behind with Colonel Dunbar, who was to follow with the heavier part of the stores, provisions, and baggage. The flyers, not being pursu'd, arriv'd at Dunbar's camp, and the panick they brought with them instantly seiz'd him and all his people; and, tho' he had now above one thousand men, and the enemy who had beaten Braddock did not at most exceed four hundred Indians and French together, instead of proceeding, and endeavoring to recover some of the lost honour, he ordered all the stores, ammunition, etc., to be destroy'd, that he might have more horses to assist his flight towards the settlements, and less lumber to remove. He was there met with requests from the governors of Virginia, Maryland, and Pennsylvania, that he would post his troops on the frontiers, so as to afford some protection to the inhabitants; but he continu'd his hasty march thro' all the country, not thinking himself safe till he arriv'd at Philadelphia, where the inhabitants could protect him. This whole transaction gave us Americans the first suspicion that our exalted ideas of the prowess of British regulars had not been well founded.

In their first march, too, from their landing till they got beyond the settlements, they had plundered and stripped the inhabitants, totally ruining some poor families, besides insulting, abusing, and confining the people if they remonstrated. This was enough to put us out of conceit of such defenders, if we had really wanted any. How different was the conduct of our French friends in 1781, who, during a march thro' the most inhabited part of our country from Rhode Island to Virginia, near seven hundred miles, occasioned not the smallest complaint for the loss of a pig, a chicken, or even an apple.

Captain Orme, who was one of the general's aids-de-camp, and, being grievously wounded, was brought off with him, and continu'd with him to his death, which happen'd in a few days, told me that he was totally silent all the first day, and at night only said, *'Who would have thought it?'* That he was silent again the following day, saying only at last, *'We shall better know how to deal with them another time'*; and dy'd in a few minutes after.

The secretary's papers, with all the general's orders, instructions, and correspondence, falling into the enemy's hands, they selected and translated into French a number of the articles, which they printed, to prove the hostile intentions of the British court before the declaration of war. Among these I saw some letters of the general to the ministry, speaking highly of the great service I had rendered the army, and recommending me to their notice. David Hume, too, who was some years after secretary to Lord Hertford, when minister in France, and afterward to General Conway, when secretary of state, told me he had seen among papers in that office, letters from Braddock highly recommending me. But, the expedition having been unfortunate, my service, it seems, was not thought of much value, for those recommendations were never of any use to me.

As to rewards from himself, I ask'd only one, which was, that he would give orders to his officers not to enlist any more of our bought servants, and that he would discharge such as had been already enlisted. This he readily granted, and several were accordingly return'd to their masters, on my application. Dunbar, when the command devolv'd on him, was not so generous. He being at Philadelphia, on his retreat, or rather flight, I apply'd to him for the discharge of the servants of three poor farmers of Lancaster county that he had enlisted, reminding him of the later general's orders on that head. He promised me that, if the masters would come to him at Trenton where he should be in a few days on his march to New York, he would there deliver their men to them. They accordingly were at the expense and trouble of going to Trenton, and there he refus'd to perform his promise, to their great loss and disappointment.

As soon as the loss of the waggons and horses was generally known, all the owners came upon me for the valuation which I had given bond to pay. Their demands gave me a great deal of trouble, my acquainting them that the money was ready in the paymaster's hands, but that orders for paying it must first be obtained from General Shirley, and my assuring them that I had apply'd to that general by letter; but, he being at a distance, an answer could not soon be receiv'd, and they must have patience, all this was not sufficient to satisfy, and some began to sue me. General Shirley at length relieved me from this terrible situation by appointing commissioners to examine the claims, and ordering payment. They amounted to near twenty thousand pound, which to pay would have ruined me.

Before we had the news of this defeat, the two Doctors Bond came to me with a subscription paper for raising money to defray the expense of a grand firework, which it was intended to exhibit at a rejoicing on receipt of the news of our taking Fort Duquesne. I looked grave, and said it would, I thought, be time enough to prepare for rejoicing when we knew we should have occasion to rejoice. They seem'd surpris'd that I did not immediately comply with their proposal. 'Why the d--l!' says one of them, 'you surely don't suppose that the fort will not be taken?' 'I don't know that it will not be taken, but I know that the events of war are subject to great uncertainty'. I gave them the reasons of my doubting; the subscription was dropt, and the projectors thereby missed the mortification they would have undergone if the firework had been prepared. Dr Bond, on some other occasion afterward, said that he did not like Franklin's forebodings.

Governor Morris, who had continually worried the Assembly with message after message before the defeat of Braddock, to beat them into the making of acts to raise money for the defense of the province, without taxing, among others, the proprietary estates, and had rejected all their bills for not having such an exempting clause, now redoubled his attacks with more hope of success, the danger and necessity being greater. The Assembly, however, continu'd firm, believing they had justice on their side, and that it would be giving up an essential right if they suffered the governor to amend their money-bills. In one of the last, indeed, which was for granting fifty thousand pounds, his propos'd amendment was only of a single word. The bill express'd 'that all estates, real and personal, were to be taxed, those of the proprietaries *not* excepted'. His amendment was, for *not* read *only*: a small, but very material alteration. However, when the news of this disaster reached England, our friends there, whom we had taken care to furnish with all the Assembly's answers to the governor's messages, rais'd a clamor against the proprietaries for their meanness and injustice in giving their governor such instructions; some going so far as to say that, by obstructing the defense of their province, they forfeited their right to it. They were intimidated by this, and sent orders to their receiver-general to add five thousand pounds of their money to whatever sum might be given by the Assembly for such purpose.

This, being notified to the House, was accepted in lieu of their share of a general tax, and a new bill was form'd, with an exempting clause, which passed accordingly. By this act I was appointed one of the commissioners for disposing of the money, sixty thousand pounds. I had been active in modelling the bill and procuring its passage, and had, at the same time, drawn a bill for establishing and disciplining a voluntary militia, which I carried thro' the House without much difficulty, as care was taken in it to leave the Quakers their liberty. To promote the association necessary to form the militia, I wrote a dialogue, stating and answering all the objections which I could think of to such a militia, which was printed, and had, as I thought, great effect.

While the several companies in the city and country were forming, and learning their exercise, the governor prevail'd with me to take charge of our North-western frontier, which was infested by the enemy, and provide for the defense of the inhabitants by raising troops and building a line of forts. I undertook this military business, tho' I did not conceive myself well qualified for it. He gave me a commission with full powers, and a parcel of blank commissions for officers, to be given to whom I thought fit. I had but little difficulty in raising men, having soon five hundred and sixty under my command. My son, who had in the preceding war been an officer in the army rais'd against Canada, was my aide-de-camp, and of great use to me. The Indians had burned Gnadenhut, a village settled by the Moravians, and massacred the inhabitants; but the place was thought a good situation for one of the forts.

In order to march thither, I assembled the companies at Bethlehem, the chief establishment of those people. I was surprised to find it in so good a posture of defense; the destruction of Gnadenhut had made them apprehend danger. The principal buildings were defended by a stockade; they had purchased a quantity of arms and ammunition from New York, and have even plac'd quantities of small paving stones between the windows of their high stone houses for their women to throw down upon the heads of any Indians that should attempt to force into them. The armed brethren, too, kept watch, and reliev'd as methodically as in any garrison town. In conversation with the bishop, Spangenberg, I mention'd this my surprise; for, knowing they had obtained an act of Parliament exempting them from military duties in the colonies, I had suppos'd they were conscientiously scrupulous of bearing arms. He answer'd me that it was not one of their established principles, but that, at the time of their obtaining that act, it was thought to be a principle with many of their people. On this occasion, however, they, to their surprise, found it adopted by but a few. It seems they were either deceiv'd in themselves, or deceiv'd the Parliament; but common sense, aided by present danger, will sometimes be too strong for whimsical opinions.

It was the beginning of January when we set out upon this business of building forts. I sent one detachment toward the Minisink, with instructions to erect one for the security of that upper part of the country, and another to the lower part, with similar instructions; and I concluded to go myself with the rest of my force to Gnadenhut, where a fort was tho't more immediately necessary. The Moravians procur'd me five waggons for our tools, stores, baggage, etc.

Just before we left Bethlehem, eleven farmers, who had been driven from their plantations by the Indians, came to me requesting a supply of firearms, that they might back and fetch off their cattle. I gave them each a gun with suitable ammunition. We had not march'd many miles before it began to rain, and it continued raining all day; there were no habitations on the road to shelter us, till we arriv'd near night at the house of a German, where, and in his barn, we were all huddled together, as wet as water could make us. It was well we were not attack'd in our march, for our arms were of the most ordinary sort, and our men could not keep their gun locks dry. The Indians are dexterous in contrivances for that purpose, which we had not. They met that day the eleven poor farmers above mentioned and killed ten of them. The one who escap'd inform'd that his and his companions' guns' would not go off, the priming being wet with the rain.

The next day being fair, we continu'd our march, and arriv'd at the desolated Gnadenhut. There was a saw-mill near, round which were left several piles of boards, with which we soon hutted ourselves; an operation the more necessary at the inclement season, as we had no tents. Our first work was to bury more effectually the dead we found there, who had been half interr'd by the country people.

The next morning our fort was plann'd and mark'd out, the circumference measuring four hundred and fifty five feet, which would require as many palisades to be made of trees, one with another, of a foot diameter each. Our axes, of which we had seventy, were immediately set to work to cut down trees, and our men being dextrous in the use of them, great despatch was made. Seeing the trees fall so fast, I had the curiosity to look at my watch when two men began to cut at a pine; in six minutes they had it upon the ground, and I found it of fourteen inches diameter. Each pine made three palisades of eighteen feet long, pointed at one end. While these were preparing, our other men dug a trench all round, of three feet deep, in which the palisades were to be planted; and our waggons, the bodys being taken off, and the fore and hind wheels separated by taking out the pin which united the two parts of the perch, we had ten carriages, with two horses each, to bring the palisades from the woods to the spot. When they were set up, our carpenters built a stage of boards all round within, about six feet high, for the men to stand on when to fire thro' the loopholes. We had one swivel gun, which we mounted on one of the angles, and fir'd it as soon as fix'd, to let the Indians know, if any were within hearing, that we had such pieces; and thus our fort, if such a magnificent name can be given to so miserable a stockade, was finish'd in a week, though it rain'd so hard every other day that the men could not work.

This gave me occasion to observe, that, when men are employ'd, they are best content'd; for on the days they worked they were good-natur'd and cheerful, and, with the consciousness of having done a good day's work, they spent the evening jollily; but on our idle days they were mutinous and quarrelsome, finding fault with their pork, the bread, etc., and in continual ill humor, which put me in mind of a sea-captain, whose rule it was to keep his men constantly at work; and, when his mate once told him that they had done every thing, and there was nothing further to employ them about, *'Oh'*, *says he*, *'make them scour the anchor'*.

This kind of fort, however contemptible, is a sufficient defense against Indians, who have no cannon. Finding ourselves now posted securely, and having a place to retreat to on occasion, we ventur'd out in parties to scour the adjacent country. We met with no Indians, but we found the places on the neighboring hills where they had lain to watch our proceedings. There was an art in their contrivance of those places that seems worth mention. It being winter, a fire was necessary for them; but a common fire on the surface of the ground would by its light have dicover'd their position at a distance. They had therefore dug holes in the ground about three feet diameter, and somewhat deeper; we saw where they had with their hatchets cut off the charcoal from the sides of burnt logs lying in the woods. With these coals they had made small fires in the bottom of the holes, and we observ'd among the weeds and grass the prints of their bodies made by their laying all round, with their legs hanging down in the holes to keep their feet warm, which, with them, is an essential point. This kind of fire, so manag'd, could not discover them, either by its light, flame, sparks, or even smoke: it appear'd that their number was not great, and it seems they saw we were too many to be attacked by them with prospect of advantage.

We had for our chaplain a zealous Presbyterian minister, Mr Beatty, who complained to me that the men did not generally attend his prayers and exhortations. When they enlisted, they were promised, besides pay and provisions, a gill of rum a day, which was punctually serv'd out to them, half in the morning, and the other half in the evening; and I observ'd they were as punctual in attending to receive it; upon which I said to Mr Beatty, 'It is, perhaps, below the dignity of your profession to act as steward of the rum, but if you were to deal it out and only just after prayers, you would have them all about you'. He liked the tho't, undertook the office, and, with the help of a few hands to measure out the liquor, executed it to satisfaction, and never were prayers more generally and more punctually attended; so that I thought this method preferable to the punishment inflicted by some military laws for non-attendance on divine service.

I had hardly finish'd this business, and got my fort well stor'd with provisions, when I receiv'd a letter from the governor, acquainting me that he had call'd the Assembly, and wished my attendance there, if the posture of affairs on the frontiers was such that my remaining there was no longer necessary. My friends, too, of the Assembly, pressing me by their letters to be, if possible, at the meeting, and my three intended forts being now compleated, and the inhabitants contented to remain on their farms under that protection, I resolved to return; the more willingly, as a New England officer, Colonel Clapham, experienced in Indian war, being on a visit to our establishment, consented to accept the command. I gave him a commission, and, parading the garrison, had it read before them, and introduc'd him to them as an officer who, from his skill in military affairs, was much more fit to command them than myself; and, giving them a little exhortation, took my leave. I was escorted as far as Bethlehem, where I rested from the fatigue I had undergone.

George Washington

1732–1799

'First in war, first in peace, first in the hearts of his countrymen'—George Washington was the first President of the United States—a legend in his own lifetime. The following extracts from his speeches and letters cover the end of the Revolutionary War when Washington was worrying about the state of the army before his final triumphant defeat of the British at Yorktown in October 1781.

THE SITUATION OF America at this time is critical. The government is without finances. Its paper credit sunk, and no expedients it can adopt capable of retrieving it. The resources of the country much diminished by a five years' war, in which it has made efforts beyond its ability. Clinton, with an army of ten thousand regular troops (aided by a considerable body of militia, whom, from motives of fear and attachment, he has engaged to take arms), in possession of one of our capital towns [New York] and a large part of the State to which it belongs. The savages desolating the frontiers. A fleet, superior to that of our allies, not only protects the enemy against any attempt of ours, but to facilitate those, which he may project against us. Lord Cornwallis, with seven or eight thousand men, in complete possession of two States, Georgia and South Carolina; a third, by recent misfortunes, at his mercy. His force is daily increasing by an accession of adherents, whom his successes naturally procure in a country inhabited a great part by emigrants from England and Scotland, who have not been long enough transplanted to exchange their ancient habits and attachments in favor of their new residence.

We are without money, and have been so for a great length of time; without provision and forage, except what is taken by impress; without clothing, and shortly shall be (in a manner) without men. In a word we have lived upon expedients till we can live no longer, and it may be truly said that the history of this war, is a history of false hopes and temporary devices, instead of system, and economy which results from it.

If we mean to continue our struggles (and it is to be hoped we shall not relinquish our claims), we must do it upon an entire new plan. We must have a permanent force, not a force that is constantly fluctuating and sliding from under us as a pedestal of ice would do from a statue on a summer's day, involving us in expense that baffles all calculation—an expense which no funds are equal to. We must at the same time contrive ways and means to aid our Taxes by loans, and put our finances upon a more certain and stable footing than they are at present. Our civil government must likewise undergo a reform—ample powers must be lodged in Congress as the head of the Federal union, adequate to all the purposes of war. Unless these things are done, our efforts will be in vain, and only serve to accumulate expense, add to our perplexities, and dissatisfy the people without a prospect of obtaining the prize in view.

I do not hesitate in giving it clearly as my opinion to you (but this opinion and this business should be concealed behind a curtain,) that the favorable movement of the Spanish operations in the Floridas ought to be improved to the utmost extent of our means; provided the Spaniards, by a junction of their maritime force with that of his Most Christian Majesty of France under the command of the Chevalier de Ternay, will give us a secure convoy, and engage not to leave us till the operations of the campaign are at an end, or it can be done by consent of parties.

The communication of His Excellency the minister is, that the Court of Spain have in contemplation two expeditions against the British settlements in the Floridas, Pensacola, and St Augustine.

The folly of temporary expedients are seen into and exploded, and vigorous efforts will be used to obtain a permanent army, and carry on the war systematically, if the obstinacy of Great Britain should compel us to continue it. We want nothing but the aid of a loan to enable us to put our finance into a tolerable train. The country does not want resources, but we the means of drawing them forth.

I shall commit to writing the result of our conferences on the present state of American affairs . . . To me it appears evident:

1st. That, considering the diffused population of these States, the consequent difficulty of drawing together its resources, the composition and temper of a part of the inhabitants, the want of a sufficient stock of national wealth as a foundation for revenue, and the almost total extinction of commerce, the efforts we have been compelled to make for carrying on the war have exceeded the natural abilities of this country, and by degrees brought it to a crisis, which renders immediate and efficacious succors from abroad indispensable to its safety.

2dly. That . . . some errors may have been committed in the administration of our finances, to which a part of our embarrassments are to be attributed; yet they are principally to be ascribed to an essential defect of means, to the want of a sufficient stock of wealth, . . . which, continuing to operate, will make it impossible by any merely interior exertions to extricate ourselves from those embarrassments, restore public credit, and furnish the funds requisite for the support of the war.

3dly. That experience has demonstrated the impracticability long to maintain a paper credit without funds for its redemption . . .

4thly. That the mode, which for want of money has been substituted for supplying the army, by assessing a proportion of the productions of the earth, has hitherto been found ineffectual, has frequently exposed the army to the most calamitous distress, and, from its novelty and incompatibility with ancient habits, is regarded by the people as burthensome and oppressive, has excited serious discontents, and in some places alarming symptoms of opposition . . .

5thly. That, from the best estimates of the annual expense of the war and the annual revenues which these States are capable of affording, there is a large balance to be supplied by public credit. The resource of domestic loans is inconsiderable, because there are properly speaking few moneyed men, and the few there are can employ their money more profitably otherwise; added to which, the instability of the currency and the deficiency of funds have impaired the public credit.

6thly. That the patience of the army, from an almost uninterrupted series of complicated distress, is now nearly exhausted, and their discontents matured to an extremity, which has recently had very disagreeable consequences, and which demonstrates the absolute necessity of speedy relief, a relief not within the compass of our means . . .

7thly. That, the people being dissatisfied with the mode of supporting the war, there is cause to apprehend, that evils actually felt in the prosecution may weaken those sentiments which began it, founded, not on immediate sufferings, but on a speculative apprehension of future sufferings from the loss of their liberties. There is danger, that a commercial and free people, little accustomed to heavy burthens, pressed by impositions of a new and odious kind, may not make a proper allowance for the necessity of the conjuncture, and may imagine they have only exchanged one tyranny for another.

8thly. That, from all the foregoing considerations result, 1st, absolute necessity of an immediate, ample, and efficacious succor in money large enough to be a foundation for substantial arrangements of finance, to revive public credit, and give vigor to future operations; 2dly, the vast importance of a decided effort of the allied arms on this continent, the ensuing campaign, to effectuate once for all the great objects of the alliance, the liberty and independence of these States. Without the first we may make a feeble and expiring effort the next campaign, in all probability the period to our opposition. With it, we should be in a condition to continue the war, as long as the obstinacy of the enemy might require. The first is essential to the latter; both combined would bring the contest to a glorious issue, crown the obligations, which America already feels to the magnanimity and generosity of her ally, and perpetuate the union by all the ties of gratitude and affection, as well as mutual advantage, which alone can render it solid and indissoluble.

9thly. That, next to a loan of money, a constant naval superiority on these coasts is the object most interesting. This would instantly reduce the enemy to a difficult defensive, and, by removing all prospect of extending their acquisitions, would take away the motives for prosecuting the war. Indeed, it is not to be conceived how they could subsist a large force in this country, if we had the command of the seas, to interrupt the regular transmission of supplies from Europe. This superiority, (with an aid in money,) would enable us to convert the war into a vigorous offensive. I say nothing of the advantages to the trade of both nations, nor how infinitely it would facilitate our supplies . . .

10thly. That an additional succor in troops would be extremely desirable. Besides a reinforcement of numbers, the excellence of French troops, that perfect discipline and order in the corps already sent, which have so happily tended to improve the respect and confidence of the people for our allies, the conciliating disposition and the zeal for the service, which distinguish every rank, sure indications of lasting harmony,—all these considerations evince the immense utility of an accession of force to the corps now here . . . But if the sending so large a succor in troops (15,000 men) should necessarily diminish the pecuniary aid, which our allies may be disposed to grant, it were preferable to diminish the aid in men; for the same sum of money, which would transport from France and maintain here a body of troops with all the necessary apparatus, being put into our hands to be employed by us, would serve to give activity to a larger force within ourselves, and its influence would pervade the whole administration.

11thly. That no nation will have it more in its power to repay what it borrows than this. Our debts are hitherto small. The vast and valuable tracts of unlocated lands, the variety and fertility of climates and soils, the advantages of every kind which we possess for commerce, insure to this country a rapid advancement in population and prosperity, and a certainty, its independence being established, of redeeming in a short term of years the comparative inconsiderable debts it may have occasion to contract.

That, notwithstanding the difficulties under which we labor, and the inquietudes prevailing among the people, there is still a fund of inclination and resource in the country, equal to great and continued exertions, provided we have it in our power to stop the progress of disgust, by changing the present system, and adopting another more consonant with the spirit of the nation, and more capable of activity and energy in public measures; of which a powerful succor of money must be the basis. The people are discontented; but it is with the feeble and oppressive mode of conducting the war, not with the war itself. They are not unwilling to contribute to its support, but they are unwilling to do it in a way that renders private property precarious; a necessary consequence of the fluctuation of the national currency, and of the inability of government to perform its engagements oftentimes coercively made. A large majority are still firmly attached to the independence of these States, abhor a reunion with Great Britain, and are affectionate to the alliance with France; but this disposition cannot supply the place of means customary and essential in war, nor can we rely on its duration amidst the perplexities, oppressions, and misfortunes, that attend the want of them.

To learn from so good authority as your information, that the distresses of the citizens of this State [New York] are maturing into complaints, which are likely to produce serious consequences, is a circumstance as necessary to be known, as it is unpleasing to hear, and I thank you for this communication. The committees now forming are at this crisis disagreeable things; and if they cannot be counteracted, or diverted from their original purposes, may outdo the views of the well-meaning members of them, and plunge this country into deeper distress and confusion, than it has hitherto experienced; though I have no doubt but that the same bountiful Providence, which has relieved us in a variety of difficulties heretofore, will enable us to emerge from them ultimately, and crown our struggles with success.

To trace these evils to their sources is by no means difficult; and errors once discovered are more than half corrected. This I hope is our case at present; but there can be no radical cure till Congress is vested, by the several States, with full and ample Powers to enact Laws for general purposes, and till the executive business is placed in the hands of able men and responsible characters. Requisitions then will be supported by Law. Jealousies, and those ruinous delays and ill-timed compliances, arising from distrust and the fear of doing more than a Sister State, will cease. Business will be properly arranged; system and order will take place; and economy must follow; but not till we have corrected the fundamental errors enumerated above.

The measure adopted by Congress of appointing Ministers of War, Finance, and for Foreign Affairs, I think a very wise one. To give efficacy to it, proper characters will, no doubt, be chosen to conduct the business of these departments. How far Col. Hamilton, of whom you ask my opinion as a financier, has turned his thoughts to that particular study, I am unable to answer, because I never entered upon a discussion of this point with him. But this I can venture to advance, from a thorough knowledge of him, that there are few men to be found, of his age, who have a more general knowledge than he possesses; and none, whose soul is more engaged in the cause, or who exceeds him in probity and sterling virtue.

I am clearly in sentiment with you, that our cause only became distressed, and apparently desperate, from an improper management of it; and that errors once discovered are more than half mended. I have no doubt of our abilities or resources, but we must not slumber nor sleep; they never will be drawn forth if we do; nor will violent exertions, which subside with the occasion, answer our purposes. It is a provident foresight, a proper arrangement of business, system and order in the execution, that is to be productive of that economy, which is to defeat the efforts and hopes of Great Britain; and I am happy, thrice happy, on private as well as public accounts, to find, that these are in train. For it will ease my shoulders of an immense burden, which the deranged and perplexed situation of our affairs, and the distresses of every department of the army, which concentered in the Commander-in-chief, had placed upon them.

I am not less pleased to hear that Maryland has acceded to the confederation, and that Virginia has relinquished its claim to the land west of the Ohio, which, for fertility of soil, pleasantness of clime, and other natural advantages, is equal to any known tract of country in the universe, of the same extent, taking the great Lakes for its northern boundary.

I wish most devoutly a happy completion to your [General Sullivan's] plan of finance, (which you say is near finished,) and much success to your scheme of borrowing coined specie and plate. But in what manner do you propose to apply the latter? As a fund to redeem its value in Paper to be emitted, or to coin it? If the latter, it will add one more to a thousand other reasons, which might be offered in proof of the necessity of vesting legislative or dictatorial powers in Congress, to make Laws of general utility for the purposes of war, so that they might prohibit, under the pains and penalty of death, specie and provisions from going to the Enemy for Goods.

The traffic with New York is immense. Individual states will not make it a felony, lest, (among other reasons) it should not become general;

and nothing short of it will ever check, much less stop a practice, which, at the same time that it serves to drain us of our provision and specie, removes the barrier between us and the enemy, corrupts the morals of our people by a lucrative traffic, by degrees weakens the opposition, affords a means for obtaining regular and perfect intelligence of every thing among us, while even in this respect we benefit nothing from a fear of discovery. Men of all descriptions are now indiscriminately engaging in it, Whig, Tory, Speculator. By its being practised by those of the latter class, in a manner with impunity, men, who two or three years ago would have shuddered at the idea of such connections, now pursue it with avidity, and reconcile it to themselves (in which their profits plead powerfully) upon a principle of equality with the Tory, who, being actuated by principle (favorable to us), and knowing that a forfeiture of the goods to the informer was all he had to dread, and that this was to be eluded by an agreement not to inform against each other, went into the measure without risk.

This is a digression; but the subject is of so serious a nature and so interesting to our wellbeing as a nation, that I never expect to see a happy termination of the war, nor great national concerns well conducted in peace, till there is something more than a recommendatory power in Congress. It is not possible in time of war that business can be conducted well without it. The last words therefore of my letter, and the first wish of my heart, concur in favor of it.

The situation of the southern States is alarming; the more so, as the measure of providing a regular and permanent force was by my last advices still unattempted, where the danger was most pressing and immediate. Unless all the states enter in good earnest upon this plan, we have little to expect but their successive subjugation. Particular successes, obtained against all the chances of war, have had too much influence, to the prejudice of general and substantial principles.

It must be a settled plan, founded in system, order, and economy, that is to carry us triumphantly through the war. Supineness and indifference to the distresses and cries of a sister State, when danger is far off, and a general but momentary resort to arms when it comes to our doors, are equally impolitic and dangerous, and prove the necessity of a controlling power in Congress to regulate and direct all matters of *general* concern—without it the great business of war can never be well conducted, if it can be conducted at all, while the powers of Congress are only recommendatory. While one state yields obedience, and another refuses it, while a third mutilates and adopts the measure in part only, and all vary in time and manner, it is scarcely possible our affairs should prosper, or that anything but disappointment can follow the best concerted plans. The willing states are almost ruined by their exertions; distrust and jealousy succeed to it. Hence proceed neglect and ill timed compliances, one state waiting to see what another will do. This thwarts all our measures after a heavy though ineffectual expense is incurred.

Do not these things show, that in the most striking point of view, the indispensable necessity, the great and good policy, of each state, sending its ablest and best men to Congress; men who have a perfect understanding of the constitution of their country, of its policy and interests; and of vesting that body with competent powers? Our Independence depends upon it, our respectability and consequence in Europe depends upon it, our greatness as a nation hereafter depends upon it. The fear of giving sufficient powers to Congress, for the purposes I have mentioned is futile, without it our Independence fails and each Assembly.

John Adams

1735–1826

*John Adams was the first Vice-President of the United
States and the second President. A fervent supporter of
Washington as military commander of the Revolutionary
forces, he became a prime mover in America's struggle to
break free of Great Britain. The following letters to Adams'
wife, Abigail Adams, trace his involvement in drafting the
Declaration of Independence for which, according to
Jefferson, he 'was the pillar of (its) support on the floor
of Congress'.*

3 JULY, 1776

YOUR FAVOR OF 17 June, dated at Plymouth, was handed me by yesterday's
post. I was much pleased to find that you had taken a long journey
to Plymouth, to see your friends, in the long absence of one whom

you may wish to see. The excursion will be an amusement, and will serve your health. How happy would it have made me to have taken this journey with you!

I was informed, a day or two before the receipt of your letter, that you was gone to Plymouth, by Mrs Polly Palmer, who was obliging enough, in your absence, to send me the particulars of the expedition to the lower harbor against the men-of-war. Her narration is executed with a precision and perspicuity, which would have become the pen of an accomplished historian.

I am very glad you had so good an opportunity of seeing one of our little American men-of-war. Many ideas new to you must have presented themselves in such a scene; and you will, in future, better understand thee relations of sea engagements.

I rejoice extremely at Dr Fulfinch's petition to open a hospital. But I hope the business will be done upon a larger scale. I hope that one hospital will be licensed in every county, if not in every town. I am happy to find you resolved to be with the children in the first class. Mr Whitney and Mrs Katy Quincy are cleverly through inoculation in this city.

The information you give me of our friend's refusing his appointment has given me much pain, grief, and anxiety. I believe I shall be obliged to follow his example. I have not fortune enough to support my family, and, what is of more importance, to support the dignity of that exalted station. It is too high and lifted up for me, who delight in nothing so much as retreat, solitude, silence, and obscurity. In private life, no one has a right to censure me for following my own inclinations in retirement, simplicity, and frugality. In public life, every man has a right to remark as he pleases. At least he thinks so.

Yesterday, the greatest question was decided which ever was debated in America, and a greater, perhaps, never was nor will be decided among men. A Resolution was passed without one dissenting Colony 'that these United Colonies are, and of right ought to be, free and independent States, and as such they have, and of right ought to have, full power to make war, conclude peace, establish commerce, and to do all other acts and things which other States may rightfully do'. You will see, in a few days, a Declaration setting forth the causes which have impelled us to this mighty revolution, and the reasons which will justify it in the sight of God and man. A plan of confederation will be taken up in a few days.

When I look back to the year 1761, and recollect the argument concerning writs of assistance in the superior court, which I have hitherto considered as the commencement of this controversy between Great Britain and America, and run through the whole period from that time to this, and recollect the series of political events, the chain of causes and effects, I am surprised at the suddenness as well as greatness of this revolution. Britain has been filled with folly, and America with wisdom; at least, this is my judgment. Time must determine. It is the will of Heaven that the two countries should be sundered forever. It may be the will of Heaven that America shall suffer calamities still more wasting, and distresses yet more dreadful. If this is to be the case, it will have this good effect at least. It will inspire us with many virtues which we have not, and correct many errors, follies, and vices which threaten to disturb, dishonor, and destroy us. The furnace of affliction produces refinement in states as well as individuals. And the new Governments we are assuming in every part will require a purification from our vices, and an augmentation of our virtues, or they will be no blessings. The people will have unbounded power, and the people are extremely addicted to corruption and venality, as well as the great. But I must submit all my hopes and fears to an overruling Providence, in which unfashionable as the faith may be, I firmly believe.

PHILADELPHIA, 3 JULY, 1776

Had a Declaration of Independence been made seven months ago, it would have been attended with many great and glorious effects. We might, before this hour, have formed alliances with foreign states. We should have mastered Quebec, and been in possession of Canada. You will perhaps wonder how such a declaration would have influenced our affairs in Canada, but if I could write with freedom, I could easily convince you that it would, and explain to you the manner how. Many gentlemen in high stations, and of great influence, have been duped by the ministerial bubble of Commissioners to treat. And in real, sincere expectation of this event, which they so fondly wished, they have been slow and languid in promoting measures for the reduction of that province. Others there are in the Colonies who really wished that our enterprise in Canada would be defeated, that the Colonies might be brought into danger and distress between two fires, and be thus induced to submit. Others really wished to defeat the expedition to Canada, lest the conquest of it should elevate the minds of the people too much to hearken to those terms of reconciliation which, they believed, would be offered us. These jarring views, wishes, and designs occasioned an opposition to many salutary measures which were proposed for the support of that expedition, and caused obstructions, embarrassments, and studied delays, which have finally lost us the province.

All these causes, however, in conjunction would not have disappointed us, if it had not been for a misfortune which could not be foreseen, and perhaps could not have been prevented; I mean the prevalence of the small-pox among our troops. This fatal pestilence completed our destruction. It is a frown of Providence upon us, which we ought to lay to heart.

But, on the other hand, the delay of this Declaration to this time has many great advantages attending it. The hopes of reconciliation which were fondly entertained by multitudes of honest and well-meaning, though weak and mistaken people, have been gradually, and at last totally extinguished. Time has been given for the whole people maturely to consider the great question of independence, and to ripen their judgment, dissipate their fears, and allure their hopes, by discussing it in newspapers and pamphlets, by debating it in assemblies, conventions, committees of safety and inspection, in town and county meetings, as well as in private conversations, so that the whole people, in every colony of the thirteen, have now adopted it as their own act. This will cement the union, and avoid those heats, and perhaps convulsions, which might have been occasioned by such a Declaration six months ago.

But the day is past. The second day of July, 1776, will be the most memorable epocha in the history of America. I am apt to believe that it will be celebrated by succeeding generations as the great anniversary festival. It ought to be commemorated as the day of deliverance, by solemn acts of devotion to God Almighty. It ought to be solemnized with pomp and parade, with shows, games, sports, guns, bells, bonfires, and illuminations, from one end of this continent to the other, from this time forward forevermore.

You will think me transported with enthusiasm, but I am not. I am well aware of the toil and blood and treasure that it will cost us to maintain this Declaration and support and defend these States. Yet, through all the gloom, I can see the rays of ravishing light and glory. I can see that the end is more than worth all the means. And that posterity will triumph in that day's transaction, even although we should rue it, which I trust in God we shall not.

PHILADELPHIA, 7 JULY, 1776.

I have this moment folded up a magazine and an Evening Post, and sent them off by an express who could not wait for me to write a single line. It always goes to my heart to send off a packet of pamphlets and newspapers without a letter, but it sometimes unavoidably happens, and I suppose you had rather receive a pamphlet or newspaper than nothing.

The design of our enemy now seems to be a powerful invasion of New York and New Jersey. The Halifax fleet and army is arrived, and another fleet and army under Lord Howe is expected to join them. We are making great preparations to meet them by marching the militia of Maryland, Pennsylvania, and New Jersey down to the scene of action, and have made large requisitions upon New England. I hope, for the honor of New England and the salvation of America our people will not be backward in marching to New York. We must maintain and defend that important post, at all events. If the enemy get possession there, it will cost New England very dear. There is no danger of the small-pox at New York. It is carefully kept out of the city and the army. I hope that your brother and mine too will go into the service of their country at this critical period of its distress.

Our army at Crown Point is an object of wretchedness enough to fill a humane mind with horror; disgraced, defeated, discontented, dis- pirited, diseased, naked, undisciplined, eaten up with vermin, no clothes, beds, blankets, no medicines, no victuals but salt pork and flour. A chaplain from that army preached a sermon here the other day from 'Cursed is he that doeth the work of the Lord deceitfully.' I knew better than he did, who the persons were who deserved these curses. But I could not help myself, nor my poor country, any more than he. I hope that measures will be taken to cleanse the army at Crown Point from the small-pox, and that other measures will be taken in New Eng- land, by tolerating and encouraging inoculation, to render that distemper less terrible.

I am solicitous to hear what figure our new Superior Court made in their eastern circuit; what business they did; whether the grand juries and petit juries were sworn; whether they tried any criminals, or any civil actions; how the people were affected at the appearance of Courts again; how the judges were treated: whether with respect or cold neglect, etc. Every colony upon the continent will soon be in the same situation. They are erecting governments as fast as children build cob-houses: but, I conjecture, they will hardly throw them down again so soon.

The practice we have hitherto been in, of ditching round about our enemies, will not always do. We must learn to use other weapons than the pick and the spade. Our armies must be disciplined, and learn to fight. I have the satisfaction to reflect that our Massachusetts people, when they have been left to themselves, have been constantly fighting and skirmishing, and always with success. I wish the same valor, prudence, and spirit had been discovered everywhere.

PHILADELPHIA, 7 JULY, 1776.
It is worth the while of a person, obliged to write as much as I do, to consider the varieties of style. The epistolary is essentially different from the oratorical and the historical style. Oratory abounds with figures. History is simple, but grave, majestic, and formal. Letters, like conversation, should be free, easy and familiar. Simplicity and familiarity are the characteristics of this kind of writing. Affectation is as disagreeable in a letter as in conversation, and therefore studied language, premeditated method, and sublime sentiments are not expected in a letter. Notwithstanding which, the sublime, as well as the beautiful and the novel, may naturally enough appear in familiar letters among friends. Among the ancients there are two illustrious examples of the epistolary style, Cicero and Pliny, whose letters present you with models of fine writing, which have borne the criticism of almost two thousand years. In these you see the sublime, the beautiful, the novel, and the pathetic, conveyed in as much simplicity, ease, freedom, and familiarity as language is capable of.

Let me request you to turn over the leaves of 'The Preceptor', to a letter of Pliny the Younger, in which he has transmitted to these days the history of his uncle's philosophical curiosity, his heroic courage, and his melancholy catastrophe. Read it, and say whether it is possible to write a narrative of facts in a better manner. It is copious and particular in selecting the circumstances most natural, remarkable, and affecting. There is not an incident omitted which ought to have been remembered, nor one inserted that is not worth remembrance. It gives you an idea of the scene, as distinct and perfect as if a painter had drawn it to the life before your eyes. It interests your passions as much as if you had been an eye-witness of the whole transaction. Yet there are no figures or art used. All is as simple, natural, easy, and familiar as if the story had been told in conversation, without a moment's premeditation.

Pope and Swift have given the world a collection of their letters; but I think in general they fall short, in the epistolary way, of their own eminence in poetry and other branches of literature. Very few of their letters have ever engaged much of my attention. Gay's letter concerning the pair of lovers killed by lightning is worth more than the whole collection, in point of simplicity and elegance of composition, and as a genuine model of the epistolary style. There is a book, which I wish you owned,—I mean Rollin's 'Belles Lettres'—in which the variations of style are explained.

Early youth is the time to learn the arts and sciences, and especially to correct the ear and the imagination, by forming a style. I wish you would think of forming the taste and judgment of your children now, before any unchaste sounds have fastened on their ears, and before any affectation or vanity is settled on their minds, upon the pure principles of nature. Music is a great advantage; for style depends, in part, upon a delicate ear. The faculty of writing is attainable by art, practice, and habit only. The sooner, therefore, the practice begins, the more likely it will be to succeed. Have no mercy upon an affected phrase, any more than an affected air, gait, dress, or manners.

Your children have capacities equal to anything. There is a vigor in the understanding and a spirit and fire in the temper of every one of them, which is capable of ascending the heights of art, science, trade, war, or politics. They should be set to compose descriptions of scenes and objects, and narrations of facts and events. Declamations upon topics and other exercises of various sorts should be prescribed to them. Set a child to form a description of a battle, a storm, a seige, a cloud, a mountain, a lake, a city, a harbor, a country seat, a meadow, a forest, or almost anything that may occur to your thoughts. Set him to compose a narration of all the little incidents and events of a day, a journey, a ride, or a walk. In this way a taste will be formed, and a facility of writing acquired.

For myself, as I never had a regular tutor, I never studied anything methodically, and consequently never was completely accomplished in anything. But, as I am conscious of my own deficiency in these respects, I should be the less pardonable if I neglected the education of my children. In grammar, rhetoric, logic, my education was imperfect, because immethodical. Yet I have perhaps read more upon these arts, and considered them in a more extensive view, than some others.

10 JULY.

You will see, by the newspapers which I from time to time inclose, with what rapidity the colonies proceed in their political manoeuvres. How many calamities might have been avoided if these measures had been taken twelve months ago, or even no longer ago than last December?

The colonies to the south are pursuing the same maxims which have heretofore governed those to the north. In constituting their new governments, their plans are remarkably popular, more so than I could ever have imagined; even more popular than the 'Thoughts on Government'; and in the choice of their rulers, capacity, spirit, and zeal in the cause supply the place of fortune, family, and every other consideration which used to have weight with mankind. My friend Archibald Bullock, Esquire, is Governor of Georgia. John Rutledge, Esquire, is Governor of South Carolina. Patrick Henry, Esquire, is Governor of Virginia, etc. Dr Franklin will be Governor of Pennsylvania. The new members of this city are all in this taste, chosen because of their inflexible zeal for independence. All the old members left out because they opposed independence, or at least were lukewarm about it. Dickinson, Morris, Allen, all fallen, like grass before the scythe, notwithstanding all their vast advantages in point of fortune, family, and abilities. I am inclined to think, however, and to wish, that these gentlemen may be restored at a fresh election, because, although mistaken in some points, they are good characters, and their great wealth and numerous connections will contribute to strengthen America and cement her union.

I wish I were at perfect liberty to portray before you all these characters in their genuine lights, and to explain to you the course of political changes in this province. It would give you a great idea of the spirit and resolution of the people, and show you, in a striking point of view, the deep roots of American independence in all the colonies. But it is not prudent to commit to writing such free speculations in the present state of things. Time, which takes away the veil, may lay open the secret springs of this surprising revolution. But I find, although the colonies have differed in religion, laws, customs, and manners, yet in the great essentials of society and government they are all alike.

PHILADELPHIA, 11 JULY, 1776.

You seem to be situated in the place of greatest tranquility and security of any upon the continent. I may be mistaken in this particular, and an armament may have invaded your neighborhood, before now. But we have no intelligence of any such design, and all that we now know of the motions, plans, operations, and designs of the enemy indicates the contrary. It is but just that you should have a little rest, and take a little breath.

I wish I knew whether your brother and mine have enlisted in the army, and what spirit is manifested by our militia for marching to New York and Crown Point. The militia of Maryland, New Jersey, Pennsylvania, and the lower counties are marching with much alacrity, and a laudable zeal to take care of Howe and his army at Staten Island. The army in New York is in high spirits, and seems determined to give the enemy a serious reception. The unprincipled and unfeeling and unnatural inhabitants of Staten Island are cordially receiving the enemy, and, deserters say, have engaged to take arms. They are an ignorant, cowardly pack of scoundrels. Their numbers are small, and their spirit less.

It is some time since I received any letter from you. The Plymouth one was the last. You must write me every week, by the post, if it is but a few lines. It gives me many spirits. I design to write to the General Court requesting a dismission, or at least a furlough. I think to propose that they choose four more members, or at least three more, so that we may attend here in rotation. Two or three or four may be at home at a time, and the Colony properly represented notwithstanding. Indeed, while the Congress were employed in political regulations, forming the sentiments of the people of the Colonies into some consistent system, extinguishing the remainders of authority under the crown, and gradually erecting and strengthening governments under the authority of the people, turning their thoughts upon the principles of polity and the forms of government, framing constitutions for the Colonies separately, and a limited and a defined Confederacy for the United Colonies, and in some other measures, which I do not choose to mention particularly, but which are now determined, or near the point of determination, I flattered myself that I might have been of some little use here. But now, these matters will be soon completed, and very little business will be to be done here but what will be either military or commercial; branches of knowledge and business for which hundreds of others in our province are much better qualified than I am. I shall therefore request my masters to relieve me.

I am not a little concerned about my health, which seems to have been providentially preserved to me, much beyond my expectations. But I begin to feel the disagreeable effects of unremitting attention to business for so long a time, and a want of exercise, and the bracing quality of my native air; so that I have the utmost reason to fear an irreparable injury to my constitution, if I do not obtain a little relaxation. The fatigues of war are much less destructive to health than the painful, laborious attention to debates and to writing, which drinks up the spirits and consumes strength.   I am, etc.

15 JULY

My very deserving friend, Mr Gerry, sets off tomorrow for Boston, worn out of health by the fatigues of this station. He is an excellent man, and an active, able statesman. I hope he will soon return hither. I am sure I should be glad to return with him, but I cannot. I must wait to have the guard relieved.

There is a most amiable, laudable, and gallant spirit prevailing in these middle colonies. The militia turn out in great numbers and in high spirits, in New Jersey, Pennsylvania, Maryland, and Delaware, so that we hope to resist Howe and his myrmidons.

Independence is, at last, unanimously agreed to in the New York Convention. You will see, by the newspapers inclosed, what is going forward in Virginia and Maryland and New Jersey. Farewell! farewell! infatuated, besotted step-dame. I have not time to add more than that I received letters from you but seldom of late. Tomorrow's post, I hope, will bring me some. So I hoped of last Saturday's and last Tuesday's.

20 JULY

I cannot omit the opportunity of writing you a line by this post. This letter will, I suppose, find you, in some degree or other, under the influence of the small-pox. The air is of very great importance. I don't know your physician, but I hope he won't deprive you of air more than is necessary.

We had yesterday an express from General Lee in Charleston, South Carolina, with an account of a brilliant little action between the armament under Clinton and Cornwallis, and a battery on Sullivan's Island, which terminated very fortunately for America. I will endeavor to inclose with this a printed account of it. It has given us good spirits here, and will have a happy effect upon our armies at New York and Ticonderoga. Surely our northern soldiers will not suffer themselves to be outdone by their brethren so nearly under the same sun. I don't yet hear of any Massachusetts men at New York. Our people must not flinch at this critical moment, when their country is in more danger than it ever will be again, perhaps. What will they say if the Howes should prevail against our forces at so important a post as New York, for want of a few thousand men from the Massachusetts? I will likewise send you by this post Lord Howe's letter and proclamation, which has let the cat out of the bag. These tricks deceive no longer. Gentlemen here, who either were or pretended to be deceived heretofore, now see or pretend to see through such artifices. I apprehend his Lordship is afraid of being attacked upon Staten Island, and is throwing out his barrels to amuse Leviathan until his reinforcements shall arrive.

20 JULY

This has been a dull day to me. I waited the arrival of the post with much solicitude and impatience, but his arrival made me more solicitous still. 'To be left at the Post Office' in your handwriting on the back of a few lines from the Dr was all that I could learn of you and my little folks. If you were too busy to write, I hoped that some kind hand would have been found to let me know something about you. Do my friends think that I have been a politician so long as to have lost all feeling? Do they suppose I have forgotten my wife and children? Or are they so panic-struck with the loss of Canada as to be afraid to correspond with me? Or have they forgotten that you have a husband, and your children a father? What have I done, or omitted to do, that I should be thus forgotten and neglected in the most tender and affecting scene of my life? Don't mistake me. I don't blame you. Your time and thoughts must have been wholly taken up with your own and your family's situation and necessities; but twenty other persons might have informed me.

I suspect that you intended to have run slyly through the small-pox with the family, without letting me know it, and then have sent me an account that you were all well. This might be a kind intention, and if the design had succeeded, would have made me very joyous. But the secret is out, and I am left to conjecture. But as the faculty have this distemper so much under command, I will flatter myself with the hope and expectation of soon hearing of your recovery.

29 JULY

How are you all this morning? Sick, weak, faint, in pain, or pretty well recovered? By this time, you are well acquainted with the small-pox. Pray, how do you like it?

We have no news. It is very hard that half a dozen or half a score armies can't supply us with news. We have a famine, a perfect dearth of this necessary article. I am, at this present writing, perplexed and plagued with two knotty problems in politics. You love to pick a political bone. So I will even throw it to you.

If a confederation should take place, one great question is, how we shall vote. Whether each colony shall count one; or whether each shall have a weight in proportion to its number, or wealth, or exports and imports, or a compound ratio of all. Another is, whether Congress shall have authority to limit the dimensions of each colony, to prevent those, which claim by charter, or proclamation, or commission to the south sea, from growing too great and powerful, so as to be dangerous to the rest?

Shall I write you a sheet upon each of these questions? When you are well enough to read, and I can find leisure enough to write, perhaps I may.

Gerry carried with him a canister for you. But he is an old bachelor, and what is worse, a politician, and what is worse still, a kind of soldier; so that I suppose he will have so much curiosity to see armies and fortifications, and assemblies, that you will lose many a fine breakfast at a time when you want them most.

Tell Betsey that this same Gerry is such another as herself, sex excepted. How is my brother and friend Cranch? How is his other self and their little selves and ours? Don't be in the dumps, above all things. I am hard put to it to keep out of them, when I look at home. But I will be gay if I can. Adieu.

3 AUGUST, 1776

The post was later than usual to-day, so that I had not yours of July 24 till this evening. You have made me very happy by the particular and favorable account you give me of all the family. But I don't understand how there are so many who have no eruptions and no symptoms.

The inflammation in the arm might do, but without these there is no small-pox. I will lay a wager, that your whole hospital has not had so much small-pox as Mrs Katy Quincy. Upon my word, she has had an abundance of it, but is finally recovered, looks as fresh as a rose, but pitted all over as thick as ever you saw anyone. I this evening presented your compliments and thanks to Mr Hancock for his polite offer of his house and likewise your compliments to his lady and Mrs Katy.

4 AUGUST

Went this morning to the Baptist meeting, in hopes of hearing Mr Stillman, but was disappointed. He was there, but another gentleman preached. His action was violent to a degree bordering on fury; his gestures unnatural and distorted. Not the least idea of grace in his motions, or elegance in his style. His voice was vociferous and boisterous, and his composition almost wholly destitute of ingenuity. I wonder extremely at the fondness of our people for scholars educated at the southward, and for southern preachers. There is no one thing in which we excel them more than in our University, our scholars and preachers. Particular gentlemen here, who have improved upon their education by travel, shine; but in general, old Massachusetts, outshines her younger sisters. Still in several particulars they have more wit than we. They have societies, the Philosophical Society particularly, which excites a scientific emulation, and propagates their fame. If ever I get through this scene of politics and war, I will spend the remainder of my days in endeavoring to instruct my countrymen in the art of making the most of their abilities and virtues; an art which they have hitherto too much neglected. A philosophical society shall be established at Boston, if I have wit and address enough to accomplish it, sometime or other. Pray set brother Cranch's philosophical head to plodding upon this project. Many of his lucubrations would have been published and preserved, for the benefit of mankind and for his honor, if such a club had existed.

My countrymen want art and address. They want knowledge of the world. They want the exterior and superficial accomplishment of gentlemen, upon which the world has set so high a value. In solid abilities and real virtues they vastly excel, in general, any people upon this continent. Our New England people are awkward and bashful, yet they are pert, ostentatious, and vain; a mixture which excites ridicule and gives disgust. They have not the faculty of showing themselves to the best advantage, nor the art of concealing this faculty; an art and faculty which some people possess in the highest degree. Our deficiencies in these respects are owing wholly to the little intercourse we have with strangers, and to our inexperience in the world. These imperfections must be remedied, for New England must produce the heroes, the statesmen, the philosophers, or America will make no great figure for some time.

Our army is rather sickly at New York, and we live in daily expectation of hearing of some great event. May God Almighty grant it may be prosperous for America. Hope is an anchor and a cordial. Disappointment, however, will not disconcert us.

If you will come to Philadelphia in September, I will stay as long as you please. I should be as proud and happy as a bridegroom. Yours.

PHILADELPHIA, 12 AUGUST, 1776.

Mr A. sets off to-day, if the rain should not prevent him, with Colonel Whipple, of Portsmouth, a brother of the celebrated Miss Hannah Whipple, a sensible and worthy man. By him I have sent you two bundles of letters, which I hope you will be careful of. I thought I should not be likely to find a safer opportunity. By them you will see that my private correspondence alone is business enough for a lazy man. I think I have answered all but a few of those large bundles.

A French vessel, a pretty large brigantine, deeply laden, arrived here yesterday from Martinique. She had fifty barrels of limes, which are all sold already, at such prices that the amount of them will be sufficient to load the brig with flour. The trade, we see, even now, in the midst of summer, is not totally interrupted by all the efforts of our enemies. Prizes are taken in no small numbers. A gentleman told me, a few days ago, that he had summed up the sugar which has been taken, and it amounted to three thousand hogsheads, since which two other ships have been taken and carried into Maryland. Thousands of schemes for privateering are afloat in American imaginations. Some are for taking the Hull ships, with woolens, for Amsterdam and Rotterdam; some are for the tin ships; some for the Irish linen ships; some for outward bound, and others for inward bound Indiamen; some for the Hudson Bay ships, and many for West India sugar ships. Out of these speculations, many fruitless and some profitable projects will grow.

We have no news from New York. All is quiet as yet. Our expectations are raised. The eyes of the world are upon Washington and Howe, and their armies. The wishes and prayers of the virtuous part of it, I hope, will be answered. If not, yet virtues grow out of affliction. I repeat my request that you would ask some of the members of the General Court if they can send me horses; and if they cannot, that you would send them. I can live no longer without a servant and a horse.

PHILADELPHIA, 12 AUGUST, 1776

Mr A. and Colonel Whipple are at length gone. Colonel Tudor went off with them. They went away about three o'clock this afternoon. I wrote by A, and Colonel Whipple too; by the latter I sent two large bundles, which he promised to deliver to you. These middle States begin to taste the sweets of war. Ten thousand difficulties and wants occur, which they had not conception of before. Their militia are as clamorous and impatient of discipline, and mutinous as ours, and more so. There has been seldom less than four thousand men in this city at a time, for a fortnight past, on their march to New Jersey. Here they wait, until we grow very angry about them, for canteens, camp kettles, blankets, tents, shoes, hose, arms, flints, and other dittoes, while we are under a very critical solicitude for our army at New York, on account of the insufficiency of men.

I want to be informed of the state of things with you; whether there is a scarcity of provisions of any kind, of West India articles, of clothing. Whether any trade is carried on, any fishery. Whether any vessels arrive from abroad, or whether any go to sea upon foreign voyages. I wish to know, likewise, what posture of defense you are in. What fortifications are at Nantasket, at Long Island, Pettick's Island, etc., and what men and officers there are to garrison them. We hear nothing from the Massachusetts, lately, in comparison of what we did when the army was before Boston.

I must not conclude without repeating my request that you would ask some of the members of the General Court to send me horses, and if they cannot, to send them yourself.

PHILADELPHIA, 14 AUGUST, 1776.

This is the anniversary of a memorable day in the history of America. A day when the principle of American resistance and independence was first asserted and carried into action. The stamp office fell before the rising spirit of our countrymen. It is not impossible that the two grateful brothers may make their grand attack this very day. If they should, it is possible it may be more glorious for this country than ever; it is certain it will become more memorable.

I am put upon a committee to prepare a device for a golden medal, to commemorate the surrender of Boston to the American arms, and upon another to prepare devices for a great seal for the confederated states. There is a gentleman here of French extraction, whose name is Du Simitiere, a painter by profession, whose designs are very ingenious, and his drawings well executed. He has been applied to for his advice. I waited on him yesterday, and saw his sketches. For the medal he proposes, Liberty, with her spear and pileus, leaning on General Washington. The British fleet in Boston harbor with all their sterns towards the town, the American troops marching in. For the seal, he proposes the arms of the several nations from whence America has been peopled, as English, Scotch, Irish, Dutch, German, etc., each in a shield. On one side of them, Liberty with her pileus, on the other, a rifler in his uniform, with his rifle-gun in one hand and his tomahawk in the other; this dress and these troops, with this kind of armor, being peculiar to America, unless the dress was known to the Romans. Dr Franklin showed me yesterday a book containing an account of the dresses of all the Roman soldiers, one of which appeared exactly like it. This M. du Simitiere is a very curious man. He has begun a collection of materials for a history of this revolution. He begins with the first advices of the tea ships. He cuts out of the newspapers every scrap of intelligence and every piece of speculation, and pastes it upon clean paper, arranging them under the head of that State to which they belong, and intends to bind them up in volumes. He has a list of every speculation and pamphlet concerning independence, and another of those concerning forms of government.

Dr F. proposes a device for a seal: Moses lifting up his wand and dividing the Red Sea, and Pharaoh, in his chariot overwhelmed with the waters. This motto, 'Rebellion to tyrants is obedience to God'.

Mr Jefferson proposed the children of Israel in the wilderness, led by a cloud by day and a pillar of fire by night; and on the other side, Hengist and Horsa, the Saxon chiefs from whom we claim the honor of being descended, and whose political principles and form of government we have assumed.

I proposed the choice of Hercules, as engraved by Gribelin, in some editions of Lord Shaftesbury's works. The hero resting on his club. Virtue pointing to her rugged mountain on one hand, and persuading him to ascend. Sloth, glancing at her flowery paths of pleasure, wantonly reclining on the ground, displaying the charms both of her eloquence and person, to seduce him into vice. But this is too complicated a group for a seal or medal, and it is not original.

I shall conclude by repeating my request for horses and a servant. Let the horses be good ones. I can't ride a bad horse so many hundred miles. If our affairs had not been in so critical a state at New York, I should have run away before now. But I am determined now to stay until some gentleman is sent here in my room, and until my horses come. But the time will be very tedious.

The whole force is arrived at Staten Island.

Ethan Allen

1738–1789

Ethan Allen, leader of the Green Mountain Boys, was a hero of the Revolutionary War. In May 1775 he gained a great victory in capturing Fort Ticonderoga but by September, after an expedition against Montreal, had been captured by the British. The following extract from his Narrative of Colonel Ethan Allen's Captivity *describes the early days of imprisonment.*

EARLY IN THE fall of the year, the little army, under the command of the generals Schuyler and Montgomery, were ordered to advance into Canada. I was at Ticonderoga, when this order arrived; and the general with most of the officers, requested me to attend them in the expedition; and though at that time, I had no commission from Congress, yet they engaged me, that I should be considered as an officer the same as though

I had a commission; and should, as occasions might require, command certain detachments of the army. This I considered as an honourable offer, and did not hesitate to comply with it, and advanced with the army to the isle Auix Noix: from whence I was ordered (by the general) to go in company with major Brown, and certain interpreters, through the woods into Canada, with letters to the Canadians, and to let them know, that the design of the army was only against the English garrisons, and not the country, their liberties, or religion; And having through much danger negociated this business, I returned to the isle Auix Noix in the fore part of September, when general Schuyler returned to Albany; and in consequence the command devolved upon general Montgomery, whom I assisted in laying a line of circumvallation round the fortress St John's: after which I was ordered by the general to make a second tour into Canada, upon nearly the same design as before; and withal to observe the disposition, designs and movement of the inhabitants of the country; this reconnoitre I undertook with reluctance, chusing rather to assist at the siege of St John's, which was then closely invested; but my esteem for the general's person, and opinion of him as a politician and brave officer, induced me to proceed.

I passed through all the parishes on the river Sorrel, to a parish at the mouth of the same, which is called by the same name, preaching politics; and went from thence across the Sorrel to the river St Lawrence, and up the river through the parishes to Longale, and so far met with good success as an itinerant. In this round, my guard was Canadians (my interpreter and some few attendants excepted). On the morning of the 24th day of September, I set out with my guard of about eighty men from Longale, to go to Lapraier; from whence I determined to go to general Montgomery's camp; but had not advanced two miles before I met with major Brown (who has since been advanced to the rank of a Col.) who desired me to halt, saying that he had something of importance to communicate to me and my confidents; upon which I halted the party, and went into an house, and took a private room with him and several of my associates, where colonel Brown proposed that, 'Provided I would return to Longale, and procure some canoes, so as to cross the river St Lawrence a little north of Montreal, he would cross it a little to the south of the town, with near two hundred men, as he had boats sufficient; and that we would make ourselves masters of Montreal.' ... This plan was readily approved by me and those in council; and in consequence of which I returned to Longale collected a few canoes, and added about thirty English Americans to my party, and crossed the river in the night of the 24th, agreeable to the before proposed plan. My whole party, at this time, consisted of about one hundred and ten men, near eighty of whom were Canadians. We were the most of the night crossing the river, as we had so few canoes that they had to pass and repass three times, to carry my party across. Soon after day break, I set a guard between me and the town, with special orders, to let no person whatever pass or repass them, and another guard on in the other end of the road, with like directions; the mean time, I reconnoitered the best ground to make a defence expecting colonel Brown's party was landed on the other side of the town, he having (the day before) agreed to give three huzzas with his men early in the morning, which signal I was to return, that we might each know that both parties were landed; but the sun by this time being near two hours high, and the sign failing, I began to conclude myself to be in a premunire, and would have crossed the river back again, but I knew the enemy would have discovered such an attempt; and as there could not more than one third part of my troops cross at one time, the other two thirds would of course fall into their hands. This I could not reconcile to my own feelings as a man, much less as an officer: I therefore concluded to maintain the ground (if possible), and all to fare alike. In consequence of this resolution, I dispatched two messengers, one to Lapraire (to Col. Brown), and the other to Lasumprion (a French settlement) to Mr Walker, who was in our interest, requesting their speedy assistance; giving them at the same time, to understand my critical situation: in the mean time, sundry persons came to my guards, pretending to be friends, but were by them taken prisoners and brought to me. These I ordered to confinement, till their friendship could be further confirmed; for I was jealous they were spies, as they proved to be afterwards: one of the principal of them making his escape, exposed the weakness of my party, which was the final cause of my misfortune; for I have been since informed that Mr Walker, agreeable to my desire, exerted himself, and had raised a considerable number of men for my assistance, which brought him into difficulty afterwards; but upon hearing of my misfortune, disbanded them again.

The town of Montreal was in a great tumult. Gen. Carlton and the royal party made every preparation to go on board their vessels of force (as I was afterwards informed), but the spy escaping from my guard to the town, occasioned an alteration in their policy, and emboldened

Gen. Carlton to send the force, which he had there collected, out against me. I had previously chosen my ground, but when I saw the number of the enemy, as they sailed out of the town, I perceived it would be a day of trouble, if not of rebuke; but I had no chance to fly, as Montreal was situated on an island, and the river St Lawrence cut off my communication to Gen. Montgomery's camp. I encouraged my soldiery to bravely defend themselves, that we should soon have help, and that we should be able to keep the ground, if no more. This, and much more I affirmed with the greatest seeming assurance, and which in reality I thought to be in some degree probable.

The enemy consisted of not more than forty regular troops, together with a mixed multitude, chiefly Canadians, with a number of English who lived in the town, and some Indians; in all to the number of 500.

The reader will notice that most of my party were Canadians; indeed it was a motley parcel of soldiery which composed both parties. However, the enemy began the attack from woodpiles, ditches, buildings, and such like places, at a considerable distance, and I returned the fire from a situation more than equally advantageous. The attack began between two and three of the clock in the afternoon, just before which I ordered a volunteer, by the name of Richard Young, with a detachment of nine men as a flank guard, which, under the cover of the bank of the river, could not only annoy the enemy, but at the same time, serve as a flank guard to the left of the main body.

The fire continued for some time on both sides; and I was confident that such a remote method of attack, could not carry the ground (provided it should be continued till night): but near half the body of the enemy began to flank round to my right: upon which I ordered a volunteer, by the name of John Dugan, who had lived many years in Canada, and understood the French language, to detach about fifty of the Canadians, and post himself at an advantageous ditch, which was on my right to prevent my being surrounded: he advanced with the detachment, but instead of occupying his post, made his escape, as did likewise Mr Young upon the left, with their detachments. I soon perceived that the enemy was in possession of the ground, which Dugan should have occupied. At this time I had but forty-five men with me; some of whom were wounded: the enemy kept closing round me, nor was it in my power to prevent it, by which means, my situation which was advantageous in the first part of the attack, ceased to be so in the last; and being almost entirely surrounded but with such vast unequal numbers,

I ordered a retreat, but found that those of the enemy, who were of the country, and their Indians, could run as fast as my men, though the regulars could not. Thus I retreated near a mile, and some of the enemy, with the savages, kept flanking me and others crowded hard in the rear: in fine I expected in a very short time, to try the world of spirits; for I was apprehensive that no quarter would be given to me, and therefore had determined to sell my life as dear as I could. One of the enemy's officers boldly pressing in the rear, discharged his fusee at me; the ball whistled near me, as did many others that day. I returned the salute, and missed him, as running had put us both out of breath; for I conclude we were not frightened, I then saluted him with my tongue in a harsh manner, and told him that inasmuch as his numbers were so far superior to mine, I would surrender, provided I could be treated with honor, and be assured of good quarter for myself and the men who were with me, and he answered I should; another officer coming up directly after, confirmed the treaty; upon which I agreed to surrender with my party, which then consisted of thirty-one effective men, and seven wounded. I ordered them to ground their arms which they did.

The officer I capitulated with, then directed me and my party to advance towards him, which was done, I handed him my sword, and in half a minute after a savage, part of whose head was shaved, being almost naked and painted, with feathers intermixed with the hair of the other side of his head, came running to me with an incredible swift-ness; he seemed to advance with more than mortal speed (as he approached near me, his hellish visage was beyond all description, snakes eyes appear innocent in comparison of his, his features extorted, malice, death, murder, and the wrath of devils and damned spirits are the emblems of his countenance) and in less than twelve feet of me, presented his firelock; at the instant, of his present, I twitched the officer to whom I gave my sword, between me and the savage, but he flew round with great fury, trying to single me out to shoot me without killing the officer; but by this time I was near as nimble as he, keeping the officer in such a position that his danger was my defence, but in less than half a minute, I was attacked by just such another imp of hell; then I made the officer fly around with incredible velocity, for a few seconds of time, when I perceived a Canadian (who had lost one eye as appeared afterwards) taking my part against the savages; and in an instant an Irishman came to my assistance with a fixed bayonet, and drove away the fiends, swearing by Jasus he would kill them. This tragic scene composed my mind. The escaping from so awful a death, made even imprisonment happy, the more so as my conquerors on the field treated me with great civility and politeness.

The regular officers said that they were very happy to see Col. Allen, I answered them that I should rather chose to have seen them at Gen. Montgomery's camp; the gentlemen replied, that they gave full credit to what I said, and as I walked to the town, which was (as I should guess) more than two miles, a British officer walking at my right hand, and one of the French noblesse at my left; the latter of which in the action, had his eyebrow carried away by a glancing shot, but was nevertheless very merry and facetious, and no abuse was offered me till I came to the barrackyard at Montreal, where I met Gen. Prescott, who asked me my name, which I told him, he then asked me, whether I was that Col. Allen, who took Ticonderoga, I told him I was the very man; then he shook his cane over my head, calling many hard names, among which he frequently used the word rebel, and put himself in a great rage. I told him he would do well not to cane me, for I was not accustomed to it, and shook my fist at him, telling him that that was the beetle of mortality for him, if he offered to strike; upon which Capt. M'Cloud of the British, pulled him by the skirt, and whispered to him (as he afterwards told me) to this import; that it was inconsistent with his honor to strike a prisoner. He then ordered a sergeant's command with fixed bayonets to come forward and kill 13 Canadians, which were included in the treaty aforesaid.

It cut me to the heart to see the Canadians in so hard a case, in consequence of their having been true to me; they were wringing their hands, saying their prayers (as I concluded), and expected immediate death. I therefore stepped between the executioners and the Canadians, opened my clothes, and told Gen. Prescott to thrust his bayonets into my breast, for I was the sole cause of the Canadians taking up arms.

The guard in the mean time, rolling their eyeballs from the General to me, as though impatient waiting his dread commands to sheath their bayonets in my heart; I could however plainly discern, that he was in a suspence and quandary about the matter: this gave me additional hopes of succeeding, for my design was not to die but save the Canadians by finesse. The General stood a minute, when he made the following reply: 'I will not execute you now, but you shall grace a halter at Tyburn, God damn ye.'

I remember I disdained his mentioning such a place, I was notwith-standing a little inwardly pleased with the expression, as it significantly conveyed to me the idea of postponing the present appearance of death; besides his sentence was by no means final, as to 'gracing a halter' although I had anxiety about it after I landed in England, as the reader will find in the course of this history. Gen. Prescott then ordered one of his officers to take me on board the *Gaspee* schooner of War, and confine me, hands and feet, in irons, which was done the same afternoon I was taken.

The action continued an hour and three quarters by the watch, and I know not to this day how many of my men were killed, though I am certain there were but few; if I remember right, seven were wounded, one of them, William Stewart by name, was wounded by a savage with a tomahawk, after he was taken prisoner and disarmed, but was rescued by some of the generous enemy; and so far recovered his wounds, that he afterwards went with the other prisoners to England.

Of the enemy were killed a major Carden, who had been wounded in eleven different battles, and an eminent merchant, Patterson of Montreal, and some others, but I never knew the whole loss, as their accounts were different. I am apprehensive that it is rare, that so much ammunition was expended, and so little execution done by it; though such of my party as stood the ground, behaved with great fortitude, much exceeding that of the enemy, but were not the best of marksmen, and I am apprehensive, were all killed or taken: the wounded were all put into the hospital at Montreal, and those that were not, were put on board different vessels in the river and shackled together in pairs, viz. two men fastened together by one hand cuff, being closely fixed to one wrist of each of them, and treated with the greatest severity, nay as criminals.

I now come to the description of the irons, which were put on me; the hand cuff was of a common size and form, but my leg irons (I should imagine) would weigh thirty pounds; the bar was eight feet long, and very substantial; the shackles which encompassed my ancles, were very tight I was told by the officer who put them on, that it was the king's plate, and I heard other of their officers say, that it would weigh forty weight. The irons were so close upon my ancles, that I could not lie down in any other manner than on my back, I was put into the lowest and most wretched part of the vessel, where I got the favour of a chest to sit on, the same answered for my bed at night, and having procured some little blocks of the guard (who day and night, with fixed bayonets, watched over me) to lay under each end of the large bar of my leg irons, to preserve my ancles from galling, while I sat on the chest, or lay back on the same, though most of the time, night and day, I sat on it; but at length having a desire to lay down on my side, which the closeness of the irons forbid, desired the Captain to loosen them for that purpose, but was denied the favor: the Captain's name was Royal, who did not seem to be an ill natured man; but often times said, that his express orders were to treat me with such severity, which was disagreeable to his own feelings; nor did he ever insult me, though many others who came on board did. One of the officers, by the name of Bradley, was very generous to me, he would often send me victuals from his own table; nor did a day fail, but that he sent me a good drink of grog.

The reader is now invited back to the time I was put in irons. I requested the privilege to write to Gen. Prescott, which was granted. I reminded him of the kind and generous manner of my treatment to the prisoners I took at Ticonderoga; the injustice and ungentleman like usage, which I had met with from him, and demanded gentleman like usage, but received no answer from him. I soon after wrote to Gen. Carlton, which met the same success. In the mean while many of those who were permitted to see me, were very insulting.

I was confined in the manner I have related, on board the *Gaspee* schooner, about six weeks; during which time I was obliged to throw out plenty of extravagant language, which answered certain purposes (at that time), better than to grace a history.

To give an instance upon being insulted, in a fit of anger I twisted off a nail with my teeth, which I took to be a ten-penny nail; it went through the mortise of the bar of my hand cuff, and at the same time I swaggered over those who abused me; particularly a Doctor Dace, who told me that I was outlawed by New York, and deserved death for several years past; was at last fully ripened for the halter, and in a fair way to obtain it: when I challenged him, he excused himself in consequence, as he said, of my being a criminal; but I flung such a flood of language at him that it shocked him and the spectators, for my anger was very great. I heard one say, damn him can he eat iron? After that a small padlock was fixed to the hand cuff, instead of the nail, and as they were mean-spirited in their treatment to me; so it appeared to me, that they were equally timorous and cowardly.

I was after sent with the prisoners taken with me to an armed vessel in the river, which lay off against Quebec, under the command of Capt. M'Cloud of the British, who treated me in a very generous and obliging manner, and according to my rank; in about twenty four hours I bid him farewell with regret; but my good fortune still continued; the name of the captain of the vessel I was put on board, was Little John, who, with his officers, behaved in a polite, generous and friendly manner. I lived with them in the cabin, and fared on the best, my irons being taken off, contrary to the order he had received from the commanding officer; but Capt. Little John swore, that a brave man should not be used as a rascal on board his ship.

Thus I found myself in possession of happiness once more, and the evils I had lately suffered, gave me an uncommon relish for it.

Captain Little John used to go to Quebec almost every day, in order to pay his respects to certain gentlemen and ladies; being there on a certain day, he happened to meet with some disagreeable treatment, as he imagined, from a lieutenant of a man of war, and one word brought on another till the lieutenant challenged him to a duel on the plains of Abraham. Captain Little John was a gentleman, who entertained a high sense of honour, and could do no less than accept the challenge.

At nine o'clock the next morning they were to fight. The Captain returned in the evening, and acquainted his lieutenant and me with the affair: his lieutenant was a high-blooded Scotchman as well as himself, who replied to his captain that he should not want for a second. With this I interrupted him, and gave the captain to understand, that since an opportunity had presented, I would be glad to testify my gratitude to him, by acting the part of a faithful second, on which he gave me his hand, and said that he wanted no better man. Says he, 'I am a king's officer, and you a prisoner under my care; you must therefore go with me to the place appointed in disguise' and added further, 'You must engage to me, upon the honour of a gentleman, that whether I die or live, or whatever happens, provided you live, that you will return to my lieutenant, on board this ship.' All this I solemnly engaged him; the combatants were to discharge each a pocket pistol, and then to fall on with their iron-hilted muckle whangers; and one of that sort was allotted for me; but some British officers, who interposed early in the morning, settled the controversy without fighting.

Now having enjoyed eight or nine days happiness, from the polite and generous treatment of Captain Little John and his officers, I was obliged to bid them farewell, parting with them in as friendly a manner as we had lived together, which, to the best of my memory, was the eleventh of November, when a detachment of Gen. Arnold's little army appeared on Point Levy, opposite Quebec, who had performed an extraordinary march through a wilderness country, with design to have surprised the capital of Canada. I was then taken on board a vessel called the *Adamant*, together with the prisoners taken with me, and put under the power of an English merchant from London, whose name was Brook Watson, a man of malicious and cruel disposition, and who was probably excited in the exercise of his malevolence, by a junto of tories, who sailed with him to England; among whom were Col. Guy Johnson, Col. Closs, and their attendants and associates, to the number of about thirty.

All the ship's crew (Col. Closs in his personal behaviour excepted) behaved towards the prisoners with that spirit of bitterness, which is the peculiar characteristic of tories, when they have the friends of America in their power, measuring their loyalty to the English king, by the barbarity, fraud and deceit which they exercise towards the whigs.

A small place in the vessel, enclosed with white-oak plank, was assigned for the prisoners, and for me among the rest; I should imagine that it was no more than twenty feet one way, and twenty-two the other. Into this place we were all, to the number of thirty-four, thrust and hand-cuffed (two prisoners more being added to our number), and were provided with two excrement tubs; in this circumference we were obliged to eat and perform the office of evacuation, during the voyage to England; and were insulted by every blackguard sailor and tory on board, in the cruelest manner; but what is the most surprising is, that not one of us died in the passage. When I was first ordered to go into the filthy inclosure, through a small sort of door, I positively refused, and endeavoured to reason the before named Brook Watson out of a conduct so derogatory to every sentiment of honour and humanity; but all to no purpose, my men being forced in the den already, and the rascal who had the charge of the prisoners commanded me to go immediately in among the rest; he further added, that the place was good enough for a rebel, that it was impertinent for a capital offender to talk of honour or humanity; that any thing short of a halter was too good for me, and that that would be my portion soon after I landed in England, for which purpose only I was sent thither. About the same time a lieutenant among the tories, insulted me in a grievous manner, saying that I ought to have been executed for my rebellion against New York, and spit in my face; upon which, though I was hand-cuffed, I sprang at him with both hands and knocked him partly down, but he scrambled along into the cabin, and I after him; there he got under the protection of some men with fixed bayonets, who were ordered to make ready to drive me into the place afore-mentioned. I challenged him to fight, notwithstanding the impediments that were on my hands, and had the exalted pleasure to see the rascal tremble for fear; his name I have forgot, but Watson ordered his guard to get me into the place with the other prisoners, dead or alive; and I had almost as leave die as do it, standing it out till they environed me round with bayonets; and brutish, prejudiced, abandoned wretches they were, from whom I could expect nothing but death or wounds: however, I told them, that they were good honest fellows, that I could not blame them, that I was only in a dispute with a callico merchant, who knew not how to behave towards a gentleman of the military establishment. This was spoke rather to appease them for my own preservation, as well as to treat Watson with contempt; but still I found that they were determined to force me into the wretched circumstances, which their prejudiced and depraved minds had prepared for me: therefore rather than die, I submitted to their indignities, being drove with bayonets into the filthy dungeon, with the other prisoners, where we were denied fresh water, except a small allowance, which was very inadequate for our wants; and in consequence of the stench of the place, each of us was soon followed with a diarrhoea and fever, which occasioned an intolerable thirst. When we asked for water, we were most commonly (instead of obtaining it) insulted and derided; and to add to all the horrors of the place, it was so dark that we could not see each other, and were overspread with body lice. We had, notwithstanding these severities, full allowance of salt provisions, and a gill of rum per day; the latter of which was of the utmost service to us, and probably was the means of saving several of our lives. About forty days we existed in this manner, when the land's end of England was discovered from the mast head; soon after which the prisoners were taken from their gloomy abode, being permitted to see the light of the sun, and breathe fresh air, which to us was very refreshing. The day following we landed at Falmouth.

A few days before I was taken prisoner, I shifted my cloaths, by which I happened to be taken in Canadian dress, viz. a short fawn skin jacket, double-breasted, an under vest and breeches of sagathy, worsted stockings, a decent pair of shoes, two plain skirts, and a red worsted cap;

this was all the cloathing I had, in which I made my appearance in England.

When the prisoners were landed, multitudes of the citizens of Falmouth, excited by curiosity, crowded together to see us, which was equally gratifying to us. I saw numbers of people on the tops of houses, and the rising adjacent grounds were covered with them of both sexes; the throng was so great, that the king's officers were obliged to draw their swords, and force a passage to Pendennis Castle, which was near a mile from the town, where we were closely confined, in consequence of orders from Gen. Carlton, who then commanded in Canada.

The rascally Brook Watson then set out for London in great haste, expecting the reward of his zeal; but the ministry received him (as I have been since informed) rather coolly; for the minority in parliament took advantage, arguing that the opposition of America to Great Britain, was not a rebellion ... 'If it is' say they, 'why do you not execute Col. Allen, according to law?' ... But the majority argued, that I ought to be executed, and that the opposition was really a rebellion, but that policy obliged them not to do it, inasmuch as the Congress had then most prisoners in their power; so that my being sent to England for the purpose of being executed, and necessity restraining them, was rather a foil on their laws and authority, and they consequently disapproved of my being sent thither ... But I never had heard the least hint of those debates in parliament, or of the working of their policy, till some time after I left England.

Consequently the reader will readily conceive I was anxious about my preservation, knowing that I was in the power of a haughty and cruel nation, and considered as such; therefore the first proposition which I determined in my own mind was, that humanity and moral suasion would not be consulted in the determination of my fate; and those that daily came in great numbers, out of curiosity to see me, both gentle and simple united in this, that I would be hanged. A gentleman from America, by the name of Temple, and who was friendly to me, just whispered me in the ear, and told me, that bets were laid in London that I would be executed; he likewise privately gave me a guinea, but durst say but little to me.

However, agreeable to my first negative proposition, that moral virtue would not influence my destiny, I had recourse to stratagem, which I was in hopes would move in the circle of their policy. I requested of the commander of the castle the privilege of writing to Congress, who, after consulting with an officer that lived in town, of a superior rank, permitted me to write. I wrote, in the fore part of the letter, a short narrative of my ill treatment; but withal let them know, that I was treated as a criminal in England, and continued in irons, together with those taken with me, yet it was in consequence of the orders which the commander of the castle received from Gen. Carlton; and therefore desired Congress to desist from matters of retaliation, till they should know the result of the government of England, respecting their treatment of me, and the prisoners with me, and govern themselves accordingly; with a particular request, that if retaliation should be found necessary, that it might be exercised not according to the smallness of my character in America, but in proportion to the importance of the cause for which I suffered . . . this is, according to my present recollection, the substance of the letter, subscribed, 'To the illustrious Continental Congress.' This letter was wrote with a view that it should be sent to the ministry at London rather than to Congress, with a design to intimidate the haughty English government, and screen my neck from the halter.

The next day the officer from whom I obtained licence to write, came to see me, and frowned on me on account of the impudence of the letter (as he phrased it) and further added, 'Do you think that we are fools in England, and would send your letter to Congress, with instructions to retaliate on our own people; I have sent your letter to Lord North.' This gave me inward satisfaction, though I carefully concealed it with a pretended resentment, for I found I had come yankee over him, and that the letter had gone to the identical person I designed it for. Nor do I know, to this day, but that it had the desired effect though I have not heard anything of the letter since.

My personal treatment by Lieutenant Hamilton, who commanded the castle, was very generous. He sent me every day a fine breakfast and dinner from his own table, and a bottle of good wine. Another aged gentleman, whose name I cannot recollect, sent me a good supper; but there was no distinction in public support between me and the privates; we all lodged on a sort of Dutch bunks, in one common apartment, and were allowed straw. The privates were well supplied with fresh provision, and, with me, took effectual measures to rid ourselves of lice.

I could not but feel inwardly extreme anxious for my fate; this I however carefully concealed from the prisoners, as well as from the enemy, who were perpetually shaking the halter at me. I nevertheless treated them with scorn and contempt; and having sent my letter to the ministry, could conceive of nothing more in my power but to keep my spirits and behave in a daring soldier-like manner, that I might exhibit a good sample of American fortitude. Such a conduct I judged would have a more probable tendency to my preservation than concession and timidity. This, therefore, was my deportment, and I had lastly determined in my own mind, that if a cruel death must inevitably be my portion, I would face it undaunted, and though I greatly rejoice that I have returned to my country and friends, and to see the power and pride of Great Britain humbled, yet I am confident that I could then die without the least appearance of dismay.

I now clearly recollect that my mind was so resolved, that I would not have trembled or shewn the least fear, nor do more than reproach my memory, make my last act despicable to my enemies, and eclipse the other actions of my life. For I reasoned thus, that nothing was more common than for men to die, with their friends round them, weeping and lamenting over them, but not able to help them, which was in reality not different in the consequence of it from such a death as I was apprehensive of; and as death was the natural consequence of animal life to which the laws of nature subject mankind, to be timorous and uneasy as to the event or manner of it was inconsistent with the character of a philosopher or soldier. The cause I was engaged in, I ever viewed worthy hazarding my life for, nor was I (at the critical moments of trouble) sorry that I engaged in it; and as to the world of spirits, though I knew nothing of the mode or manner of it, expected nevertheless, when I should arrive at such a world, that I should be as well treated as other gentlemen of my merit.

Among the great numbers of people, who came to the castle to see the prisoners, some gentlemen told me, that they had come 50 miles on purpose to see me, and desired to ask me a number of questions, and to make free with me in conversation. I gave for answer, that I chose freedom in every sense of the word: then one of them asked me what my occupation in life had been? I answered him, that in my younger days I had studied divinity, but was a conjurer by passion. He replied, that I conjured wrong at the time I was taken; and I was obliged to own, that I mistook a figure at that time, but that I had conjured them out of Ticonderoga. This was a place of great notoriety in England, so that the joke seemed to go in my favour.

It was a common thing for me to be taken out of close confinement, into a spacious green in the castle, or rather parade, where numbers of gentlemen and ladies were ready to see and hear me. I often entertained such audiences, with harangues on the impracticability of Great Britain's conquering the (then) colonies of America. At one of these times I asked a gentleman for a bowl of punch, and he ordered his servant to bring it, which he did, and offered it me, but I refused to take it from the hand of his servant; he then gave it to me with his own hand, refusing to drink with me in consequence of my being a state criminal: however I took the punch and drank it all down at one draught, and handed the gentleman the bowl: this made the spectators as well as myself merry.

I expatiated on American freedom: this gained the resentment of a young beardless gentleman of the company, who gave himself very great airs, and replied, that he 'knew the Americans very well' and was certain that they could 'not bear the smell of powder.' I replied, that I accepted it as a challenge, and was ready to convince him on the spot, that an American could bear the smell of powder; at which he answered he should not put himself on a par with me. I then demanded of him to treat the character of the Americans with due respect: he answered that I was an Irishman; but I assured him, that I was a *full blooded Yankee*, and in fine, bantered him so much, that he left me in possession of the ground, and the laugh went against him. Two clergymen came to see me, and inasmuch as they behaved with civility, I returned them the same: we discoursed on several parts of moral philosophy and christianity; and they seemed to be surprized, that I should be acquainted with such topics, or that I should understand a syllogism or regular mood of argumentation. I am apprehensive my Canadian dress contributed not a little to the surprize, and excitement of curiosity: to see a gentleman in England, regularly dressed and well behaved, would be no sight at all; but such a rebel, as they were pleased to call me, it is probable was never before seen in England.

The prisoners were landed at Falmouth a few days before Christmas, and ordered on board of the *Solebay* frigate, Captain Symonds, the eighth day of January, 1776, when our hand irons were taken off. This remove was in consequence (as I have been since informed) of a writ of habeas corpus, which had been procured by some gentlemen in England, in order to obtain me my liberty.

The *Solebay* with several other men of war, and about forty transports, rendezvoused at the cove of Cork, in Ireland, to take in provision and water.

When we were first brought on board, Captain Symonds ordered all the prisoners, and most of the hands on board, to go on the deck, and caused to be read in their hearing, a certain code of laws, or rules for the regulation and ordering of their behaviour; and then in a sovereign manner, ordered the prisoners, me in particular, off the deck, and never to come on it again; for said he, this is a place for gentlemen to walk. So I went off, an officer following me, who told me, that he would shew me the place allotted for me, and took me down to the cable tire, saying to me, this is your place.

Prior to this I had taken cold, by which I was in an ill state of health, and did not say much to the officer; but stayed there that night, consulted my policy, and found I was in an evil case; that a Captain of a man of war was more arbitrary than a king, as he could view his territory with a look of his eye, and a movement of his finger commanded obedience ... I felt myself more desponding than I had done at any time before; for I concluded it to be a governmental scheme, to do that clandestinely, which policy forbid me to be done under sanction of public justice and law.

However, two days after I shaved and cleansed myself as well as I could, and went on deck. The Captain spoke to me in a great rage, and said 'Did I not order you not to come on deck?' I answered him, that at the same time he said, 'That it was a place for gentlemen to walk;' That I was Colonel Allen, but had not been properly introduced to him. He replied, 'G-d damn you, Sir, be careful not to walk the same side of the deck that I do.' This gave encouragement, and ever after that I walked in the manner he had directed, except when he (at certain times afterwards) ordered me off in a passion, and then would directly afterwards go on again, telling him to command his slaves, that I was a gentleman, and had a right to walk the deck; yet when he expressly ordered me off, I obeyed, not out of obedience to him, but to set an example to his ship's crew, who ought to obey him—

To walk to the windward side of the deck, is according to custom the prerogative of the Captain of the man of war, though he oftentimes, nay commonly walks with his Lieutenants, when no strangers are by; when a captain from some other man of war, comes on board, the Captains walk to the windward side, and the other gentlemen to the leeward.

It was but a few nights I lodged in the cable tire, before I gained acquaintance with the master of arms; his name was Gillegin, an Irishman, who was a generous and well disposed man, and in a friendly manner, made me a proffer of lying with him in a little birth, which was allotted him between decks, and enclosed with canvas; his preferment on board was about equal to that of a sergeant in a regiment, I was comparatively happy in the acceptance of his clemency, and lived with him in friendship, till the frigate anchored in the harbour of cape Fear, North Carolina, in America.

Abigail Adams

1744–1818

*Wife of the second President of the United States and
mother of the sixth, Abigail Adams was involved in many
of the turbulent events of 1776 through her brave refusal
to leave Boston during the troubles. The following letters
to her husband give a vivid insight into the uncertainties
of those times.*

PLYMOUTH, 17 JUNE, 1776, A REMARKABLE DAY.

I THIS DAY received by the hands of our worthy friend a large packet,
which has refreshed and comforted me. Your own sensations have ever
been similar to mine. I need not then tell you how gratified I am at
the frequent tokens of remembrance with which you favor me, nor how
they rouse every tender sensation of my soul, which sometimes will
find vent at my eyes. Nor dare I describe how earnestly I long to fold

to my fluttering heart the object of my warmest affections; the idea soothes me. I feast upon it with a pleasure known only to those whose hearts and hopes are one.

The approbation you give to my conduct in the management of our private affairs is very grateful to me, and sufficiently compensates for all my anxieties and endeavors to discharge the many duties devolved upon me in consequence of the absence of my dearest friend. Were they discharged according to my wishes, I should merit the praises you bestow.

You see I date from Plymouth. I came upon a visit to our amiable friends, accompanied by my sister Betsey, a day or two ago. It is the first night I have been absent since you left me. Having determined upon this visit for some time, I put my family in order and prepared for it, thinking I might leave it with safety. Yet, the day I set out I was under many apprehensions, by the coming in of ten transports, which were seen to have many soldiers on board, and the determination of the people to go and fortify upon Long Island, Pettick's Island, Nantasket, and Great Hill. It was apprehended they would attempt to land somewhere, but the next morning I had the pleasure to hear they were all driven out, *Commodore* and all; not a transport, a ship, or tender to be seen. This shows what might have been long ago done. Had this been done in season, the ten transports, with many others, in all probability would have fallen into our hands; but the progress of wisdom is slow.

Since I arrived here I have really had a scene quite novel to me. The brig *Defence*, from Connecticut, put in here for ballast. The officers, who are all from thence, and who are intimately acquainted at Dr Lathrop's, invited his lady to come on board, and bring with her as many of her friends as she could collect. She sent an invitation to our friend, Mrs Warren, and to us. The brig lay about a mile and a half from town. The officers sent their barge, and we went. Every mark of respect and attention which was in their power, they showed us. She is a fine brig, mounts sixteen guns, twelve swivels, and carries one hundred and twenty men. A hundred and seventeen were on board, and no private family ever appeared under better regulation than the crew. It was as still as though there had been only half a dozen; not a profane word among any of them. The captain himself is an exemplary man (Harden his name); has been in nine sea engagements; says if he gets a man who swears, and finds he cannot reform him, he turns him on shore, yet is free to confess that it was the sin of his youth. He has one lieutenant, a very fine fellow, Smelden by name. We spent a very agreeable afternoon, and drank tea on board. They showed us their arms, which were sent by Queen Anne, and everything on board was a curiosity to me. They gave us a mock engagement with an enemy, and the manner of taking a ship. The young folks went upon the quarter-deck and danced. Some of their Jacks played very well upon the violin and German flute. The brig bears the Continental colors, and was fitted out by the Colony of Connecticut. As we set off from the brig, they fired their guns in honor of us, a ceremony I would very readily have dispensed with.

I pity you, and feel for you under all the difficulties you have to encounter. My daily petitions to Heaven for you are that you may have health, wisdom, and fortitude sufficient to carry you through the great and arduous business in which you are engaged, and that your endeavors may be crowned with success. Canada seems a dangerous and ill-fated place. It is reported here that General Thomas is no more, that he took the small-pox and died with it. Every day some circumstance arises which shows me the importance of having the distemper in youth. Dr Bulfinch has petitioned the General Court for leave to open a hospital somewhere, and it will be granted him. I shall, with all the children, be one of the first class, you may depend upon it.

I have just this moment heard that the brig which I was on board of on Saturday, and which sailed yesterday morning from this place, fell in with two transports, having each of them a hundred and fifty men on board, and took them, and has brought them into Nantasket Roads, under cover of the guns which are mounted there. I will add further particulars as soon as I am informed.

I am now better informed, and will give you the truth. The brig *Defence*, accompanied by a small privateer sailed in concert Sunday morning. About twelve o'clock they discovered two transports, and made for them. Two privateers, which were small, had been in chase of them, but finding the enemy was of much larger force, had run under Cohasset rocks. The *Defence* gave a signal gun to bring them out. Captain Burk, who accompanied the *Defence*, being a prime sailer, he came up first, and poured a broadside on board a sixteen gun brig. The *Defence* soon attacked her upon her bows. An obstinate engagement ensued. There was a continual blaze upon all sides for many hours, and it was near midnight before they struck. In the engagement, the *Defence* lost one man, and five wounded. With Burk, not one man received any damage; on board the enemy, fourteen killed, among whom was a major, and sixty wounded. They are part of the Highland soldiers. The other transport mounted six guns. When the fleet sailed out of this harbor last week, they blew up the lighthouse. They met six transports coming in, which they carried off with them. I hope we shall soon be in such a posture of defense as to bid them defiance.

I feel no great anxiety at the large armament designed against us. The remarkable interpositions of Heaven in our favour cannot be too gratefully acknowledged. He who fed the Israelites in the wilderness, 'who clothes the lilies of the field, and feeds the young ravens when they cry' will not forsake a people engaged in so righteous a cause, if we remember his loving-kindness. We wanted powder,—we have a supply. We wanted arms,—we have been favored in that respect. We wanted hard money,—twenty-two thousand dollars, and an equal value in plate, are delivered into our hands.

You mention your peas, your cherries and your strawberries, etc. Ours are but just in blossom. We have had the coldest spring I ever knew. Things are three weeks behind what they generally used to be. The corn looks poor. The season now is rather dry. I believe I did not understand you, when in a former letter you said, 'I want to resign my office, for a thousand reasons.' If you mean that of judge, I know not what to say. I know it will be a difficult and arduous station; but, divesting myself of private interest, which would lead me to be against your holding that office, I know of no person who is so well calculated to discharge the trust, or who I think would act a more conscientious part.

BOSTON, 13 JULY, 1776.

I must begin with apologizing to you for not writing since the 17th of June. I have really had so many cares upon my hands and mind, with a bad inflammation in my eyes, that I have not been able to write. I now date from Boston, where I yesterday arrived and was with all of our little ones innoculated for the small-pox . . .

As to news, we have taken several prizes since I wrote you, as you will see by the newspapers. The present report is of Lord Howe's coming with unlimited powers. However, suppose it is so, I believe he little thinks of treating with us as Independent States. How can any person yet dream of a settlement, accommodation, etc? They have neither the spirit nor the feeling of men. Yet I see some who never were called

Tories gratified with the idea of Lord Howe's being upon his passage with such powers!

SUNDAY, 14 JULY

By yesterday's post I received two letters dated 3d and 4th of July, and though your letters never fail to give me pleasure, be the subject what it will, yet it was greatly heightened by the prospect of the future happiness and glory of our country. Nor am I a little gratified when I reflect that a person so nearly connected with me has had the honor of being a principal actor in laying a foundation for its future greatness.

May the foundation of our new Constitution be Justice, Truth, Righteousness! Like the wise man's house, may it be founded upon these rocks, and then neither storms nor tempests will overthrow it!

I cannot but be sorry that some of the most manly sentiments in the Declaration are expunged from the printed copy. Perhaps wise reasons induced it.

I shall write you now very often. Pray inform me constantly of every important action. Every expression of tenderness is a cordial to my heart. Important as they are to the rest of the world, to me they are *everything*.

I suppose you have heard of a fleet which came up pretty near the Light and kept us all with our mouths open, ready to catch them, but after staying near a week, and making what observations they could, set sail and went off, to our great mortification, who were for them in every respect. If our ship of thirty-two guns which was built at Portsmouth, and waiting only for guns, and another at Plymouth in the same state, had been in readiness, we should in all probability have been masters of them. Where the blame lies in that respect I know not. 'Tis laid upon Congress, and Congress is also blamed for not appointing us a General. But Rome was not built in a day.

All our friends desire to be remember to you, and foremost in that number stands your

PORTIA.

BOSTON, 21 JULY, 1776

Last Thursday, after hearing a very good sermon, I went with the multitude into King Street to hear the Proclamation for Independence read and proclaimed. Some field-pieces with the train were brought there. The troops appeared under arms, and all the inhabitants assembled there (the small-pox prevented many thousands from the country), when Colonel Crafts read from the balcony of the State House the proclamation. Great attention was given to every word. As soon as he ended, the cry from the balcony was, 'God save our American States' and then three cheers which rent the air. The bells rang, the privateers fired, the forts and batteries, the cannon were discharged, the platoons followed, and every face appeared joyful. Mr Bowdoin then gave a sentiment, 'Stability and perpetuity to American independence.' After dinner, the King's Arms were taken down from the State House, and every vestige of him from every place in which it appeared, and burnt in King Street. Thus ends royal authority in this State. And all the people shall say Amen.

I have been a little surprised that we collect no better accounts with regard to the horrid conspiracy at New York; and that so little mention has been made of it here. It made a talk for a few days, but now seems all hushed in silence. The Tories say that it was not a conspiracy, but an association. And pretend that there was no plot to assassinate the General. Even their hardened hearts feel—the discovery—we have in George a match for 'a Borgia or a Catiline'—a wretch callous to every humane feeling. Our worthy preacher told us that he believed one of our great sins, for which a righteous God has come out in judgement against us, was our bigoted attachment to so wicked a man. May our repentance be sincere.

BOSTON, 14 AUGUST, 1776

Mr Smith called upon me to-day and told me he should set out to-morrow for Philadelphia; desired I would write by him. I have shown him all the civility in my power, since he has been here, though not all I have wished to. I was much pleased with the account he gave us of the universal joy of his province upon the establishment of their new government, and the harmony subsisting between every branch of it. This State seems to be behindhand of their neighbors. We want some master workman here. Those who are capable seem backward in this work, and some who are so tenacious of their own particular plan as to be loath to give it up. Some who are for abolishing both House and Council, affirming business was never so well done as in the provincial Congress, and they perhaps never so important.

Last Sunday, after service, the Declaration of Independence was read from the pulpit by order of Council. The Dr concluded with asking a blessing 'upon the United States of America even until the final restitution of all things.'

Dr Chauncy's address pleased me. The good man after having read it, lifted his eyes and hands to heaven. 'God bless the United States of America, and let all the people say Amen.'

One of his audience told me it universally struck them.

I have no news to write you. I am sure it will be none to tell you I am ever   Yours   PORTIA

14 AUGUST, 1776

Your letter of August 3 came by this day's post. I find it very convenient to be so handy. I can receive a letter at night, sit down and reply to it, and send it off in the morning.

You remark upon the deficiency of education in your countrymen. It never, I believe, was in a worse state, at least for many years. The college is not in the state one could wish. The scholars complain that their professor in philosophy is taken off by public business, to their great detriment. In this town I never saw so great a neglect of education. The poorer sort of children are wholly neglected, and left to range the streets, without schools, without business, given up to all evil. The town is not, as formerly, divided into wards. There is either too much business left upon the hands of a few, or too little care to do it. We daily see the necessity of a regular government.

You speak of our worthy brother. I often lament it, that a man so peculiarly formed for the education of youth, and so well qualified as he is in many branches of literature, excelling in philosophy and the mathematics, should not be employed in some public station. I know not the person who would make half so good a successor to Dr Winthrop. He has a peculiar, easy manner of communicating his ideas to youth; and the goodness of his heart and the purity of his morals, without an affected austerity, must have a happy effect upon the minds of pupils.

If you complain of neglect of education in sons, what shall I say with regard to daughters, who every day experience the want of it? With regard to the education of my own children, I find myself soon out of my depth, destitute and deficient in every part of education.

I most sincerely wish that some more liberal plan might be laid and executed for the benefit of the rising generation, and that our new Constitution may be distinguished for encouraging learning and virtue. If we mean to have heroes, statesmen, and philosophers, we should have learned women. The world perhaps would laugh at me and accuse me of vanity, but you, I know, have a mind too enlarged and liberal to disregard the sentiment. If much depends, as is allowed, upon the early education of youth, and the first principles which are instilled take the deepest root, great benefit must arise from literary accomplishments in women.

Excuse me. My pen has run away with me. I have no thoughts of coming to Philadelphia. The length of time I have and shall be detained here would have prevented me, even if you had no thoughts of returning till December; but I live in daily expectation of seeing you here. Your health I think, requires your immediate return. I expected Mr G—— would have set off before now, but he perhaps finds it very hard to leave his mistress. I won't say harder than some do to leave their wives. Mr Gerry stood very high in my esteem. What is meat for one is not for another. No accounting for fancy. She is a queer dame and leads people wild dances.

But hush! Post, don't betray your trust and lose my letter.

PORTIA.

BOSTON, 25 AUGUST, 1776

I sent Johnny last evening to the post-office for letters. He soon returned, and pulling one from under his gown gave it me. The young rogue, smiling and watching mamma's countenance, draws out another and then another, highly gratified to think he had so many presents to bestow.

I took the liberty of sending my compliments to General Lincoln, and asking him some questions which you proposed to me, but which I was totally unable to answer, and he has promised a particular reply to them.

As to provisions, there is no scarcity. 'Tis true they are high, but that is more owing to the advanced price of labor than the scarcity. English goods of every kind are not purchasable, at least by me. They are extravagantly high. West India goods articles are very high, all except sugars, which have fallen half since I came into town. Our New England rum is four shillings per gallon; molasses the same price; loaf sugar two and fourpence; cotton-wool four shillings per pound; sheep's wool two shillings; flax one and sixpence. In short, one hundred pounds two years ago would purchase more than two would now.

House rent in this town is very low. Some of the best and genteelest houses rent for twenty pounds a year. Ben Hallowell's has been offered for ten and Mr Chardon's for thirteen pounds six shillings and eight pence.

The privateer *Independence,* which sailed from Plymouth about three weeks ago, has taken a Jamaica man laden with sugars, and sent her into Marblehead last Saturday. I hear the *Defence* has taken another. I think we made a fine haul of prizes.

Colonel Quincy desires me to ask you whether you have received a letter from him; he wrote you some time ago.

I like Dr Franklin's device for a seal. It is such a one as will please most; at least it will be most agreeable to the spirit of New England.

We have not any news here—anxiously waiting the event, and in daily expectation of hearing tidings from New York. Heaven grant they may be glorious for our country and countrymen. Then will I glory in being an American. Ever, Ever yours,   PORTIA.

PS. We are in such want of lead as to be obliged to take down the leads from the windows in this town.

BOSTON, 29 AUGUST, 1776

I have spent the three days past almost entirely with you. The weather has been stormy. I have had little company, and I amused myself in my closet, reading over the letters I have received from you since I have been here.

I have possession of my aunt's chamber, in which, you know, is a very convenient, pretty closet, with a window which looks into her flower garden. In this closet are a number of bookshelves, which are but poorly furnished. However I have a pretty little desk or cabinet here, where I write all my letters and keep my papers, unmolested by any one. I do not covet my neighbor's goods, but I should like to be the owner of such conveniences. I always had a fancy for a closet with a window, which I could more particularly call my own.

I feel anxious for a post day, and am full as solicitous for two letters a week, and as uneasy if I do not get them, as I used to be when I got but one in a month or five weeks. Thus do I presume upon indulgence, and this is human nature. It brings to my mind a sentiment of one of your correspondents, to wit, that 'man is the only animal who is hungry with his belly full.'

Last evening Dr Cooper came in and brought me your favor, from the post-office, of August 16, and Colonel Whipple arrived yesterday morning and delivered to me the two bundles you sent and a letter of the 12th of August. They have already afforded me much amusement, and I expect much more from them.

I am sorry to find from your last, as well as from some others of your letters, that you feel so dissatisfied with the office to which you are chosen. Though in your acceptance of it I know you were actuated by the purest motives, and I know of no person here so well qualified to discharge the important duties of it, yet I will not urge you to it. In accepting of it you must be excluded from all other employments. There never will be a salary adequate to the importance of the office or to support you and your family from penury. If you possessed a fortune I would urge you to it, in spite of all the fleers and gibes of minds which themselves are incapable of acting a disinterested part, and have no conception that others can. I have never heard any one speak about it, nor did I know that such insinuations had been thrown out.

Pure and disinterested virtue must ever be its own reward. Mankind are too selfish and too depraved to discern the pure gold from the baser metal.

I wish for peace and tranquility. All my desire and all my ambition is to be esteemed and loved by my partner, to join with him in the education and instruction of our little ones, to sit under our own vines in peace, liberty and safety.

Adieu, my dearest friend! Soon, soon return to your most affectionate

PORTIA.

PS. A very odd report has been propagated in Braintree, namely, that you were poisoned upon your return, at New York.

BRAINTREE, 9 SEPTEMBER, 1776

This night our good uncle came from town and brought me yours of August 20, 21, 25, 27, and 28, for all of which I most sincerely thank you. I have felt uneasy to hear from you. The report of your being dead has no doubt reached you by Bass, who heard enough of it before he came away. It took its rise among the Tories, who, as Swift said of himself, 'By their fears betray their hopes.' How they should ever take it into their heads that you was poisoned at New York, a fortnight before that we heard anything of that villain Zedwitz's plan of poisoning the waters of the city, I cannot tell. I am sometimes ready to suspect that there is a communication between the Tories of every State; for they seem to know all news that is passing before it is known by the Whigs.

We have had many stories concerning engagements upon Long Island this week; of our lines being forced and of our troops returning to New York. Particulars we have not yet obtained. All we can learn is that we have been unsuccessful there; having lost many men as prisoners, among whom are Lord Stirling and General Sullivan.

But if we should be defeated, I think we shall not be conquered. A people fired like the Romans with love of their country and of liberty, a zeal for the public good, and a noble emulation of glory, will not be disheartened or dispirited by a succession of unfortunate events. But like them may we learn by defeat the power of becoming invincible!

I hope to hear from you by every post till you return. The herbs you mention I never received. I was upon a visit to Mrs S. Adams about a week after Mr Gerry returned, when she entertained me with a very fine dish of green tea. The scarcity of the article made me ask her where she got it. She replied that her *sweetheart* sent it to her by Mr Gerry. I said nothing, but thought my sweetheart might have been equally kind, considering the disease I was visited with, and that was recommended a bracer. A little after, you mentioned a couple of bundles sent. I supposed one of them might contain the article, but found they were letters. How Mr Gerry should make such a mistake I know not. I shall take the liberty of sending for what is left of it, though I suppose it is half gone, as it was very freely used. If you had mentioned a single word of it in your letter, I should have immediately found out the mistake.

It is said that the efforts of our enemies will be to stop the communication between the Colonies by taking possession of Hudson's Bay. Can it be effected? The *Milford* frigate rides triumphant in our bay, taking vessels every day, and no colony or Continental vessel has yet attempted to hinder her. She mounts twenty-eight guns, but is one of the finest sailers in the British navy. They complain we have not weighty metal enough, and I suppose truly. The rage for privateering is as great here as anywhere, and I believe the success has been as great.

15 SEPTEMBER, 1776

I have been so much engaged with company this week, that though I never cease to think of you I have not had leisure to write. It has been High Court week with us. Judge Cushing and lady kept here.

The judges all dined with me one day and the bar another day. The Court sit till Saturday night and then are obliged to continue many causes. The people seem to be pleased and gratified at seeing justice returning into its old regular channel again.

I this week received two letters, one dated 27th and one 29th July. Where they have been these two months I cannot conceive. I hear of another by the express, but have not yet been able to find it. I write now not knowing where to direct to you; whether you are in the American Senate or on board the British fleet, is a matter of uncertainty. I hear to-day that you are one of a committee sent by Congress to hold a conference with Lord Howe. Some say to negotiate an exchange of General Sullivan. Others say you are charged with other matters.

May you be as wise as serpents. I wish to hear from you. The 28th of August was the last date. I may have letters at the post-office. The town is not yet clear of the small-pox, which makes it difficult for me to get a conveyance from there unless I send on purpose.

I only write now to let you know we are all well, anxiously longing for your return.

As this is a child of chance, I do not choose to say anything more than I am   Sincerely Yours.

29 SEPTEMBER, 1776

Not since the 6th of September have I had one line from you, which makes me very uneasy. Are you all this time conferring with his Lordship? Is there no communication? or are the post-riders all dismissed? Let the cause be what it will, not hearing from you has given me much uneasiness.

We seem to be kept in total ignorance of affairs at York. I hope you at Congress are more enlightened. Who fell, who are wounded, who prisoners, or their number, is as undetermined as it was the day after the battle. If our army is in ever so critical a state I wish to know it, and the worst of it. If all America is to be ruined and undone by a pack of cowards and knaves, I wish to know it. Pitiable is the lot of their commander. Caesar's tenth legion never was forgiven. We are told for truth that a regiment of Yorkers refused to quit the city, and that another regiment behaved like a pack of cowardly villains by quitting their posts. If they are unjustly censured, it is for want of proper intelligence.

I am sorry to see a spirit so venal prevailing everywhere. When our men were drawn out for Canada, a very large bounty was given them; and now another call is made upon us; no one will go without a large bounty, though only for two months, and each town seems to think its honor engaged in outbidding the others. The province pay is forty shillings. In addition to that, this town voted to make it up six pounds. They then drew out the persons most unlikely to go, and they are obliged to give three pounds to hire a man. Some pay the whole fine, ten pounds. Forty men are now drafted from this town. More than half, from sixteen to fifty, are now in the service. This method of conducting will create a general uneasiness in the Continental army. I hardly think you can be sensible how much we are thinned in this province.

The rage for privateering is as great here as anywhere. Vast numbers are employed in that way. If it is necessary to make any more drafts upon us, the women must reap the harvests. I am willing to do my part. I believe I could gather corn, and husk it; but I should make a poor figure at digging potatoes.

There has been a report that a fleet was seen in our bay yesterday. I cannot conceive from whence, nor do I believe the story.

'Tis said you have been upon Staten Island to hold your conference. 'Tis a little odd that I have never received the least intimation of it from you. Did you think I should be alarmed? Don't you know me better than to think me a coward? I hope you will write me everything concerning this affair. I have a great curiosity to know the result.

As to government, nothing is yet done about it. The Church is opened here every Sunday, and the King prayed for, as usual, in open defiance of the Congress.

If the next post does not bring me a letter, I think I will leave off writing, for I shall not believe you get mine.

Adieu.   Yours,

PS. Master John has become post-rider from Boston to Braintree.

12 FEBRUARY, 1777.

Mr Bromfield was so obliging as to write me word that he designed a journey to the Southern States and would take particular care of a letter to you. I rejoice in so good an opportunity of letting you know that I am well as usual, but that I have not yet got reconciled to the great distance between us. I have many melancholy hours, when the best company is tiresome to me and solitude the greatest happiness I can enjoy.

I wait most earnestly for a letter to bring me the welcome tidings of your safe arrival. I hope you will be very particular and let me know how you are, after your fatiguing journey; how you are accommodated; how you like Maryland; what state of mind you find the Congress in. You know how little intelligence we received during your stay here with regard to what was passing there or in the army. We know no better now. All communication seems to be embarrassed. I got more knowledge from a letter written to you from your namesake, which I received since you left me, than I had before obtained since you left Philadelphia. I find by that letter that six Hessian officers, together with Colonel Campbell had been offered in exchange for General Lee. I fear he receives very ill treatment. The terms were not complied with, as poor Campbell finds. He was much surprised when the officers went to take him and begged to know what he had been guilty of. They told him it was no crime of his own, but they were obliged, though reluctantly, to commit him to Concord Jail, in consequence of the ill treatment of General Lee. He then begged to know how long his confinement was to last. They told him that was impossible for them to say, since it laid wholly in the power of General Howe to determine it.

By a vessel from Bilbao, we have accounts of the safe arrival of Dr Franklin in France, ten days before she sailed. A French gentleman who came passenger says we may rely upon it that two hundred thousand Russians will be here in the spring.

A lethargy seems to have seized our countrymen. I hear no more of molesting Great Britain. We just begin to talk of raising men for the standing army. I wish to know whether the reports may be credited of the Southern regiments being full.

You will write me by the bearer of this letter, to whose care you may venture to commit anything you have liberty to communicate. I have wrote to you twice before this; hope you have received them.

The children all desire to be remembered. So does your

PORTIA.

2 APRIL, 1777.

I sit down to write, though I feel very languid. The approach of spring unstrings my nerves, and the south winds have the same effect upon me which Brydone says the sirocco winds have upon the inhabitants of Sicily. It gives the vapors—blows away all their gayety and spirits, and gives a degree of lassitude both to the body and mind which renders them absolutely incapable of performing their usual functions.

He adds that 'it is not surprising that it should produce these effects upon a phlegmatic English constitution; but that he had just had an instance that all the mercury of France must sink under the weight of this horrid leaden atmosphere. A smart Parisian Marquis came to Naples about ten days ago. He was so full of animal spirits that the people thought him mad. He never remained a moment in the same place, but at their grave conversations used to skip from room to room with such amazing elasticity that the Italians swore he had got springs in his shoes. I met him this morning walking with the step of a philosopher, a smelling bottle in his hand and all his vivacity extinguished. I asked what was the matter. 'Ah, mon ami' said he, ''je m'ennuie á la mort—moi, qui n'ai jamais sçu l'ennui. Mais cet exécrable vent m'accable; et deux jours de plus, et je me pend.'''

I think the author of 'Common Sense' somewhere says that no persons make use of quotations but those who are destitute of ideas of their own. Though this may not at all times be true, yet I am willing to acknowledge it at present.

Yours of the 9th of March received by the post. 'Tis said here that Howe is meditating another visit to Philadelphia. If so, I would advise him to taking down all the doors, that the panels may not suffer for the future.

'Tis said here that General Washington has but eight thousand troops with him. Can it be true? That we have but twelve hundred at Ticonderoga? I know not who has the care of raising them here, but this I know, we are very dilatory about it. All the troops which were stationed upon Nantasket and at Boston are dismissed this week, so that we are now very fit to receive an enemy. I have heard some talk of routing the enemy at Newport; but if anything was designed against them, believe me 'tis wholly laid aside. Nobody seems to consider them as dangerous, or indeed to care anything about them. Where is General Gates? We hear nothing of him.

The Church doors were shut up last Sunday in consequence of a presentiment; a farewell sermon preached and much weeping and wailing; persecuted, but sure, but not for righteousness' sake. The conscientious parson had taken an oath upon the Holy Evangelists to pray for his most gracious Majesty as his sovereign lord, and having no father confessor to absolve him, he could not omit it without breaking his oath.

Who is to have the command at Ticonderoga? Where is General Lee? How is he treated? Is there a scarcity of grain in Philadelphia. How is flour sold there by the hundred?

We are just beginning farming business. I wish most sincerely you were here to amuse yourself with it and to unbend your mind from the cares of State. I hope your associates are more to your mind that they have been in times past. Suppose you will be joined this month by two from this State. Adieu.   Yours.

20 APRIL, 1777.

The post is very regular, and faithfully brings me all your letters, I believe. If I do not write so often as you do, be assured that 'tis because I have nothing worth your acceptance to write. Whilst the army lay this way I had constantly something by way of intelligence to write. Of late there has been a general state of tranquility, as if we had no contending armies.

There seems to be something preparing against Newport at last. If we are not wise too late, it will be well. Two thousand militia are ordered to be drafted for that place, and last week the independent company marched very generally; expect to tarry six weeks, till the militia are collected.

Your obliging favors of various dates came safe to hand last week, and contain a fine parcel of agreeable intelligence, for which I am much obliged, and I feel very important to have such a budget to communicate.

As to the town of Boston, I cannot give you any very agreeable account of it. It seems to be really destitute of the choice spirits which once inhabited it, though I have not heard any particular charges of Toryism against it. No doubt you had your intelligence from better authority than I can name. I have not been into town since your absence, nor do I desire to go till a better spirit prevails. If 'tis not Toryism it is a spirit of avarice and contempt of authority, an inordinate love of gain, that prevails not only in town but everywhere I look or hear from. As to dissipation, there was always enough of it in the town, but I believe not more now that when you left us.

There is a general cry against the merchants, against monopolizers, etc., who, 'tis said, have created a partial scarcity. That a scarcity prevails of every article, not only of luxury but even the necessaries of life, is a certain fact. Everything bears an exorbitant price. The Act, which was in some measure regarded and stemmed the torrent of oppression, is now no more heeded than if it had never been made. Indian corn at five shillings; rye, eleven and twelve shillings, but scarcely any to be had even at that price; beef, eightpence; veal, sixpence and eightpence; butter, one and sixpence; mutton, none; lamb, none; pork, none; mean sugar, four pounds per hundred; molasses, none; cotton-wool, none; New England rum, eight shillings per gallon; coffee, two and sixpence per pound; chocolate, three shillings.

What can be done? Will gold and silver remedy this evil? By your accounts of board, horsekeeping, etc., I fancy you are not better off than we are here. I live in hopes that we see the most difficult time we have to experience. Why is Carolina so much better furnished than any other State, and at so reasonable prices?

I hate to tell a story unless I am fully informed of every particular. As it happened yesterday, and to-day is Sunday, I have not been so fully informed as I could wish. About eleven o'clock yesterday William Jackson, Dick Green, Harry Perkins, and Sargent, of Cape Ann, and A. Carry, of Charlestown, were carted out of Boston under the direction of Joice junior, who was mounted on horseback, with a red coat, a white wig, and a drawn sword, with drum and fife following. A concourse of people to the amount of five hundred followed. They proceeded as far as Roxbury, when he ordered the cart to be tipped up, then told them if they were ever caught in town again it should be at the expense of their lives. He then ordered his gang to return, which they did immediately without any disturbance.

Whether they had been guilty of any new offense I cannot learn. 'Tis said that a week or two ago there was a public auction at Salem, when these five Tories went down and bid up the articles to an enormous price, in consequence of which they were complained of by Salem Committee. Two of them, I hear, took refuge in this town last night.

I believe we shall be the last State to assume government. Whilst we harbor such a number of designing Tories amongst us, we shall find government disregarded and every measure brought into contempt by secretly undermining and openly contemning them. We abound with designing Tories and ignorant, avaricious Whigs.

MONDAY, 21ST.

Have now learned the crime of the carted Tories. It seems they have refused to take paper money, and offered their goods lower for silver than for paper; bought up articles at a dear rate, and then would not part with them for paper.

Yesterday arrived two French vessels—one a twenty, some say thirty-six gun frigate; dry goods, and four hundred stand of arms, 'tis said they contain. I believe I wrote you that Manly had sailed, but it was only as far as Cape Ann. He and MacNeal both lie at anchor in the harbor.

6 MAY, 1777.

'Tis ten days, I believe, since I wrote you a line, yet not ten minutes pass without thinking of you. 'Tis four months wanting three days since we parted. Every day of the time I have mourned the absence of my friend, and felt a vacancy in my heart which nothing, nothing can supply. In vain the spring blooms or the birds sing. Their music has not its former melody, nor the spring its usual pleasures. I look around with a melancholy delight and sigh for my absent partner. I fancy I see you worn down with cares, fatigued with business, and solitary amidst a multitude.

And I think it probable before this reaches you that you may be driven from the city by our barbarous and hostile foes, and the city sharing the fate of Charlestown and Falmouth, Norfolk and Danbury. So vague and uncertain are the accounts with regard to the latter, that I shall not pretend to mention them. 'Tis more than a week since the event, yet we have not accounts which can be depended upon. I wish it may serve the valuable purpose of arousing our degenerated countrymen from that state of security and torpitude into which they seem to be sunk.

9 MAY.

I have been prevented writing for several days by company from town. Since I wrote you I have received several letters; two of the 13th of April, one of the 19th, and one of the 22d. Though some of them were very short, I will not complain. I rejoice to hear from you though you write but a line.

Since the above we have some account of the affair at Danbury, and of the loss of General Wooster. That they had no more assistance, 'tis said, was owing to six expresses being stopped by the Tories. We shall never prosper till we fall upon some method to extirpate that blood-thirsty set of men. Too much lenity will prove our ruin. We have rumors too of an action at Brunswick much to our advantage, but little credit is yet given to the report. I wish we may be able to meet them in the field, to encounter and conquer so vile an enemy.

The two Continental frigates lie windbound, with three brigs of twenty guns and some others, which are all going out in company. The wind has been a long time at east and prevented the vessels from going out.

I was mistaken in my brother's going with MacNeal. He is going in the *Darter*, a vessel which mounts twenty-four guns, is private property, but sails with the fleet.

I cannot write you half so much as I would. I have left company because I would not lose an opportunity of sending this. Believe me, etc.

I must add a little more. A most horrid plot has been discovered of a band of villains counterfeiting the Hampshire currency to a great amount. No person scarcely but what has more or less of these bills. I am unlucky enough to have about five pounds L.M. of it, but this is not the worst of it. One Colonel Farrington, who has been concerned in the plot, was taken sick and has confessed not only the counterfeiting, but says they had engaged and enlisted near two thousand men, who, upon the troop's coming to Boston, were to fall upon the people and make a general havoc.

How much more merciful God is than man, in thus providentially bringing to light these horrid plots and schemes. I doubt not Heaven will still continue to favor us unless our iniquities prevent. The Hampshire people have been stupid enough to let one of the principal plotters, Colonel Holland, out upon bail, and he has made his escape.

SUNDAY, 18 MAY, 1777.

I think myself very happy that not a week passes but what I receive a letter or two, sometimes more, from you; and though they are no longer in coming than formerly, owing, I suppose, to the post being obliged to travel farther round, yet I believe they all faithfully reach me; even the curious conversation between Mr Burne and your honor arrived safe, and made me laugh very heartily.

I think before this time many of our troops must have arrived at head-quarters, for though we have been dilatory in this and the neighboring towns, others, I hear, have done their duty better. Not an hour in the day but what we see soldiers marching. The sure way to prevent their distressing us here would be to have a strong army with the General. There are a number, not more than half, I believe though, of this town's proportion, enlisted. The rest were to be drawn at our May meeting, but as nothing was done in that way, they concluded to try a little longer to enlist them. The town send but one representative this year, and that is Mr N———s, of the middle parish. Give him his pipe and let him laugh, he will not trouble anybody.

Phileleutheros I suppose will be chosen into the Council, since he finds that the plan for making them lackeys and tools to the House was not so acceptable as he expected.

> 'Then let me have the highest post,
> Suppose it but an inch at most.'

I should feel more unhappy and anxious than ever if I realized our being again invaded by wickedness and cruelty of our enemies. The recital of the inhuman and brutal treatment of those poor creatures who have fallen into their hands freezes me with horror.

'Tis an observation of Bishop Butler's that they who have lost all tenderness and fellow-feeling for others have withal contracted a certain callousness of heart which renders them insensible to all other satisfactions but those of the grossest kind. Our enemies have found the truth of the observation in every instance of their conduct. Is it not astonishing what men may at last bring themselves to by suppressing passions and affections of the best kind, and suffering the worst to rule over them in their full strength?

Infidelity has been a growing part of the British character for many years. It is not so much to be wondered at that those who pay no regard to a Supreme Being should throw off all regard to their fellow-creatures and to those precepts and doctrines which require peace and good will to men, and in a particular manner distinguish the followers of Him who hath said, 'By this shall all men know that ye are my disciples, if ye have love one towards another.'

Let them reproach us ever so much for our kindness and tenderness to those who have fallen into our hands, I hope it will never provoke us to retaliate their cruelties. Let us put it as much as possible out of their power to injure us, but let us keep in mind the precepts of Him who hath commanded us to love our enemies and to exercise towards them acts of humanity, benevolence, and kindness, even when they despitefully use us.

And here suffer me to quote an authority which you greatly esteem, Dr Tillotson:—

'It is commonly said that revenge is sweet, but to a calm and considerate mind patience and forgiveness are sweeter, and do afford a much more rational and solid and durable pleasure than revenge. The monuments of our mercy and goodness are a far more pleasing and delightful spectacle than of our rage and cruelty, and no sort of thought does usually haunt men with more terror than the reflection upon what they have done in the way of revenge.'

If our cause is just, it will be best supported by justice and righteousness. Though we have many other crimes to answer for, that of cruelty to our enemies is not chargeable upon Americans, and I hope never will be. If we have erred it is upon the side of mercy; and we have exercised so much lenity to our enemies as to endanger our friends. But their malice and wicked designs against us have and will oblige every State to proceed against them with more rigor. Justice and self-preservation are duties as much incumbent upon Christians as forgiveness and love of enemies.

Adieu. I have devoted an hour this day to you. I dare say you are not in debt.

Ever remember with the tenderest affection one whose greatest felicity consists in the belief of a love unabated either by years or absence.

PORTIA.

David Crockett

1786–1836

Frontier hero, Congressman and hero of the valiant defense of the Alamo, Davy Crockett was a backwoodsman who became a national legend. The following extract from A Narrative of the Life of David Crockett, of the State of Tennessee *celebrates his Indian-fighting days.*

I WAS LIVING ten miles below Winchester when the Creek war commenced; and as military men are making so much fuss in the world at this time, I must give an account of the part I took in the defense of the country. If it should make me president, why I can't help it; such things will sometimes happen; and my pluck is, never 'to seek, nor decline office.'

It is true, I had a little rather not; but yet, if the government can't get on without taking another president from Tennessee, to finish the work of 'retrenchment and report' why, then, I reckon I must go in for it. But I must begin about the war, and leave the other matter for the people to begin on.

The Creek Indians had commenced their open hostilities by a most bloody butchery at Fort Mimms. There had been no war among us for so long, that but few, who were not too old to bear arms, knew any thing about the business. I, for one, had often thought about war, and had often heard it described; and I did verily believe in my own mind, that I couldn't fight in that way at all; but my after experience convinced me that this was all a notion. For when I heard of the mischief which was done at the fort, I instantly felt like going, and I had none of the dread of dying that I expected to feel. In a few days a general meeting of the militia was called for the purpose of raising volunteers; and when the day arrived for that meeting, my wife, who had heard me say I meant to go the war, began to beg me not to turn out. She said she was a stranger in the parts where we lived, had no connexions living near her, and that she and our little children would be left in a lonesome and unhappy situation if I went away. It was mighty hard to go against such arguments as these; but my countrymen had been murdered, and I knew that the next thing would be, that the Indians would be scalping the women and children all about there, if we didn't put a stop to it. I reasoned the case with her as well as I could, and told her, that if every man would wait till his wife got willing for him to go to war, there would be no fighting done, until we would all be killed in our own houses; that I was as able to go as any man in the world; and that I believed it was a duty I owed to my country. Whether she was satisfied with this reasoning or not, she did not tell me; but seeing I was bent on it, all she did was to cry a little, and turn about to her work. The truth is, my dander was up, and nothing but war could bring it right again.

I went to Winchester, where the muster was to be, and a great many people had collected, for there was as much fuss among the people about the war as there is now about moving the deposites. When the men were paraded, a lawyer by the name of Jones addressed us, and closed by turning himself and enquiring, at the same time, who among us felt like we could fight Indians? This was the same Mr Jones who afterwards served in Congress, from the state of Tennessee. He informed us he wished to raise a company, and that then the men should meet and elect their own officers. I believe I was about the second or third man that step'd out; but on marching up and down the regiment a few times, we found we had a large company. We volunteered for sixty days, as it was supposed our services would not be longer wanted. A day or two after this we met and elected Mr Jones our captain, and also elected our other officers. We then received orders to start on the next Monday week; before which time, I had fixed as well as I could to go, and my wife had equip'd me as well as she was able for the camp. The time arrived; I took a parting farewell of my wife and my little boys, mounted my horse, and set sail, to join my company. Expecting to be gone only a short time, I took no more clothing with me than I supposed would be necessary, so that if I got into an Indian battle, I might not be pestered with any unnecessary plunder, to prevent my having a fair shake with them. We all met and went ahead, till we passed Huntsville, and camped at a large spring called Beaty's spring. Here we staid for several days, in which time the troops began to collect from all quarters. At last we mustered about thirteen hundred strong, all mounted volunteers, and all determined to fight, judging from myself, for I felt wolfish all over. I verily believe the whole army was of the real grit. Our captain didn't want any other sort; and to try them he several times told his men, that if any of them wanted to go back home, they might do so at any time, before they were regularly mustered into the service. But he had the honour to command all his men from first to last, as not one of them left him.

Gen'l Jackson had not yet left Nashville with his old foot volunteers, that had gone with him to Natchez in 1812, the year before. While we remained at the spring, a Major Gibson came, and wanted some volunteers to go with him across the Tennessee river and into the Creek nation, to find out the movements of the Indians. He came to my captain, and asked for two of his best woodsmen, and such as were best with a rifle. The captain pointed me out to him, and said he would be security that I would go as far as the major would himself, or any other man. I willingly engaged to go with him, and asked him to let me choose my own mate to go with me, which he said I might do. I chose a young man by the name of George Russell, a son of old Major Russell, of Tennessee. I called him up, but Major Gibson said he thought he hadn't beard enough to please him,—he wanted men, and not boys. I must confess I was a little nettled at this; for I know'd George Russell, and I know'd there was no mistake in him; and I didn't think that courage ought to be measured by the beard, for fear a goat would have the preference over a man. I told the major he was on the wrong scent; that Russell could go as far as he could, and I must have him along. He saw I was a little wrathy, and said I had the best chance of knowing, and agreed that it should be as I wanted it. He told us to be ready early in the morning for a start; and so we were. We took our camp equipage, mounted our horses, and, thirteen in number, including the major, we cut out. We went on, and crossed the Tennessee river at a place called Ditto's Landing; and then traveled about seven miles further, and took up camp for the night. Here a man by the name of John Haynes overtook us. He had been an Indian trader in that part of the nation, and was well acquainted with it. He went with us as a pilot. The next morning, however, Major Gibson and myself concluded we should separate and take different directions to see what discoveries we could make; so he took seven of the men, and I five, making thirteen in all, including myself. He was to go by the house of a Cherokee Indian, named Dick Brown, and I was to go by Dick's father's; and getting all the information we could we were to meet that evening where the roads came together, fifteen miles the other side of Brown's. At old Mr Brown's I got a half blood Cherokee to agree to go with me, whose name was Jack Thompson. He was not then ready to start, but was to fix that evening, and overtake us at the fork road where I was to meet Major Gibson. I know'd it wouldn't be safe to camp right at the road; and so I told Jack, that when he got to the fork he must holler like an owl, and I would answer him in the same way; for I know'd it would be night before he got there. I and my men then started, and went on to the place of meeting, but Major Gibson was not there. We waited till almost dark, but still he didn't come. We then left the Indian trace a little distance, and turning into the head of a hollow, we struck up camp. It was about ten o'clock at night, when I heard my owl, and I answered him. Jack soon found us, and we determined to rest there during the night. We staid also next morning till after breakfast; but in vain, for the major didn't still come.

I told the men we had set out to hunt a fight, and I wouldn't go back in that way; that we must go ahead, and see what the red men were at. We started, and went to a Cherokee town about twenty miles off; and after a short stay there, we pushed on to the house of a man by the name of Radcliff. He was a white man, but had married a Creek woman, and lived just in the edge of the Creek nation. He had two sons, large likely fellows, and a great deal of potatoes and corn, and, indeed, almost every thing else to go on; so we fed our horses and got dinner with him, and seemed to be doing mighty well. But he was bad scared all the time. He told us there had been ten painted warriors at his house only an hour before, and if we were discovered there, they would kill us, and his family with us. I replied to him, that my business was to hunt for just such fellows as he had described, and I was determined not to go back until I had done it. Our dinner being over, we saddled up our horses, and made ready to start. But some of my small company were disposed to return. I told them, if we were to go back then, we should never hear the last of it; and I was determined to go ahead. I knowed some of them would go with me, and that the rest were afraid to go back by themselves; and so we pushed on to the camp of some of the friendly Creeks, which was distant about eight miles. The moon was about the full, and the night was clear; we therefore had the benefit of her light from night to morning, and I knew if we were placed in such danger as to make a retreat necessary, we could travel by night as well as in the day time.

We had not gone very far, when we met two negroes, well mounted on Indian ponies, and each with a good rifle. They had been taken from their owners by the Indians, and were running away from them, and trying to get back to their masters again. They were brothers, both very large and likely, and could talk Indian as well as English. One of them I sent to Ditto's Landing, the other I took back with me. It was after dark when we got to the camp, where we found about forty men, women and children.

They had bows and arrows, and I turned in to shooting with their boys by a pine light. In this way we amused ourselves very well for a while; but at last the negro, who had been talking to the Indians, came to me and told me they were very much alarmed, for the 'red sticks', as they called the war party of the Creeks, would come and find us there; and, if so, we should all be killed. I directed him to tell them that I would watch, and if one would come that night, I would carry the skin of his head home to make me a mockasin. When he made this communication, the Indians laughed aloud. At about ten o'clock at night we all concluded to try to sleep a little; but that our horses might be ready for use, as the treasurer said of the drafts on the United States' bank, on certain 'contingences' we tied them up with our saddles on them, and every thing to our hand, if in the night our quarters should get uncomfortable. We lay down with our guns in our arms, and I had just gotten into a dose of sleep, when I heard the sharpest scream that ever escaped the throat of a human creature. It was more like a wrathy painter than any thing else. The negro understood it, and he sprang to me; for tho' I heard the noise well enough, yet I wasn't wide awake enough to get up. So the negro caught me, and said the red sticks was coming. I rose quicker then, and asked what was the matter? Our negro had gone and talked with the Indian who had just fetched the scream, as he come into camp, and learned from him, that the war party had been crossing the Coosa river all day at the Ten islands; and were going on to meet Jackson, and this Indian had come as a runner. This news very much alarmed the friendly Indians in camp, and they were all off in a few minutes. I felt bound to make this intelligence known as soon as possible to the army we had left at the landing; and so we all mounted our horses, and put out in a long loop to make our way back to that place. We were about sixty-five miles off. We went on to the same Cherokee town we had visited on our way out, having first called at Radcliff's who was off with his family; and at the town we found large fires burning, but not a single Indian was to be seen. They were all gone. These circumstances were calculated to lay our dander a little, as it appeared we must be in great danger; though we could easily have licked any force of not more than five to one. But we expected the whole nation would be on us, and against such fearful odds we were not so rampant for a fight.

We therefore staid only a short time in the light of the fires about the town, preferring the light of the moon and the shade of the woods. We pushed on till we got again to old Mr Brown's, which was still about thirty miles from where we had left the main army. When we got there, the chickens were just at the first crowing for day. We fed our horses, got a morsel to eat ourselves, and again cut out. About ten o'clock in the morning we reached the camp, and I reported to Colonel Coffee the news. He didn't seem to mind my report a bit, and this raised my dander higher than ever; but I knowed I had to be on my best behaviour, and so I kept it all to myself; though I was so mad that I was burning inside like a tarkiln, and I wonder that the smoke hadn't been pouring out of me at all points.

Major Gibson hadn't yet returned, and we all began to think he was killed; and that night they put out a double guard. The next day the major got in, and brought a worse tale than I had, though he stated the same facts, so far as I went. This seemed to put our colonel all in a fidget; and it convinced me, clearly, of one of the hateful ways of the world. When I made my report, it wasn't believed, because I was no officer; I was no great man, but just a poor soldier. But when the same thing was reported by Major Gibson!! why, then, it was all as true as preaching, and the colonel believed it every word.

He, therefore, ordered breastworks to be thrown up, near a quarter of a mile long, and sent an express to Fayetteville, where General Jackson and his troops was, requesting them to push on like the very mischief, for fear we should all be cooked up to a cracklin before they could get there. Old Hickory-face made a forced march on getting the news; and on the next day, he and his men got into camp, with their feet all blistered from the effects of their swift journey. The volunteers, therefore, stood guard together, to let them rest.

About eight hundred of the volunteers, and of that number I was one, were now sent back, crossing the Tennessee river, and on through Huntsville, so as to cross the river again at another place, and to get on the Indians in another direction. After we passed Huntsville, we struck on the river at the Muscle Shoals, and at a place on them called Melton's Bluff. This river is here about two miles wide, and a rough bottom; so much so, indeed, in many places, as to be dangerous; and in fording it this time, we left several of the horses belonging to our men, with their feet fast in the crevices of the rocks. The men, whose horses were thus left, went ahead on foot. We pushed on till we got to what was called the Black Warrior's town, which stood near the very spot where Tuscaloosa now stands, which is the seat of government for the state of Alabama.

This Indian town was a large one; but when we arrived we found the Indians had all left it. There was a large field of corn standing out, and a pretty good supply in some cribs. There was also a fine quantity of dried beans, which were very acceptable to us; and without delay we secured them as well as the corn, and then burned the town to ashes; after which we left the place.

In the field where we gathered the corn we saw plenty of fresh Indian tracks, and we had no doubt they had been scared off by our arrival.

We then went on to meet the main army at the fork road, where I was first to have met Major Gibson. We got that evening as far back as the encampment we had made the night before we reached the Black Warrior's town, which we had just destroyed. The next we were entirely out of meat. I went to Colonel Coffee, who was then in command of us, and asked his leave to hunt as we marched. He gave me leave, but told me to take mighty good care of myself. I turned aside to hunt, and had not gone far when I found a deer that had just been killed and skinned, and his flesh was still warm and smoking. From this I was sure that the Indian who had killed it had been gone only a very few minutes; and though I was never much in favour of one hunter stealing from another, yet meat was so scarce in camp, that I thought I must go in for it. So I just took up the deer on my horse before me, and carried it on till night. I could have sold it for almost any price I would have asked; but this wasn't my rule, neither in peace nor war. Whenever I had any thing, and saw a fellow suffering, I was more anxious to relieve him than to benefit myself. And this is one of the true secrets of my being a poor man to this day. But it is my way; and while it has often left me with an empty purse, which is as near the devil as any thing else I have seen, yet it has never left my heart empty of consolations which money couldn't buy,—the consolations of having sometimes fed the hungry and covered the naked.

I gave all my deer away, except a small part I kept for myself, and just sufficient to make a good supper for my mess; for meat was getting to be a rarity to us all. We had to live mostly on parched corn. The next day we marched on, and at night took up camp near a large cane brake. While here, I told my mess I would again try for some meat; so I took my rifle and cut out, but hadn't gone far, when I discovered a large gang of hogs. I shot one of them down in his tracks, and the rest broke directly towards the camp. In a few minutes, the guns began to roar, as bad as if the whole army had been in an Indian battle; and the hogs to squeal as bad as the pig did, when the devil turned barber. I shouldered my hog, and went on to the camp; and when I got there I found they had killed a good many of the hogs, and a fine fat cow into the bargain, that had broke out of the cane brake. We did very well that night, and the next morning marched on to a Cherokee town, where our officers stop'd and gave the inhabitants an order on Uncle Sam for their cow, and the hogs we had killed. The next day we met the main army, having had, as we thought, hard times, and a plenty of them, though we had yet seen hardly the beginning of trouble.

After our meeting we went on to Radcliff's where I had been before while out as a spy; and when we got there, we found he had hid all his provisions. We also got into the secret, that he was the very rascal who had sent the runner to the Indian camp, with the news that the 'red sticks' were crossing at the Ten Islands; and that his object was to scare me and my men away, and send us back with a false alarm.

To make some atonement for this, we took the old scoundrell's two big sons with us, and made them serve in the war.

We then marched to a place, which we called Camp Wills; and here it was that Captain Cannon was promoted to a colonel and a Colonel Coffee to a general. We then marched to the Ten Islands, on the Coosa river, where we established a fort; and our spy companies were sent out. They soon made prisoners of Bob Catala and his warriors, and in a few days afterwards, we heard of some Indians in a town about eight miles off. So we mounted our horses, and put out for that town, under the direction of two friendly Creeks we had taken for pilots. We had also a Cherokee colonel, Dick Brown, and some of his men with us. When we got near the town we divided; one of our pilots going with each division. And so we passed on each side of the town, keeping near to it, until our lines met on the far side. We then closed up at both ends, so as to surround it completely; and then we sent Captain Hammond's company of rangers to bring on the affray. He had advanced near the town, when the Indians saw him, and they raised the yell, and came running at him like so many red devils. The main army was now formed in a hollow square around the town, and they pursued Hammond till they came in reach of us. We then gave them a fire, and they returned it, and then ran back into their town. We began to close on the town by making our files closer and closer, and the Indians soon saw they were our property. So most of them wanted us to take them prisoners; and their squaws and all would run and take hold of any of us they could, and give themselves up. I saw seven squaws have hold of one man, which made me think of the Scriptures. So I hollered out the Scriptures was fulfilling; that there were seven women holding to one man's coat tail. But I believe it was a hunting-shirt all the time. We took them all prisoners that came out to us in this way; but I saw some warriors run into a house, until I counted forty-six of them. We pursued them until we got near the house, when we saw a squaw sitting in the door, and she placed her feet against the bow she had in her hand, and then took an arrow, and, raising her feet, she drew with all her might, and let fly at us, and she killed a man, whose name, I believe, was Moore. He was a lieutenant, and his death so enraged us all, that she was fired on, and had at least twenty balls blown through her. This was the first man I ever saw killed with a bow and arrow. We now shot them like dogs; and then set the house on fire, and burned it up with the forty-six warriors in it. I recollect seeing a boy who was shot down near the house. His arm and thigh was broken, and he was so near the burning house that the grease was stewing out of him. In this situation he was still trying to crawl along; but not a murmur escaped him, though he was only about twelve years old. So sullen is the Indian, when his dander is up, that he had sooner die than make a noise, or ask for quarters.

The number that we took prisoners, being added to the number we killed, amounted to one hundred and eighty six; though I don't remember the exact number of either. We had five of our men killed. We then returned to our camp, at which our fort was erected, and known by the name of Fort Strother. No provisions had yet reached us, and we had now been for several days on half rations. However we went back to our Indian town on the next day, when many of the carcasses of the Indians were still be seen. They looked very awful, for the burning had not entirely consumed them, but given them a very terrible appearance, at least what remained of them. It was, somehow or other, found out that the house had a potatoe cellar under it, and an immediate examination was made, for we were all as hungry as wolves. We found a fine chance of potatoes in it, and hunger compelled us to eat them, though I had rather not, if I could have helped it, for the oil of the Indians we had burned up on the day before had run down on them, and they looked like they had been stewed with fat meat. We then again returned to the army, and remained there for several days almost starving, as all our beef was gone. We commenced eating the beef hides, and continued to eat every scrap we could lay out hands on. At length an Indian came to our guard one night and hollered, and said he wanted to see 'Captain Jackson'. He was conducted to the general's markee, into which he entered, and in a few minutes we received orders to prepare for marching.

In an hour we were all ready, and took up the line of march. We crossed the Coosa river, and went on in the direction of Fort Taladega. When we arrived near the place, we met eleven hundred painted warriors, the very choice of the Creek nation. They had encamped near the fort, and had informed the friendly Indians who were in it, that if they didn't come out, and fight with them against the whites, they would take their fort and all their ammunition and provision. The friendly party asked three days to consider of it, and agreed that if on the third day they didn't come out ready to fight with them, they might take their fort. Thus they put them off. They then immediately started their runner to General Jackson, and he and the army pushed over, as I have just before stated.

The camp of warriors had their spies out, and discovered us coming, some time before we got to the fort. They then went to the friendly Indians, and told them Captain Jackson was coming, and had a great many fine horses, and blankets, and guns, and every thing else; and if they would come out and help to whip him, and to take his plunder, it should all be divided with those in the fort. They promised that when Jackson came, they would then come out and help to whip him. It was about an hour by sun in the morning, when we got near the fort. We were piloted by friendly Indians, and divided as we had done on a former occasion, so as to go the right and left of the fort, and consequently, of the warriors who were camped near it. Our lines marched on, as before, till they met in front, and then closed in the rear, forming again into a hollow square. We then sent on old Major Russell, with his spy company, to bring on the battle; Captain Evans' company went also. When they got near the fort, the top of it was lined with the friendly Indians crying out as loud as they could roar, 'How-dy-do, brother, how-dy-do?' They kept this up till Major Russel had passed by the fort, and was moving on towards the warriors. They were all painted as red as scarlet, and were just as naked as they were born. They had concealed themselves under the bank of a branch that ran partly around the fort, in the manner of a half moon. Russel was going right into their circle, for he couldn't see them, while the Indians on the top of the fort were trying every plan to show him his danger. But he couldn't understand them. At last, two of them jumped from it, and ran, and took his horse by the bridle, and pointing to where they were, told him there were thousands of them lying under the bank. This brought them to a halt, and about this moment the Indians fired on them, and came rushing forth like a cloud of Egyptian locusts, and screaming like all the young devils had been turned loose, with the old devil of all at their head. Russel's company quit their horses and took into the fort, and their horses ran up to our line, which was then in full view. The warriors then came yelling on, meeting us, and continued till they were within shot of us, when we fired and killed a considerable number of them. They then broke like a gang of steers, and ran across to our other lines, where they were again fired on; and so we kept them running from one line to the other, constantly under a heavy fire, until we had killed upwards of four hundred of them. They fought with guns, and also with their bows and arrows; but at length they made their escape through a part of our line, which was made up of drafted militia, which broke ranks, and they passed. We lost fifteen of our men, as brave fellows as ever lived or died. We buried them all in one grave, and started back to our fort; but before we got there, two more of our men died of wounds they had received; making our loss seventeen good fellows in that battle.

We now remained at the fort a few days, but no provision came yet, and we were all likely to perish. The weather also began to get very cold; and our clothes were nearly worn out, and horses getting very feeble and poor. Our officers proposed to General Jackson to let us return home and get fresh horses, and fresh clothing, so as to be better prepared for another campaign; for our sixty days had long been out, and that was the time we entered for.

But the general took 'the responsibility' on himself, and refused. We were, however, determined to go, as I am to put back the deposites, *if I can*. With this, the general issued his orders against it, as he has against the bank. But we began to fix for a start, as provisions were too scarce; just as Clay, and Webster, and myself are preparing to fix bank matters, on account of the scarcity of money. The general went and placed his cannon on a bridge we had to cross, and ordered out his regulars and drafted men to keep us from crossing; just as he has planted his Globe and K.C. to alarm the bank men, while his regulars and militia in Congress are to act as artillery men. But when the militia started to guard the bridge, they would holler back to us to bring their knapsacks along when we come, for they wanted to go as bad as we did; just as many a good fellow now wants his political knapsack brought along, that if, when we come to vote, he sees he has a *fair shake to go*, he may join in and help us to take back the deposites.

We got ready and moved on till we came near the bridge, where the general's men were all strung along on both sides, just like the office-holders are now, to keep us from getting along to the help of the country and the people. But we all had our flints ready picked, and our guns ready primed, that if we were fired on we might fight our way through, or all die together; just as we are now determined to save the country from ready ruin, or to sink down with it. When we came still nearer the bridge we heard the guards cocking their guns, and we did the same; just as we have had it in Congress, while the 'government' regulars and the people's volunteers have all been setting their political triggers. But, after all, we marched boldly on, and not a gun was fired, nor a life lost; just as I hope it will be again, that we shall not be afraid of the general's Globe, nor his K.C., nor his regulars, nor their trigger snapping; but just march boldly over the executive bridge, and take the deposites back where the law placed them, and where they ought to be. When we had passed, no further attempt was made to stp us; but the general said, we were, 'the damned'st volunteers he had ever seen in his life; that we would volunteer and go and fight, and then at our pleasure would *volunteer* and go home again, in spite of the devil.' But we went on; and near Huntsville we met a reinforcement who were going on to join the army. It consisted of a regiment of volunteers, and was under the command of some one whose name I can't remember. They were sixty-day volunteers.

We got home pretty safely, and in a short time we had procured fresh horses and a supply of clothing better suited for the season; and then we returned to Fort Deposite, where our officers held a sort of '*national convention*' on the subject of a message they had received from General Jackson,—demanding that on our return we should serve out *six months*. We had already served three months instead of two, which was the time we had volunteered for. On the next morning the officers reported to us the conclusions they had come to; and told us, if any of us felt bound to go on and serve out the six months, we could do so; but they intended to go back home. I knowed if I went back home I couldn't rest, for I felt it my duty to be out; and when out was, somehow or other, always delighted to be in the very thickest of the danger. A few of us, therefore, determined to push on, and join the army. The number I do not recollect, but it was very small.

When we got out there, I joined Major Russel's company of spies. Before we reached the place, General Jackson had started. We went on likewise, and overtook him at a place where we established a fort, called Fort Williams, and leaving men to guard it, we went ahead; intending to go to a place called the Horse-shoe bend of the Talapoosa river. When we came near that place, we began to find Indian sign plenty, and we struck up camp for the night. About two hours before day, we heard our guard firing, and we were all up in little or no time. We mended up our camp fires, and then fell back in the dark, expecting to see the Indians pouring in; and intending, when they should do so, to shot them by the light of our own fires. But it happened that they did not rush in as we had expected, but commenced a fire on us as we were. We were encamped in a hollow square, and we not only returned the fire, but continued to shoot as well as we could in the dark, till day broke, when the Indians disappeared. The only guide we had in shooting was to notice the flash of their guns, and then shoot as directly at the place as we could guess.

In this scrape we had four men killed, and several wounded; but whether we killed any of the Indians or not we never could tell, for it is their custom always to carry off their dead, if they can possibly do so. We buried ours, and then made a large log heap over them, and set it on fire, so that the place of their deposite might not be known to the savages, who, we knew, would seek for them, that they might scalp them. We made some horse litters for our wounded, and took up a retreat. We moved on till we came to a large creek which we had to cross; and about half of our men had crossed, when the Indians commenced firing on our left wing, and they kept it up very warmly. We had left Major Russel and his brother at the camp we had moved from that morning, to see what discovery they could make as to the movements of the Indians; and about this time, while a warm fire was kept up on our left, as I have just stated, the major came up in our rear, and was closely pursued by a large number of Indians, who immediately commence a fire on our artillery men. They hid themselves behind a large log, and could kill one of our men almost every shot, they being in open ground and exposed. The worst of all was, two of our colonels just as this trying moment left their men, and by a *forced march*, crossed the creek out of the reach of the fire. Their names, at this late day, would do the world no good, and my object is history alone, and not the slightest interference with character. An opportunity was now afforded for Governor Carroll to distinguish himself, and on this occasion he did so, by greater bravery than I ever saw any other man display. In truth, I believe, as firmly as I do that General Jackson is president, that if it hadn't been for Carroll, we should all have been genteely licked that time, for we were in a devil of a fix; part of our men on one side of the creek, and part on the other, and the Indians all the time pouring it on us, as hot as fresh mustard to a sore shin. I will not say exactly that the old general was whip'd; but I will say, that if we escaped it at all, it was like old Henry Snider going to heaven, 'mit a tam tite squeeze.' I think he would confess himself, that he was nearer whip'd this time than he wa at any other, for I know that all the world couldn't make him acknowledge that he was *pointedly* whip'd. I know I was mighty glad when it was over, and the savages quit us, for I had begun to think there was one behind every tree in the woods.

We buried our dead, the number of whom I have also forgotten;and again made horse litters to carry our wounded, and so we put out, and returned to Fort Williams, from which place we had started. In the mean time, my horse had got crippled, and was unfit for service, and as another reinforcement had arrived, I thought they could get along without me for a short time; so I got a furlough and went home, for we had had hard times again on this hunt, and I began to feel as though I had done Indian fighting enough for one time. I remained at home until after the army had returned to Horse-shoe bend, and fought the battle there. But not being with them at that time, of course no history of that fight can be expected of me.

Soon after this, an army was to be raised to go to Pensacola, and I determined to go again with them, for I wanted a small taste of British fighting, and I supposed they would be there.

Here again the entreaties of my wife were thrown in the way of my going, but all in vain; for I always had a way of just going ahead, at whatever I had a mind to. One of my neighbours, hearing I had determined to go, came to me, and offered me a hundred dollars to go in his place as a substitute, as he had been drafted. I told him I was better raised than to hire myself out to be shot at; but that I would go, and he should go too, and in that way the government would have the services of us both. But we didn't call General Jackson 'the government' in those days, though we used to go and fight under him in the war.

I fixed up, and joined old Major Russel again; but we couldn't start with the main army, but followed on, in a little time, after them. In a day or two, we had a hundred and thirty men in our company; and we went over and crossed the Muscle Shoals at the same place where I had crossed when first out, and when we burned the Black Warrior's town. We passed through the Choctaw and Chickesaw nations, on to Fort Stephens, and from thence to what is called the Cut-off, at the junction off the Tom-Bigby with the Alabama river. This place is near the old Fort Mimms, where the Indians committed the great butchery at the commencement of the war.

We were here about two days behind the main army, who had left their horses at the Cut-off, and taken it on foot; and they did this because there was no chance for forage between there and Pensacola. We did the same, leaving men enough to take care of our horses, and cut out on foot for that place. It was about eighty miles off; but in good heart we shouldered our guns, blankets, and provisions, and trudged merrily on. About twelve o'clock the second day, we reached the encampment of the main army, which was situated on a hill, overlooking the city of Pensacola. My commander, Major Russel, was a great favourite with General Jackson, and our arrival was hailed with great applause, though we were a little after the feast; for they had taken the town and fort before we got there. That evening we went down into the town, and could see the British fleet lying in sight of the place. We got some liquor, and took a 'horn' or so, and went back to the camp. We remained there that night, and in the morning we marched back towards the Cut-off. We pursued this direction till we reached old Fort Mimms, where we remained two or three days. It was here that Major Russel was promoted from his command, which was only that of a captain of spies, to the command of a major in the line. He had been known long before at home as old Major Russel, and so we all continued to call him in the army. A Major Childs, from East Tennessee, also commanded a battalion, and his and the one Russel was now appointed to command, composed a regiment, which, by agreement with General Jackson, was to quit his army and to go to the south, to kill up the Indians on the Scamby river.

General Jackson and the main army set out the next morning for New Orleans, and a Colonel Blue took command of the regiment which I have before described. We remained, however, a few days after the general's departure, and then started also on our route.

As it gave rise to so much war and bloodshed, it may not be improper here to give a little description of Fort Mimms, and the manner in which the Indian war commenced. The fort was built right in the middle of a large field, and in it the people had been forted so long and so quietly, that they didn't apprehend any danger at all, and had, therefore, become quite careless. A small negro boy, whose business it was to bring up the calves at milking time, had been out for that purpose, and on coming back, he said he saw a great many Indians. At this the inhabitants took the alarm, and closed their gates and placed out their guards, which they continued for a few days. But finding that no attack was made, they concluded the little negro had lied; and again threw their gates open, and set all their hands out to work their fields. The same boy was out again on the same errand, when, returning in great haste and alarm, he informed them he had seen the Indians as thick as trees in the woods. He was not believed, but was tucked up to receive a flogging for the supposed lie; and was actually getting badly licked at the very moment when the Indians came in a troop, loaded with rails, with which they stop'd all the port holes of the fort on one side except the bastion; and then they fell in to cutting down the picketing. Those inside the fort had only the bastion to shoot from, as all the other holes were spiked up; and they shot several of the Indians, while engaged in cutting. But as fast as one would fall, another would seize up the axe and chop away, until they succeeded in cutting down enough of the picketing to admit them to enter. They then began to rush through, and continued until they were all in. They immediately commenced scalping, without regard to age or sex; having forced the inhabitants up to one side of the fort, where they carried on the work of death as a butcher would in a slaughter pen.

The scene was particularly described to me by a young man who was in the fort when it happened, and subsequently went on with us to Pensacola. He said that he saw his father, and mother, his four sisters, and the same number of brothers, all butchered in the most shocking manner, and that he made his escape by running over the heads of the crowd, who were against the fort wall, to the top of the fort, and then jumping off, and taking to the woods. He was closely pursued by several Indians, until he came to a small bay, across which there was a log. He knew the log was hollow on the under side, so he slip'd under the log and hid himself. He said he heard the Indians walk over him several times back and forward. He remained, nevertheless, still till night, when he came out, and finished his escape. The name of this young man has entirely escaped my recollection, though his tale greatly excited my feelings. But to return to my subject. The regiment marched from where General Jackson had left us to Fort Montgomery, which was distant from Fort Mimms about a mile and a half, and there we remained for some days.

Here we supplied ourselves pretty well with beef, by killing wild cattle which had formerly belonged to the people who perished in the fort, but had gone wild after their massacre.

When we marched from Fort Montgomery, we went some distance

back towards Pensacola; then we turned to the left, and passed through a poor piny country, till we reached the Scamby river, near which we encamped. We had about one thousand men and as a part of that number, one hundred and eighty-six Chickesaw and Choctaw Indians with us. That evening a boat landed from Pensacola, bringing many articles that were both good and necessary; such as sugar and coffee, and liquors of all kinds. The same evening, the Indians we had along proposed to cross the river, and the officers thinking it might be well for them to do so, consented; and Major Russell went with them, taking sixteen white men, of which number I was one. We camped on the opposite bank that night, and early in the morning we set out. We had not gone far before we came to a place where the whole country was covered with water, and looked like a sea. We didn't stop for this, tho', but just put in like so many spaniels, and waded on, sometimes up to our armpits, until we reached the pine hills, which made our distance through the water about a mile and a half. Here we struck up a fire to warm ourselves, for it was cold, and we were chilled through by being so long in the water. We again moved on, keeping our spies out; two to our left near the bank of the river, two straight before us, and two others on our right. We had gone in this way about six miles up the river, when our spies on the left came to us leaping the brush like so many old bucks, and informed us that they had discovered a camp of Creek Indians, and that we must kill them. Here we paused for a few minutes, and the prophets pow-wowed over their men awhile, and then got out their paint, and painted them, all according to their custom when going into battle. They then brought their paint to old Major Russell, and said to him that as he was an officer, he must be painted too. He agreed, and they painted him just as they had done themselves. We let the Indians understand that we white men would first fire on the camp, and then fall back, so as to give the Indians a chance to rush in and scalp them. The Chickasaws marched on our left hand, and the Choctaws on our right, and we moved on till we got in hearing of the camp, where the Indians were employed in beating up what they called chainy briar root. On this they mostly subsisted. On a nearer approach we found they were on an island and that we could not get to them. While we were chatting about this matter, we heard some guns fired, and in a very short time after a keen whoop, which satisfied us, that wherever it was, there was war on a small scale. With that we all broke, like quarter horses, for the firing; and when we got there we found it was our two front spies, who related to us the following story:—As they were moving on, they had met with two Creeks who were out hunting their horses; as they approached each other, there was a large cluster of bay green bushes exactly between them, so that they were within a few feet of meeting before either was discovered. Our spies walked up to them, and speaking in the Shawness tongue, informed them that General Jackson was at Pensacola, and they were making their escape, and wanted to know where they could get something to eat. The Creeks told them that nine miles up the Conaker, the river they were then on, there was a large camp of Creeks, and they had cattle and plenty to eat; and further, that their own camp was on an island about a mile off, and just below the mouth of the Conaker. They held their conversation and struck up a fire, and smoked together, and shook hands, and parted. One of the Creeks had a gun, the other had none; and as soon as they had parted, our Choctaws turned round and shot down the one that had the gun, and the other attempted to run off. They snapped several times at him, but the gun still missing fire, they took after him, and overtaking him, one of them struck him over the head with his gun, and followed up his blows till he killed him.

The gun was broken in the combat, and they then fired off the gun of the Creek they had killed, and raised the war-whoop. When we reached them, they had cut off the heads of both the Indians; and each of those Indians with us would walk up to one of the heads, and taking his war club would strike on it. This was done by every one of them; and when they had got done, I took one of their clubs, and walked up as they had done, and struck it on the head also. At this they all gathered round me, and patting me on the shoulder, would call me 'Warrior—warrior.'

They scalped the heads, and then we moved on a short distance to where we found a trace leading in towards the river. We took this trace and pursued it, till we came to where a Spaniard had been killed and scalped, together with a woman, who we supposed to be his wife, and also four children. I began to feel mighty ticklish along about this time, for I knowed if there was no danger then, there had been; and I felt exactly like there still was. We, however, went on till we struck the river, and then continued down it till we came opposite to the Indian camp, where we found they were still beating their roots.

It was now late in the evening, and they were in a thick cane brake.

We had some few friendly Creeks with us who said they could decoy them. So we all hid behind trees and logs, while the attempt was made. The Indians would not agree that we should fire, but pick'd out some of their best gunners, and placed them near the river. Our Creeks went down to the river's side, and we hailed the camp in Creek language. We heard an answer, and an Indian man started down towards the river, but didn't come in sight. He went back and again commenced beating his roots, and sent a squaw. She came down, and talked with our Creeks until dark came on. They told her they wanted her to bring them a canoe. To which she replied, that their canoe was on our side; that two of their men had gone out to hunt their horses and hadn't yet returned. They were the same two we had killed. The canoe was found, and forty of our picked Indian warriors were crossed over to take the camp. There was at last only one man in it, and he escaped; and they took two squaws, and ten children, but killed none of them of course.

We had run nearly out of provisions, and Major Russell had determined to go up the Conaker to the camp we had heard of from the Indians we had killed. I was one that he selected to go down the river that night for provisions, with the canoe, to where we had left our regiment. I took with me a man by the name of John Guess, and one of the friendly Creeks, and set out. It was very dark, and the river was so full that it overflowed the banks and the adjacent low bottoms. This rendered it very difficult to keep the channel, and particularly as the river was very crooked. At about ten o'clock at night we reached the camp, and were to return by morning to Major Russell, with provisions for his trip up the river; but on informing Colonel Blue of this arrangement, he vetoed it as quick as General Jackson did the bank bill; and said, if Major Russell didn't come back the next day, it would be bad times for him. I found we were not to go up the Conaker to the Indian camp, and a man of my company offered to go up in my place to inform Major Russell. I let him go; and they reached the major, as I was told, about sunrise in the morning, who immediately returned with those who were with him to the regiment, and joined us where we crossed the river, as hereafter stated.

The next morning we all fixed up, and marched down the Scamby to a place called Miller's Landing, where we swam our horses across, and sent on two companies down on the side of the bay opposite to Pensacola, where the Indians had fled when the main army first marched to that place. One was the company of Captain William Russell, a son of the old major, and the other was commanded by a Captain Trimble. They went on, and had a little skirmish with the Indians. They killed some, and took all the balance prisoners, though I don't remember the numbers. We again met those companies in a day or two, and sent the prisoners they had taken on to Fort Montgomery, in charge of some of our Indians.

I did hear that after they left us, the Indians killed and scalped all the prisoners, and I never heard the report contradicted. I cannot positively say it was true, but I think it entirely probable, for it is very much like the Indian character.

When we made a move from the point where we met the companies, we set out for Chatahachy, the place for which we had started when we left Fort Montgomery. At the start we had taken only twenty days' rations of flour, and eight days' rations of beef; and it was now thirty-four days before we reached that place. We were, therefore, in extreme suffering for want of something to eat, and exhausted with our exposure and the fatigues of our journey. I remember well, that I had not myself tasted bread but twice in nineteen days. I had bought a pretty good supply of coffee from the boat that had reached us from Pensacola, on the Scamby, and on that we chiefly subsisted. At length, one night our spies came in, and informed us they had found Holm's village on the Chatahachy river; and we made an immediate push for that place. We traveled all night, expecting to get something to eat when we got there. We arrived about sunrise, and near the place prepared for battle. We were all so furious, that even the certainty of a pretty hard fight could not have restrained us. We made a furious charge on the town, but to our great mortification and surprise, there wasn't a human being in it. The Indians had all run off and left it. We burned the town, however; but, melancholy to tell, we found no provision whatever. We then turned about, and went back to the camp we had left the night before, as nearly starved as any set of poor fellows ever were in the world.

We staid there only a little while, when we divided our regiment; and Major Childs, with his men, went back the way we had come for a considerable distance, and then turned to Baton-Rouge, where they joined General Jackson and the main army on their return from New Orleans. Major Russell and his men struck for Fort Decatur, on the Talapoosa river. Some of our friendly Indians, who knew the country, went on ahead of us, as we had no trail except the one they made to follow. With them we sent some of our ablest horses and men, to get us some provisions, to prevent us from absolutely starving to death. As the army marched, I hunted every day, and would kill every hawk, bird, and squirrel that I could find. Others did the same; and it was a rule with us that when we stop'd at night, the hunters would throw all they had killed in a pile, and then we would make a general division among all the men. One evening I came in, having killed nothing that day. I had a very sick man in my mess, and I wanted something for him to eat, even if I starved myself. So I went to the fire of Captain Cowen, who commanded my company after the promotion of Major Russell, and informed him that I was on the hunt of something for a sick man to eat. I knowed the captain was as bad off as the rest of us, but I found him broiling a turkey's gizzard. He said he had divided the turkey out among the sick, that Major Smiley had killed it, and that nothing else had been killed that day. I immediately went to Smiley's fire, where I found him broiling another gizzard. I told him, that it was the first turkey I had ever seen have two gizzards. But so it was, I got nothing for my sick man. And now seeing that every fellow must shift for himself, I determined that in the morning, I would come up missing; so I took my mess and cut out to go ahead of the army. We know'd that nothing more could happen to us if we went than if we staid, for it looked like it was to be starvation any way; we therefore determined to go on the old saying, root hog or die. We passed two camps, at which our men that had gone on before us, had killed Indians. At one they had killed nine, and at the other three. About daylight we came to a small river, which I thought was the Scamby; but we continued on for three days, killing little or nothing to eat; till, at last, we all began to get nearly ready to give up the ghost, and lie down and die; for we had no prospect of provision, and we knew we couldn't go much further without it.

We came to a large prairie, that was about six miles across it, and in this I saw a trail which I knowed was made by bear, deer, and turkeys. We went on through it till we came to a large creek, and the low grounds were all set over with wild rye, looking as green as a wheat field. We here made a halt, unsaddled our horses, and turned them loose to graze.

One of my companions, a Mr Vanzant, and myself, then went up the low grounds to hunt. We had gone some distance, finding nothing; when at last, I found a squirrel, which I shot, but he got into a hole in the tree. The game was small, but necessity is not very particular; so I thought I must have him, and I climbed that tree thirty feet high, without a limb, and pulled him out of his hole. I shouldn't relate such small matters, only to show what lengths a hungry man will go to, to get something to eat. I soon killed two other squirrels, and fired at a large hawk. At this a large gang of turkeys rose from the cane brake, and flew across the creek to where my friend was, who had just before crossed it. He soon fired on a large gobler, and I heard it fall. By this time my gun was loaded again, and I saw one sitting on my side of the creek, which had flew over when he fired; so I blazed away, and down I brought him. I gathered him up, and a fine turkey he was. I now began to think we had struck a breeze of luck, and almost forgot our past sufferings, in the prospect of once more having something to eat. I raised the shout, and my comrade came to me, and we went on to our camp with the game we had killed. While we were gone two of our mess had been out, and each of them had found a bee tree. We turned into cooking some of our game, but we had neither salt nor bread. Just at this moment, on looking down the creek, we saw our men, who had gone on before us for provisions, coming to us. They came up, and measured out to each man a cupful of flower. With this, we thickened our soup, when our turkey was cooked, and our friends took dinner with us, and then went on.

We now took our tomahawks and went and cut our bee trees, out of which we got a fine chance of honey; though we had been starving so long that we feared to eat much at a time, till, like the Irish by hanging, we got used to it again. We rested that night without moving our camp; and the next morning myself and Vanzant again turned out to hunt. We had not gone far, when I wounded a fine buck very badly; and while pursuing him, I was walking on a large tree that had fallen down, when from the top of it, a large bear broke out and ran off. I had no dogs; and I was sorry enough for it; for of all the hunting I ever did, I have always delighted most in bear hunting. Soon after this, I killed a large buck; and we had just gotten him to camp, when our poor starved army came up. They told us, that to lessen their sufferings as much as possible, Captain William Russell had had his horse led up to be shot for them to eat, just at that moment they saw our men returning, who had carried on the flour.

We were now about fourteen miles from Fort Decatur, and we gave away all our meat, and honey, and went on with the rest of the army.

When we got there, they could give us only one ration of meat, but not a mouthful of bread. I immediately got a canoe, and taking my gun, crossed over the river, and went to the Big Warrior's town. I had a large hat, and offered an Indian a silver dollar for my hat full of corn. He told me that his corn was all 'shuestea' which in English means, it was all gone. But he showed me where an Indian lived, who, he said, had corn. I went to him, and made the same offer. He could talk a little broken English, and said to me, 'You got any powder? You got bullet?' I told him I had. He then said, 'Me swap my corn, for powder and bullet.' I took out about ten bullets, and showed him; and he proposed to give me a hat full of corn for them. I took him up, mighty quick. I then offered to give him ten charges of powder for another hat full of corn. To this he agreed very willingly. So I took off my hunting-shirt, and tied up my corn; and though it had cost me very little of my powder and lead, yet I wouldn't have taken fifty silver dollars for it. I returned to the camp, and the next morning we started for the Hickory Ground, which was thirty miles off. It was here that General Jackson met the Indians, and made peace with the body of the nation.

We got nothing to eat at this place, and we had yet to go forty-nine miles over a rough and wilderness country, to Fort Williams. Parched corn, and but little even of that, was our daily subsistence. When we reached Fort Williams, we got one ration of pork and one of flour, which was our only hope until we could reach Fort Strother.

I pursued on, by myself, till some time after night, when I came up with the rest of the army. That night my company and myself did pretty well, as I divided out my corn among them. The next morning we met the East Tennessee troops, who were on their road to Mobile, and my youngest brother was with them. They had plenty of corn and provisions, and they gave me what I wanted for myself and my horse. I remained with them that night, though my company went across the Coosa river to the fort, where they also had the good fortune to find plenty of provisions. Next morning, I took leave of my brother and all my old neighbours, for there were a good many of them with him, and crossed over to my men at the fort. Here I had enough to go on, and after remaining a few days, cut out for home. Nothing more, worthy of the reader's attention, transpired till I was safely landed at home once more with my wife and children. I found them all well and doing well; and though I was only a rough sort of backwoodsman, they seemed mighty glad to see me, however little the quality folks might suppose it. For I do reckon we love as hard in the backwood country, as any people in the whole creation.

But I had been home only a few days, when we received orders to start again, and go on to the Black Warrior and Cahawba rivers, to see if there was no Indians there. I know'd well enough there was none, and I wasn't willing to trust my craw any more where there was neither any fighting to do, nor any thing to go on; and so I agreed to give a young man, who wanted to go, the balance of my wages if he would serve out my time, which was about a month. He did so, and when they returned, sure enough they hadn't seen an Indian any more than if they had been all the time chopping wood in my clearing. This closed my career as a warrior, and I am glad of it, for I like life now a heap better than I did then; and I am glad all over that I lived to see these times, which I should not have done if I had kept fooling along in war, and got used up at it. When I say I am glad, I just mean I am glad I am alive, for there is a confounded heap of things I an't glad of at all. I an't glad, for example, that the 'government' moved the deposites, and if my military glory should take such a turn as to make me president after the general's time, I'll move them back; yes, I, the 'government' will 'take the responsibility' and move them back again. If I don't, I wish I may be shot.

But I am glad that I am now through war matters, and I reckon the reader is too, for they have no fun in them at all; and less if he had had to pass through them first, and then to write them afterwards. But for the dullness of their narrative, I must try to make amends by relating some of the curious things that happened to me in private life, and when *forced* to become a public man, as I shall have to be again, if ever I consent to take the presidential chair.

Ralph Waldo Emerson

1803–1882

Poet, essayist and Transcendentalist philosopher, Ralph Waldo Emerson was described by Walt Whitman as 'A just man, poised on himself, all-loving, all-inclosing, and sane and clear as the sun.' This extract from his journals demonstrates the inquiring, profound and perceptive range of his interests.

JAN. 1858

I found Henry T. yesterday in my woods. He thought nothing to be hoped from you, if this bit of mould under your feet was not sweeter to you to eat, than any other in this world, or in any world. We talked of the willows. He says, 'tis impossible to tell when they push the bud (which so marks the arrival of spring) out of its dark scales. It is done & doing all winter. It is begun in the previous autumn. It seems one steady push from autumn to spring. I say, How divine these studies! Here there is no taint of mortality.

JAN.? 1858

Why do we not say, We are abolitionists of the most absolute abolition, as every man that is a man must be? Only the Hottentots, only the barbarous or semibarbarous societies are not. We do not try to alter your laws in Alabama, nor yours in Japan, or the Fee Jee Islands; but we do not admit them or permit a trace of them here. Nor shall we suffer you to carry your Thuggism north, south, east, or west into a single rod of territory which we control. We intend to set & keep a *cordon sanitaire* all around the infected district, & by no means suffer the pestilence to spread.

Minds of low & surface power pounce on some fault of expression, of rhetoric, or petty mis-statement of fact, and quite lose sight of the main purpose. I knew a lady who thought she knew she had heard my discourse before, because the word *'Arena'* was in both of the two discourses.

JAN.–MAY 1858
1858
<u>1776</u>

82 years count the age of the Union, and yet they say the nation is as old & infirm as a man is with those years. Now a building is not in its prime till after 500 years. Nor should a nation be; and we aged at 80!

All the children born in the last three years or 8 years should be charged with love of liberty, for their parents have been filled with Kansas & antislavery.

You are too historical by half. I show you a grievance, & you proceed to inquire, not if it is mischievous, but if it is old. I point the redress, & you inquire about a constitutional precedent for the redress. That which only requires perception, mischiefs that are rank & intolerable, which only need to be seen, to be hated & attacked, with you are ground for argument, & you are already preparing to defend them. The reliance on simple perception constitutes genius & heroism; and that is the religion before us.

MAY 11, 1858

Yesterday with Henry T. at the pond . . . I hear the account of the man who lives in the wilderness of Maine with respect, but with despair . . . Henry's hermit, 45 miles from the nearest house, [is not] important, until we know what he is now, what he thinks of it on his return & after a year. Perhaps he has found it foolish & wasteful to spend a tenth or a twentieth of his active life with a muskrat & fried fishes.

My dear Henry,

A frog was made to live in a swamp, but a man was not made to live in a swamp. Yours ever,

R.

MAY–JUNE 1858

We are all better in attack than in defence. It is very easy to make acute objections to any style of life, but the objector is quite as vulnerable. Greenough wittily called my speculations *masturbation*; but the artist life seems to me intolerably thin & superficial. I feel the reasonableness of what the lawyer or merchant or laborer has to allege against readers & thinkers, until I look at each of their wretched industries, and find them without end or aim.

Nature overloads the bias, overshoots the mark, to hit the mark. Her end of reproduction & care of young is so dear to her, that she demoralizes the universe of men with this immense superfluity of attraction in all directions to woman: & see what carnage in relations results! Nothing is so hypocritical as the abuse in all journals—& at the South, especially—of Mormonism & Free-Love Socialism. These men who write the paragraphs in the *Herald* & *Observer*, have just come from their brothel, or, in Carolina, from their Mulattoes. How then can you say, that, in nature is always a minimum of force to effect a change? It is a maximum.

FEB.? 1859

My sheriff ought not to be forgotten down in Maine, who had once tasted a cordial, but did not know the name of it, at some hotel in New York, many years before, & had been testing liquors at all places in all the United States ever since in the faint hope that he might yet cry *Eureka*, it is the same.

SPRING? 1859

'Tis very important in writing that you do not lose your presence of mind. Despair is no muse, & he who finds himself hurried, & gives up carrying his point this time, writes in vain. Goethe had the *'urkraftige behagen'* the stout comfortableness, the stomach for the fight, and you must.

I am a natural reader, & only a writer in the absence of natural writers. In a true time, I should never have written.

The village of Amherst is eagerly discussing the authorship of a paper signed Bifid which appeared in the College Magazine. 'Tis said, if the Faculty knew his name, the author would be expelled from the college. Ten miles off, nobody ever heard of the magazine, or ever will hear of it. In London 'tis of equal interest today whether Lord Palmerston wrote the leader in Wednesday's Times.

I have now for more than a year, I believe, ceased to write in my Journal, in which I formerly wrote almost daily. I see few intellectual persons, & even those to no purpose, & sometimes believe that I have no new thoughts, and that my life is quite at an end. But the magnet that lies in my drawer for years, may believe it has no magnetism, and, on touching it with steel, it shows the old virtue; and, this morning, came by a man with knowledge & interests like mine, in his head, and suddenly I had thoughts again.

Why do I hide in a library, read books, or write them & skulk in the woods, & not dictate to these fellows, who, you say, dictate to me, as they should not? Why? but because in my bones is none of the magnetism which flows in theirs. They inundate all men with their streams. I have a reception & a perception, which they have not, but it is rare & casual, and yet drives me forth to watch these workers, if so be I may derive from their performance a new insight for mine. But there are no equal terms for me & them. They all unwittingly perform for me the part of the gymnotus on the fish.

The number of conceited people is so great, that it must subserve great uses in nature, like sexual passion.

1. You shall be somebody.
2. You shall have catholicity.
3. You shall know the power of the imagination.

You shall come from the Azure.

You shall be intellectual.

I delight in persons who clearly perceive the transcendant superiority of Shakspeare to all other writers. I delight in the votaries of the genius of Plato. Because this clear love does not consist with self-conceit.

Not so, when I see youths coming to me with their books & poems. I soon discover that they are egotists & wish my homage.

I have been writing & speaking what were once called novelties, for twenty five or thirty years, & have not now one disciple. Why? Not that what I said was not true; not that it has not found intelligent receivers but because it did not go from any wish in me to bring men to me, but to themselves. I delight in driving them from me. What could I do, if they came to me? they would interrupt & encumber me. This is my boast that I have no school & no follower. I should account it a measure of the impurity of insight, if it did not create independence.

A man finds out that there is somewhat in him that knows more than he does.
Then he come presently to the curious question, who's who? which of these two is really me? the one that knows more, or the one that knows less? the little fellow, or the big fellow?

No man's egotism covers his personality.

What a Critic is the Age! Calvinism how coherent! how sufficing! how poetic! It stood well every test but the telescope. When that showed the Copernican system to be true, it was too ridiculous to pretend that our little spec of an earth was the central point of nature, &c.

When India was explored, & the wonderful riches of Indian theologic literature found, that dispelled once for all the dream about Christianity being the sole revelation—for, here in India—there in China, were the same principles, the same grandeurs, the like depths moral & intellectual.

Well, we still maintained that we were the true men—we were believers—the rest were heathen. Now comes this doctrine of the pseudospiritists to explain to us that we are not Christians, are not believers, but totally unbelieving.

Now & then, rarely comes a stout man like Luther, Montaigne, Pascal, Herbert, who utters a thought or feeling in a virile manner, and it is unforgettable. Then follow any number of spiritual eunuchs and women who talk about that thought, imply it, in pages & volumes . . . .

Great bands of female souls who only receive the spermatic aura & brood on the same but add nothing.

People live like these boys who watch for a sleigh-ride & mount on the first that passes, & when they meet another that they know, swing themselves on to that, & ride in another direction, until a third passes, & they change again; 'tis no matter where they go, as long as there is snow & company.

Shall I blame my mother, whitest of women, because she was not a gipsy, & gave me no swarthy ferocity? or my father, because he came of a lettered race, & had no porter's shoulders?

MAY 25, 1859
The warblers at this season make much of the beauty & interest of the woods. They are so elegant in form & coat, and many of them here but for a short time; the Blackburnian warbler rarely seen by HDT; the trees still allowing you to see far. Their small leaflets do not vie with the spaces of the sky—but let in the vision high—and (yesterday) Concord was all Sicily.

MAY? 1859

'Tis pity to see egotism for its poverty. All must talk about themselves, for 'tis all they know, but genius never needs to allude to his personality, as every person & creature he has seen serves him as an exponent of his private experience. So he communicates all his secrets, and endless autobiography, & never lets on that he means himself.

Dante cannot utter a few lines but I am informed what transcendent eyes he had, as, for example,

> 'un foco
> Ch'emisperio di tenebre vincia.'

How many millions would have looked at candles, lamps, & fires, & planets, all their days, & never noticed this measure of their illuminating force, 'of conquering a hemisphere of the darkness.' Yet he says nothing about his own eyes.

What marks right mental action is always newness, ignoring of the past; & the elasticity of the present object—which makes all the magnitudes & magnates quite unnecessary. This is what we mean when we say your subject is absolutely indifferent. You need not write the History of the World, nor the Fall of Man, nor King Arthur, nor Iliad, nor Christianity; but write of hay, or of cattleshows, or trade sales, or of a ship, or of Ellen, or Alcott, or of a couple of schoolboys, if only you can be the fanatic of your subject, & find a fibre reaching from it to the core of your heart, so that all your affection & all your thought can freely play.

MAY–AUG.? 1859

T. Appleton says, that he thinks that all Bostonians, when they die, if they are good, go to Paris.

AUG. 16–19, 1859

Am I not, one of these days, to write consecutively of the beatitude of intellect? It is too great for feeble souls, and they are overexcited. The wineglass shakes, & the wine is spilled. What then? The joy which will not let me sit in my chair, which brings me bolt upright to my feet, & sends me striding around my room, like a tiger in his cage, and I cannot have composure & concentration enough even to set down in English words the thought which thrills me— is not that joy a certificate of the elevation? What if I never write a book or a line? For a moment, the eyes of my eyes were opened, the affirmative experience remains, & consoles through all suffering.

On Wachusett, I sprained my foot. It was slow to heal, & I went to the doctors. Dr H. Bigelow said, 'a splint, & absolute rest;' Dr Russell said, 'rest yes; but a splint, no.' Dr Bartlett said, 'neither splint nor rest, but go & walk.' Dr Russell said, 'Pour water on the foot, but it must be warm.' Dr Jackson said, 'stand in a trout brook all day.'

AUG. 20, 1859

Home is a good place in August. We have plenty of sopsavines, & Moscow Transparents, & the sweet apple we call Early Bough . . . .

AUG.–SEPT. 1859

Mr Crump. The unfortunate days of August & September, when the two cows were due from the Temple Pasture, & did not arrive, & we learn that they strayed on the way, & are lost. When the Muster approached bringing alarms to all housekeepers & orchard-owners. When the foot was lame, & the hand was palsied, & the foot mending was lame again. When a strong southwest wind blew in vicious gusts, all day, stripping every loaded pear tree of its fruit, just six weeks too early. The beggars arrive every day, some on foot, the Sardinians & Sicilians, who cannot argue the questions of labor & mendicity with you, since they do not speak a word of English; then the Monumentals, who come in landaus or barouches, & wish your large aid to Mt Vernon; Plymouth; Ball's Webster; or President Quincy in marble; then the chipping lady from the Cape who has three blind sisters, & I know not how many dumb ones, & she had been advised to put them in the Poor House. No, not she. As long as she had health, she would go about & sell these books for them, which I am to buy, and she tosses her head, & expects my praise & tears for her heroic resolution; though I had a puzzled feeling, that, if there was sacrifice anywhere it was in me, if I should buy them; & I am sure I was very little inclined to toss my head on the occasion.

Mr Crump remarked that he hated lame folks: there was no telling how hypocritical they were. They are dreadful lame when you see them, but the lamest of them, if he wants something, & there's nobody will help him to it, will manage to get it himself, though it were a mile off; *if you are not by.*

I think wealth has lost much of its value, if it have not wine. I abstain from wine only on account of the expense. When I heard that Mr Sturgis had given up wine, I had the same regret that I had lately in hearing that Mr Bowditch had broken his hip; a millionaire without wine, & a millionaire that must lie on his bed.

Dr Johnson is a good example of the force of temperament. 'Tis surprising how often I am reminded of my Aunt Mary E. in reading Boswell lately. Johnson impresses his company as she does, not only by the points of the remark, but also when the point fails, because he makes it. Like hers, his obvious religion or superstition, his deep wish that they should think so or so, weighs with them, so rare is depth of feeling, or a constitutional value for a thought or opinion, among the lightminded men & women who make up society. And this, though in both cases, their companions know that there is a degree of shortcoming, & of insincerity, & of talking for victory. Yet the existence of character and habitual reverence of principles over talent or learning is felt by the frivolous.

FALL? 1859
The resistance to slavery—it is the old mistake of the slaveholder to impute the resistance to Clarkson or Pitt, to Channing or Garrison, or to some John Brown whom he has just captured, & to make a personal affair of it; & he believes, whilst he chains & chops him, that he is getting rid of his tormentors; and does not see that the air which this man breathed is liberty, & is breathed by thousands & millions; that men of the same complexion as he, will look at slaveholders as felons who have disentitled themselves to the protection of law, as the burglar has, whom I see breaking into my neighbor's house; and therefore no matter how many Browns he can catch & kill, he does not make the number less, for the air breeds them, every school, every church, every domestic circle, every home of courtesy, genius, & conscience is educating haters of him & his misdeeds.

We talk of Sparta & Rome, we dilettanti of liberty.
But the last thing a brave man thinks of is Sparta or Scythia or the

Gauls: he is up to the top of his boots in his own meadow, & can't be bothered with histories. That will do for a winter evening with school-boys. As soon as a man talks Washington & Putnam & General Jackson to me, I detect the coxcomb & charlatan. He is a frivolous nobody who has no duties of his own.

Anna Ward was at a loss in talking with me, because I had no church whose weakness she could show up, in return for my charges upon hers. I said to her, Do you not see that though I have no eloquence & no flow of thought, yet that I do not stoop to accept any thing less than truth? that I sit here contented with my poverty, mendicity, & deaf & dumb estate, from year to year, from youth to age, rather than adorn myself with any red rag of false church or false association? My low & lonely sitting here by the wayside, is my homage to truth, which I see is sufficient without me; which is honored by my abstaining, not by superserviceableness. I see how grand & selfsufficing it is; how it burns up, & will none of your shifty patchwork of additions & ingenuities.

Brown shows us, said HDT, another school to send our boys to—that the best lesson of oratory is to speak the truth. A lesson rarely learned—To stand by the truth. We stand by our party, our trade, our reputation, our talent, but these each lead away from the truth. That is so volatile & vital, evanescing instantly from all but dedication to it.

And yet inspiration is that, to be so quick as truth; to drop the load of Memory & of Futurity, Memory & Care, & let the moment suffice us: then one discovers that the first thought is related to all thought & carries power & fate in its womb.

Mattie Griffith says, if Brown is hung, the gallows will be sacred as the cross.

APRIL–MAY 1860

The teaching of politics is that the Government which was set for protection & comfort of all good citizens, becomes the principal obstruction & nuisance, with which we have to contend. Wherever we look, whether to Kansas, to Utah, to the frontier—as Mexico & Cuba, or to laws & contracts for internal improvement, the capital enemy in the way is always this ugly government.

We could manage very well by private enterprise, for carrying the mails, associations for emigration, & emigrant aid, for local police & defence, & for prevention of crime; but the cheat & bully & malefactor we meet everywhere is the Government.

This can only be counteracted by magnifying the local powers at its cost. Take from the U.S. the appointment of postmasters & let the towns elect them, and you deprive the Federal Government of half a million defenders.

Death. When our friends die, we not only lose them, but we lose a great deal of life which in the survivors was related to them.

Advantages of old age. I reached the other day the end of my fifty seventh year, and am easier in my mind than hitherto. I could never give much reality to evil & pain. But now when my wife says, perhaps this tumor on your shoulder is a cancer, I say, what if it is? It would not make the gentleman on his way in a cart to the gallows very unhappy, to tell him that the pain in his knee threatened a white swelling.

OCT. 1860 EARTHQUAKE 17 OCT. AT 6 A.M.
Queenie's private earthquake. We had disputed about the duration of the vibrations, which I thought lasted 12 seconds, and she insisted returned at intervals of two minutes. Of course our accounts could not agree; but, yesterday, it chanced to turn out, that her earthquake was *in the afternoon*, & that of the rest of the world at 6 in the morning.

NOV. 15, 1860
The news of last Wednesday morning (7th) was sublime, the pronunciation of the masses of America against Slavery. And now on Tuesday 14th I attended the dedication of the Zoological Museum at Cambridge, an auspicious & happy event, most honorable to Agassiz & to the State. On Wednesday 7th, we had Charles Sumner here at Concord & my house. Yesterday eve I attended at the Lyceum in the Town Hall the Exhibition of Stereoscopic views magnified on the wall, which seems to me the last & most important application of this wonderful art: for here was London, Paris, Switzerland, Spain &, at last, Egypt, brought visibly & accurately to Concord, for authentic examination by women & children, who had never left their state. Cornelius Agrippa was fairly outdone. And the lovely manner in which one picture was changed for another beat the faculty of dreaming. Edward thought that 'the

thanks of the town should be presented to Mr Munroe, for carrying us to Europe, & bringing us home, without expense.' An odd incident of yesterday was that I received a letter or envelope mailed from Frazer, Pennsylvania enclosing no letter but a blank envelope containing a Ten dollar bank note.

JAN. 4, 1861
I hear this morning, whilst it is snowing fast, the chicadee singing.

JAN.? 1861
We can easily come up to the average culture & performance; not easily go beyond it. I often think of the poor caterpillar, who, when he gets to the end of a straw or a twig in his climbing, throws his head uneasily about in all directions; he is sure he has legs & muscle & head enough to go further indefinitely—but what to do? he is at the end of his twig.

JAN. 1861
We have no guess what we are doing, even then when we do our best; perhaps it will not appear for an age or two yet: then, the dim outline of the reef & new continent we madrepores were making, will sketch itself to the eyes of the dullest sailer. Luther would cut his hand off sooner than write theses against the Pope, if he suspected that he was bringing on with all his might the pale negations of Boston Unitarianism.

The furious slaveholder does not see that the one thing he is doing, by night & by day, is, to destroy slavery. They who help & they who hinder are all equally diligent in hastening its downfall. Blessed be the inevitabilities.

The best thing I heard yesterday was Henry James's statement, that, in the spiritual world, the very lowest function was Governing. In heaven, as soon as one wishes to rule, or despises others he is thrust out at the door.

Another fine spiritual statement which he made, was, to the effect, that all which men value themselves for as religious progress—going alone, renouncing, & self mortifying, to attain a certain religious superiority—was the way *from*, not the way *to* what they seek; for, it is only as our existence is shared, not as it is self-hood, that it is divine.

JAN.–FEB. 1861

I know no more irreconcilable persons ever brought to annoy & confound each other in one room than are sometimes actually lodged by nature in one man's skin. Thus I knew a saint of a woman who lived in ecstasies of devotion, 'a pensive nun devout & pure' and who, moved by pity for a poor schoolmistress, undertook one day to give her a little vacation which she sorely needed, & took her place in the school: but, when the children whispered, or did not mind their book, she stuck a pin into their arms, & never seemed to suspect the cruelty. I knew a gentle imaginative soul, all poetry & sympathy, who hated every inmate of his house, & drove away his dog, by starving him. Rousseau left his children at the Foundling Hospital. Mrs Ripley at Brook Farm, said the hard selfishness of the socialists ruined the Community. Hawthorne, I believe, sued the members for their debt to him. Howard the great philanthropist was harsh to his children, & Sterne the sentimentalist had a bad name for hardness to his mother.

Overture of the Quintette Club last evening.

> Tuttle tuttle lira
> tuttle tuttle liro
> tuttle tuttle polywog po
> tuttle tuttle up the stairs

Robert E. Lee

1807–1870

*General Robert E. Lee was the distinguished commander
of the Virginia troops in the Confederate Army during the
Civil War. He gained notable successes in the battles of
Antietam, Fredericksburg and Chancellorsville before being
checked at Gettysburg and finally defeated at Appomattox.
Lee has remained famous for his chivalry, honesty and
courage, qualities demonstrated in this extract from his
son's volume* Recollections and Letters of General
Robert E. Lee.

HIS HEADQUARTERS CONTINUED all the winter at the same place, and with
stove and fire-places in the tents, the General and his military family
managed to keep fairly comfortable. On February 6, 1863, he wrote to
his daughter, Agnes, from this camp:

'CAMP FREDERICKSBURG, FEBRUARY 6, 1863.

'... I read yesterday, my precious daughter, your letter, and grieved very much when last in Richmond at not seeing you. My movements are so uncertain that I cannot be relied on for anything. The only place I am to be found is in camp, and I am so cross now that I am not worth seeing anywhere. Here you will have to take me with the three stools—the snow, the rain, and the mud. The storm of the last twenty-four hours has added to our stock of all, and we are now in a floating condition. But the sun and the wind will carry all off in time, and then we shall appreciate our relief. Our horses and mules suffer the most. They have to bear the cold and rain, tug through the mud, and suffer all the time with hunger. The roads are wretched, almost impassable. I heard of Mag lately. One of our scouts brought me a card of Margaret Stuart's with a pair of gauntlets directed to 'Cousin Robert.' ... I have no news. General Hooker is obliged to do something. I do not know what it will be. He is playing the Chinese game, trying what frightening will do. He runs out his guns, starts his wagons and troops up and down the river, and creates an excitement generally. Our men look on in wonder, give a cheer, and all again subsides *in statu quo ante bellum*. I wish you were here with me today. You would have to sit by this little stove, look out at the rain, and keep yourself dry. But here come, in all the wet, the adjutants general with the papers. I must stop and go to work. See how kind God is; we have plenty to do in good weather and bad ....'

'Your devoted father,
'R. E. LEE.'

On February 23rd, he writes to Mrs Lee:

'CAMP FREDERICKSBURG, FEBRUARY 23, 1863.

'The weather is now very hard upon our poor bushmen. This morning the whole country is covered with a mantle of snow fully a foot deep. It was nearly up to my knees as I stepped out this morning, and our poor horses were enveloped. We have dug them out and opened our avenues a little, but it will be terrible and the roads impassable. No cars from Richmond yesterday. I fear our short rations for man and horse will have to be curtailed. Our enemies have their troubles too. They are very strong immediately in front, but have withdrawn their troops above and below us back toward Acquia Creek. I owe Mr F.J.

Hooker no thanks for keeping me here. He ought to have made up his mind long ago what to do—24th. The cars have arrived and brought me a young French officer, full of vivacity, and ardent for service with me. I think the appearance of things will cool him. If they do not, the night will, for he brought no blankets.

'R. E. LEE.'

The dreary winter gradually passed away. Toward the last of April, the two armies, which had been opposite each other for four months, began to move, and, about the first of May, the greatest of General Lee's battles was fought. My command was on the extreme left, and, as Hooker crossed the river, we followed a raiding party of the enemy's cavalry over toward the James River above Richmond; so I did not see my father at any time during the several days' fighting. The joy of our victory at Chancellorsville was saddened by the death of 'Stonewall' Jackson. His loss was the heaviest blow the Army of Northern Virginia ever sustained. To Jackson's note telling him he was wounded, my father replied:

'I cannot express my regret at the occurrence. Could I have directed events, I should have chosen for the good of the country to have been disabled in your stead. I congratulate you on the victory, which is due to your skill and energy.'

Jackson said, when this was read to him,
'Better that ten Jacksons should fall than one Lee.'
Afterward, when it was reported that Jackson was doing well, General Lee playfully sent him word:
'You are better off than I am, for while you have only lost your *left*, I have lost my *right* arm.'
Then, hearing that he was worse, he said:
'Tell him that I am praying for him as I believe I have never prayed for myself.'
After his death, General Lee writes to my mother, on May 11th:

'. . . In addition to the deaths of officers and friends consequent upon the late battles, you will see that we have to mourn the loss of the great and good Jackson. Any victory would be dear at such a price.

His remains go to Richmond today. I know not how to replace him. God's will be done! I trust He will raise up some one in his place . . .'

Jones, in his Memoirs, says: 'To one of his officers, after Jackson's death, he [General Lee] said: "I had such implicit confidence in Jackson's skill and energy that I never troubled myself to give him detailed instructions. The most general suggestions were all that he needed."'

To one of his aides, who came to his tent, April 29th, to inform him that the enemy had crossed the Rappahannock River in heavy force, General Lee made the playful reply:

'Well, I heard firing, and I was beginning to think it was time some of you lazy young fellows were coming to tell me what it was all about. Say to General Jackson that he knows just as well what to do with the enemy as I do.'

Jackson said of Lee, when it was intimated by some, at the time he first took command, that he was slow:

'He is cautious. He ought to be. But he is *not* slow. Lee is a phenomenon. He is the only man whom I would follow blindfold.'

As the story of these great men year by year is made plainer to the world, their love, trust, and respect for each other will be better understood. As commander and lieutenant they were exactly suited. When General Lee wanted a movement made and gave Jackson an outline of his plans and the object to be gained, it was performed promptly, well, and thoroughly, if it was possible for flesh and blood to do it.

At the end of May, the Army of Northern Virginia, rested and strengthened, was ready for active operations. On May 31st General Lee writes to Mrs Lee:

'. . . General Hooker has been very daring this past week, and quite active. He has not said what he intends to do, but is giving out by his movements that he designs crossing the Rappahannock. I hope we may be able to frustrate his plans, in part, if not in whole. . . . I pray that our merciful Father in Heaven may protect and direct us! In that case, I fear no odds and no numbers.'

About June 5th most of the army was gathered around Culpeper. Its efficiency, confidence, and *morale* were never better. On June 7th the entire cavalry corps was reviewed on the plain near Brandy Station in

Culpeper by General Lee. We had been preparing ourselves for this event for some days, cleaning, mending and polishing, and I remember we were very proud of our appearance. In fact, it was a grand sight—about eight thousand well-mounted men riding by their beloved commander, first passing him in a walk and then in a trot. He writes to my mother next day—June 8, 1863:

'. . . I reviewed the cavalry in this section yesterday. It was a splendid sight. The men and horses looked well. They have recuperated since last fall. Stuart was in all his glory. Your sons and nephews were well and flourishing. The country here looks very green and pretty, notwithstanding the ravages of war. What a beautiful world God, in His loving kindness to His creatures, has given us! What a shame that men endowed with reason and knowledge of right should mar His gifts . . . '

The next day, June 9th, a large force of the enemy's cavalry, supported by infantry, crossed the Rappahannock and attacked General Stuart. The conflict lasted until dark, when

'The enemy was compelled to recross the river, with heavy loss, leaving about five hundred prisoners, three pieces of artillery, and several colours in our hands.'

During the engagement, about 3 p.m., my brother, General W. H. F. Lee, my commanding officer, was severely wounded. In a letter dated the 11th of the month, my father writes to my mother:

'. . . My supplications continue to ascend for you, my children, and my country. When I last wrote I did not suppose that Fitzhugh would be so soon sent to the rear disabled, and I hope it will be for a short time. I saw him the night after the battle—indeed, met him on the field as they were bringing him from the front. He is young and healthy, and I trust will soon be up again. He seemed to be more concerned about his brave men and officers, who had fallen in the battle, than about himself . . . .'

It was decided, the next day, to send my brother to 'Hickory Hill' the home of Mr W. F. Wickham, in Hanover County, about twenty miles from Richmond, and I was put in charge of him to take him there and to be with him until his wound should heal. Thus it happened that I did not meet my father again until after Gettysburg had been fought, and the army had recrossed into Virginia, almost to the same place I had left it. My father wrote my brother a note the morning after he was wounded, before he left Culpeper. It shows his consideration and tenderness:

'*My Dear Son:* I send you a despatch, received from C. last night. I hope you are comfortable this morning. I wish I could see you, but I cannot. Take care of yourself, and make haste and get well and return. Though I scarcely ever saw you, it was a great comfort to know that you were near and with me. I could think of you and hope to see you. May we yet meet in peace and happiness . . .'

In a letter to my brother's wife, written on the 11th, his love and concern for both of them are plainly shown:

'I am so grieved, my dear daughter, to send Fitzhugh to you wounded. But I am so grateful that his wound is of a character to give us full hope of a speedy recovery. With his youth and strength to aid him, and your tender care to nurse him, I trust he will soon be well again. I know that you will unite with me in thanks to Almighty God, who has so often sheltered him in the hour of danger, for his recent deliverance, and lift up your whole heart in praise to Him for sparing a life so dear to us, while enabling him to do his duty in the station in which He had placed him. Ask him to join us in supplication that He may always cover him with the shadow of His almighty arm, and teach him that his only refuge is in Him, the greatness of whose mercy reacheth unto the heavens, and His truth unto the clouds. As some good is always mixed with the evil in this world, you will now have him with you for a time, and I shall look to you to cure him soon and send him back to me . . .'

My brother reached 'Hickory Hill' quite comfortably, and his wound commenced to heal finely. His wife joined him, my mother and sisters came up from Richmond, and he had all the tender care he could wish.

In a letter dated Culpeper, July 26th, to my brother's wife, my father thus urges resignation:

'I received, last night, my darling daughter, your letter of the 18th from ''Hickory Hill.'' ... You must not be sick while Fitzhugh is away, or he will be more restless under his separation. Get strong and hearty by his return, that he may the more rejoice at the sight of you .... I can appreciate your distress at Fitzhugh's situation. I deeply sympathize with it, and in the lone hours of the night I groan in sorrow at his captivity and separation from you. But we must bear it, exercise all our patience, and do nothing to aggravate the evil. This, besides injuring ourselves, would rejoice our enemies and be sinful in the eyes of God. In His own good time He will relieve us and make all things work together for our good, if we give Him our love and place in Him our trust. I can see no harm that can result from Fitzhugh's capture, except his detention. I feel assured that he will be well attended to. He will be in the hands of old army officers and surgeons, most of whom are men of principle and humanity. His wound, I understand, has not been injured by his removal, but is doing well. Nothing would do him more harm than for him to learn that you were sick and sad. How could he get well? So cheer up and prove your fortitude and patriotism ... You may think of Fitzhugh and love him as much as you please, but do not grieve over him or grow sad.'

From Williamsport, to my mother, he thus writes of his son's capture:

'I have heard with great grief that Fitzhugh has been captured by the enemy. Had not expected that he would be taken from his bed and carried off, but we must bear this additional affliction with fortitude and resignation, and not repine at the will of God. It will eventuate in some good that we know not of now. We must bear our labours and hardships manfully. Our noble men are cheerful and confident. I constantly remember you in my thoughts and prayers.'

On July 12th, from near Hagerstown, he writes again about him:

'The consequences of war are horrid enough at best, surrounded by all the ameliorations of civilization and Christianity. I am very sorry for the injuries done the family at Hickory Hill, and particularly that our dear old Uncle Williams, in his eightieth year, should be subjected to such treatment. But we cannot help it, and must endure it. You will, however, learn before this reaches you that our success at Gettysburg was not so great as reported—in fact, that we failed to drive the enemy from his position, and that our army withdrew to the Potomac. Had the river not unexpectedly risen, all would have been well with us; but God, in His all-wise providence, willed otherwise, and our communications have been interrupted and almost cut off. The waters have subsided to about four feet, and, if they continue, by tomorrow, I hope, our communications will be open. I trust that a merciful God, our only hope and refuge, will not desert us in this hour of need, and will deliver us by His almighty hand, that the whole world may recognize His power and all hearts be lifted up in adoration and praise of His unbounded loving kindness. We must, however, submit to His almighty will, whatever that may be. May God guide and protect us all is my constant prayer.'

In 1868, in a letter to Major Wm. M. McDonald, of Berryville, Clarke County, Virginia, who was intending to write a school history, and had written to my father, asking for information about some of his great battles, the following statement appears:

'As to the battle of Gettysburg, I must again refer you to the official accounts. Its loss was occasioned by a combination of circumstances. It was commenced in the absence of correct intelligence. It was continued in the effort to overcome the difficulties by which we were surrounded, and it would have been gained could one determined and united blow have been delivered by our whole line. As it was, victory trembled in the balance for three days, and the battle resulted in the infliction of as great an amount of injury as was received and in frustrating the Federal campaign for the season.'

After my brother's capture I went to Richmond, taking with me his horses and servants. After remaining there a short time, I mounted my mare and started back to the army, which I found at its old camping ground in Culpeper. I stopped at first for a few days with my father. He was very glad to see me, and I could tell him all about my mother and sisters, and many other friends whom I had just left in Richmond. He appeared to be unchanged in manner and appearance. The disappointment in the Gettysburg campaign, to which he alludes in his letter to my mother, was not shown in anything he said or did. He was calm and dignified with all, at times bright and cheerful, and always had a playful smile and a pleasant word for those about him. The army lay inactive, along the line of the Rappahannock and the Rapidan for two months, watching the enemy, who was in our front. We were very anxious to attack or to be attacked, but each general desired to fight on ground of his own choosing.

During this period, and indeed at all times, my father was fully employed. Besides the care of his own immediate command, he advised with the President and Secretary of War as to the movements and dispositions of the other armies in the Confederacy. In looking over his correspondence one is astonished at the amount of it and at its varied character. He always answered all letters addressed to him, from whatever source, if it was possible. During this winter he devoted himself especially to looking after the welfare of his troops, their clothing, shoes, and rations, all three of which were becoming very scarce. Often, indeed, his army had only a few days' rations in sight. Here are some letters written to the authorities, showing how he was hampered in his movements by the deficiencies existing in the quartermaster's and commissary departments. To the Quartermaster-General, at Richmond, he writes, October, 1863, after his movement around General Meade's right, to Manassas:

'. . . The want of the supplies of shoes, clothing and blankets is very great. Nothing but my unwillingness to expose the men to the hardships that would have resulted from moving them into Loudoun in their present condition induced me to return to the Rappahannock. But I was averse to marching them over the rough roads of that region, at a season, too, when frosts are certain and snows probable, unless they were better provided to encounter them without suffering. I should, otherwise, have endeavoured to detain General Meade near the Potomac, if I could not throw him to the north side.'

In a letter of the same time to the Honourable James A. Seddon, Secretary of War:

'. . . If General Meade is disposed to remain quiet where he is, it was my intention, provided the army could be supplied with clothing, again to advance and threaten his position. Nothing prevented my continuing in his front but the destitute condition of the men, thousands of whom are barefooted, a greater number partially shod, and nearly all without overcoats, blankets, or warm clothing. I think the sublimest sight of war was the cheerfulness and alacrity exhibited by this army in the pursuit of the enemy under all the trials and privations to which it was exposed . . . '

Later on, in January, when the severe weather commenced, he again writes to the Quartermaster-General on the same subject:

'GENERAL:
The want of shoes and blankets in this army continues to cause much suffering and to impair its efficiency. In one regiment I am informed that there are only fifty men with serviceable shoes, and a brigade that recently went on picket was compelled to leave several hundred men in camp, who were unable to bear the exposure of duty, being destitute of shoes and blankets. . . . The supply, by running the blockade, has become so precarious that I think we should turn our attention chiefly to our own resources, and I should like to be informed how far the latter can be counted upon . . . I trust that no efforts will be spared to develop our own resources of supply, as a further dependence upon those from abroad can result in nothing but increase of suffering and want. I am, with great respect,

'Your obedient servant,
R. E. LEE, General.'

There was at this time a great revival of religion in the army. My father became much interested in it, and did what he could to promote in his camps all sacred exercises. Reverend J.W. Jones, in his 'Personal Reminiscences of General R.E. Lee' says:

'General Lee's orders and reports always gratefully recognized "The Lord of Hosts" as the "Giver of Victory" and expressed an humble dependence upon and trust in Him.'

All his correspondence shows the same devout feeling.
On August 13, 1863, he issued the following order:

'HEADQUARTERS, ARMY NORTHERN VIRGINIA,
'AUGUST 13, 1863.
'The President of the Confederate States has, in the name of the people,
appointed August 21st as a day of fasting, humiliation, and prayer. A
strict observance of the day is enjoined upon the officers and soldiers
of this army. All military duties, except such as are absolutely necessary,
will be suspended. The commanding officers of brigades and regiments
are requested to cause divine services, suitable to the occasion, to be
performed in their respective commands. Soldiers! we have sinned
against Almighty God. We have forgotten His signal mercies, and have
cultivated a revengeful, haughty, and boastful spirit. We have not
remembered that the defenders of a just cause should be pure in His
eyes; that 'our times are in His hands' and we have relied too much
on our own arms for the achievement of our independence. God is
our only refuge and our strength. Let us humble ourselves before Him.
Let us confess our many sins, and beseech Him to give us a higher
courage, a purer patriotism, and more determined will; that He will
convert the hearts of our enemies; that He will hasten the time when
war, with its sorrows and sufferings, shall cease, and that He will give
us a name and place among the nations of the earth.

'R. E. LEE, General.'

His was a practical, every-day religion, which supported him all
through his life, enabled him to bear with equanimity every reverse
of fortune, and to accept her gifts without undue elation. During this
period of rest, so unusual to the Army of Northern Virginia, several
reviews were held before the commanding general. I remember being
present when that of the Third Army Corps, General A.P. Hill commanding, took place. . . .
It was a most imposing sight. After it was all over, my father rode
up to several carriages whose occupants he knew and gladdened them
by a smile, a word, or a shake of the hand. He found several of us
young officers with some pretty cousins of his from Richmond, and
he was very bright and cheerful, joking us young people about each
other. His letters to my mother and sister this summer and fall help
to give an insight into his thoughts and feelings. On July 15th, from
Bunker Hill, in a letter to his wife, he says:

'. . . The army has returned to Virginia. Its return is rather sooner

than I had originally contemplated, but, having accomplished much of
what I proposed on leaving the Rappahannock—namely, relieving the
valley of the presence of the enemy and drawing his army north of
the Potomac—I determined to recross the latter river. The enemy, after
centering his forces in our front, began to fortify himself in his position
and bring up his troops, militia, etc.—and those around Washington
and Alexandria. This gave him enormous odds. It also circumscribed
our limits for procuring subsistence for men and animals, which, with
the uncertain state of the river, rendered it hazardous for us to continue
on the north side. It has been raining a great deal since we first crossed
the Potomac, making the roads horrid and embarrassing our operations.
The night we recrossed it rained terribly, yet we got all over safe, save
such vehicles as broke down on the road from the mud, rocks, etc.
We are all well. I hope we will yet be able to damage our adversaries
when they meet us. That it should be so, we must implore the forgiveness
of God for our sins, and the continuance of His blessings. There is
nothing but His almighty power that can sustain us. God bless you
all . . .'

Later, July 26th, he writes from Camp Culpeper:

'. . . After crossing the Potomac, finding that the Shenandoah was
six feet above the fording stage, and, having waited for a week for it
to fall, so that I might cross into Loudoun, fearing that the enemy might
take advantage of our position and move upon Richmond, I determined
to ascend the Valley and cross into Culpeper. Two corps are here with
me. The third passed Thornton's Gap, and I hope will be in striking
distance tomorrow. The army has laboured hard, endured much, and
behaved nobly. It has accomplished all that could be reasonably
expected. It ought not to have been expected to perform impossibilities,
or to have fulfilled the anticipations of the thoughtless and unreasonable.'

On August 2nd, from the same camp, he again writes to my mother:

'. . . I have heard of some doctor having reached Richmond, who had
seen our son at Fortress Monroe. He said that his wound was improving,
and that he himself was well and walking about on crutches. The
exchange of prisoners that had been going on has, for some cause, been

suspended, owing to some crotchet or other, but I hope will soon be resumed, and that we shall have him back soon. The armies are in such close proximity that frequent collisions are common along the outposts. Yesterday the enemy laid down two or three pontoon bridges across the Rappahannock and crossed his cavalry, with a big force of his infantry. It looked at first as if it were the advance of his army, and, as I had not intended to deliver battle, I directed our cavalry to retire slowly before them and to check their too rapid pursuit. Finding, later in the day, that their army was not following, I ordered out the infantry and drove them back to the river. I suppose they intended to push on to Richmond by this or some other route. I trust, however, they will never reach there . . . '

On August 23rd, from the camp near Orange Court House, General Lee writes to Mrs Lee:

'. . . My camp is near Mr Erasmus Taylor's house, who has been very kind in contributing to our comfort. His wife sends us, every day, buttermilk, loaf bread, ice, and such vegetables as she has. I cannot get her to desist, though I have made two special visits to that effect. All the brides have come on a visit to the army: Mrs Ewell, Mrs Walker, Mrs Heth, etc. General Meade's army is north of the Rappahannock along the Orange and Alexandria Railroad. He is very quiet . . . '

'September 4, 1863.
'. . . You see I am still here. When I wrote last, the indications were that the enemy would move against us any day; but this past week he has been very quiet, and seems at present to continue so. I was out looking at him yesterday, from Clarke's Mountain. He has spread himself over a large surface and looks immense . . . '

And on September 18th, from the same camp:

'. . . The enemy state that they have heard of a great reduction in our forces here, and are now going to drive us back to Richmond. I trust they will not succeed; but our hope and our refuge is in our merciful Father in Heaven . . . '

On October 9th, the Army of Northern Virginia was put in motion, and was pushed around Meade's right. Meade was gradually forced back to a position near the old battlefield at Manassas. Although we had hard marching, much skirmishing, and several severe fights between the cavalry of both armies, nothing permanent was accomplished, and in about ten days we were back on our old lines. In a letter of October 19, 1863, to his wife, my father says:

'. . . I have returned to the Rappahannock. I did not pursue with the main army beyond Bristoe or Broad Run. Our advance went as far as Bull Run, where the enemy was entrenched, extending his right as far as 'Chantilly' in the yard of which he was building a redoubt. I could have thrown him farther back, but saw no chance of bringing him to battle, and it would only have served to fatigue our troops by advancing farther. I should certainly have endeavoured to throw them north of the Potomac; but thousands were barefooted, thousands with fragments of shoes, and all without overcoats, blankets, or warm clothing. I could not bear to expose them to certain suffering and an uncertain issue . . .'

On October 25th, from 'Camp Rappahannock' he writes again to my mother:

'. . . I moved yesterday into a nice pine thicket, and Perry is today engaged in constructing a chimney in front of my tent, which will make it warm and comfortable. I have no idea when Fitzhugh will be exchanged. The Federal authorities still resist all exchanges, because they think it is to our interest to make them. Any desire expressed on our part for the exchange of any individual magnifies the difficulty, as they at once think some great benefit is to result to us from it. His detention is very grievous to me, and, besides, I want his services. I am glad you have some socks for the army. Send them to me. They will come safely. Tell the girls to send all they can. I wish they could make some shoes, too. We have thousands of barefooted men. There is no news. General Meade, I believe, is repairing the railroad, and I presume will come on again. If I could only get some shoes and clothes for the men, I would save him the trouble . . .'

One can see from these letters of my father how deeply he felt for the sufferings of his soldiers, and how his plans were hindered by inadequate supplies of food and clothing. I heard him constantly allude to these troubles; indeed, they seemed never absent from his mind.

Abraham Lincoln

1809–1865

Abraham Lincoln, the sixteenth President of the United States, has become a symbol of American democracy and the importance of the Union. This selection of speeches and letters demonstrates the uniquely American quality of the man—a compound of simple dignity, practical compassion, lucid philosophy and backwoods humor.

A Letter to Mrs O.H. Browning.
Springfield, Illinois. April 1, 1838

DEAR MADAM,

Without apologizing for being egotistical, I shall make the history of so much of my life as has elapsed since I saw you the subject of this letter. And, by the way, I now discover that in order to give a full and intelligible account of the things I have done and suffered since I saw you, I shall necessarily have to relate some that happened before.

It was, then, in the autumn of 1836 that a married lady of my acquaintance, and who was a great friend of mine, being about to pay a visit to her father and other relatives residing in Kentucky, proposed to me that on her return she would bring a sister of hers with her on condition that I would engage to become her brother-in-law with all convenient dispatch. I, of course, accepted the proposal, for you know I could not have done otherwise had I really been averse to it; but privately, between you and me, I was most confoundedly well pleased with the project. I had seen the said sister some three years before, thought her intelligent and agreeable, and saw no good objection to plodding life through hand-in-hand with her. Time passed on, the lady took her journey, and in due time returned, sister in company, sure enough. This astonished me a little, for it appeared to me that her coming so readily showed that she was a trifle too willing, but on reflection it occurred to me that she might have been prevailed on by her married sister to come, without anything concerning me having been mentioned to her, and so I concluded that if no other objection presented itself, I would consent to waive this. All this occurred to me on hearing of her arrival in the neighbourhood—for, be it remembered, I had not yet seen her, except about three years previous, as above mentioned. In a few days we had an interview, and, although I had seen her before, she did not look as my imagination had pictured her. I knew she was over-size, but she now appeared a fair match for Falstaff. I knew she was called an 'old maid' and I felt no doubt of the truth of at least half of the appellation, but now, when I beheld her, I could not for my life avoid thinking of my mother; and this, not from withered features,—for her skin was too full of fat to permit of its contracting into wrinkles—but from her want of teeth, weather-beaten appearance in general, and from a kind of notion that ran in my head that nothing could have commenced at the size of infancy and reached her present bulk in less than thirty-five or forty years; and, in short, I was not at all pleased with her. But what could I do? I had told her sister that I would take her for better or for worse, and I made a point of honour and conscience in all things to stick to my word, especially if others had been induced to act on it, which in this case I had no doubt they had, for I was now fairly convinced that no other man on earth would have her, and hence the conclusion that they were bent on holding me to my bargain. 'Well' thought I, 'I have said it, and, be the consequences what they may, it shall not be my fault if I fail to do it.' At once I determined to consider her my wife, and this done, all my powers of discovery were put to work in search of perfections in her which might be fairly set off against her defects. I tried to imagine her handsome, which, but for her unfortunate corpulency, was actually true. Exclusive of this, no woman that I have ever seen has a finer face. I also tried to convince myself that the mind was much more to be valued than the person, and in this she was not inferior, as I could discover, to any with whom I had been acquainted.

Shortly after this, without attempting to come to any positive understanding with her, I set out for Vandalia, when and where you first saw me. During my stay there I had letters from her which did not change my opinion of either her intellect or intention, but, on the contrary, confirmed it in both.

All this while, although I was fixed 'firm as the surge-repelling rock' in my resolution, I found I was continually repenting the rashness which had led me to make it. Through life I have been in no bondage, either real or imaginary, from the thraldom of which I so much desired to be free. After my return home, I saw nothing to change my opinion of her in any particular. She was the same, and so was I. I now spent my time in planning how I might get along in life after my contemplated change of circumstances should have taken place, and how I might procrastinate the evil day for a time, which I really dreaded as much, perhaps more, than an Irishman does the halter.

After all my sufferings upon this deeply interesting subject, here I am, wholly, unexpectedly, completely out of the 'scrape' and I now want to know if you can guess how I got out of it—out, clear, in every sense of the term—no violation of word, honour, or conscience. I don't believe you can guess, and so I might as well tell you at once. As the lawyer says, it was done in the manner following, to wit: After I had delayed the matter as long as I thought I could in honour do (which, by the way, had brought me round into the last fall), I concluded I might as well bring it to a consummation without further delay, and so I mustered my resolution and made the proposal to her direct; but, shocking to relate, she answered, No. At first I supposed she did it through an affectation of modesty, which I thought but ill became her under the peculiar circumstances of the case, but on my renewal of the charge I found she repelled it with greater firmness than before. I tried it again and again, but with the same success, or rather with the same want of success.

I finally was forced to give it up, at which I very unexpectedly found myself mortified almost beyond endurance. I was mortified, it seemed to me, in a hundred different ways. My vanity was deeply wounded by the reflection that I had so long been too stupid to discover her intentions, and at the same time never doubting that I understood them perfectly; and also that she, whom I had taught myself to believe nobody else would have, had actually rejected me with all my fancied greatness. And, to cap the whole, I then for the first time began to suspect that I was really a little in love with her. But let it all go! I'll try and outlive it. Others have been made fools of by the girls, but this can never in truth be said of me. I most emphatically, in this instance, made a fool of myself. I have now come to the conclusion never again to think of marrying, and for this reason—I can never be satisfied with any one who would be blockhead enough to have me.

When you receive this, write me a long yarn about something to amuse me. Give my respects to Mr Browning.

EXTRACTS FROM LETTER TO JOSHUA F. SPEED.

AUGUST 24, 1855

You suggest that in political action now, you and I would differ. I suppose we would; not quite so much however, as you may think. You know I dislike slavery, and you fully admit the abstract wrong of it. So far there is no cause of difference. But you say that sooner than yield your legal right to the slave, especially at the bidding of those who are not themselves interested, you would see the Union dissolved. I am not aware that any one is bidding you yield that right; very certainly I am not. I leave that matter entirely to yourself. I also acknowledge your rights and my obligations under the Constitution in regard to your slaves. I confess I hate to see the poor creatures hunted down and caught and carried back to their stripes and unrequited toil; but I bite my lips and keep quiet. In 1841, you and I had together a tedious low-water trip on a steamboat, from Louisville to St. Louis. You may remember, as I well do, that from Louisville to the mouth of the Ohio, there were on board ten or a dozen slaves shackled together with irons. That sight was a continued torment to me, and I see something like it every time I touch the Ohio or any other slave border. It is not fair for you to assume that I have no interest in a thing which has, and continually exercises, the power of making me miserable. You ought rather to appreciate how much the great body of the Northern people do crucify their feelings in order to maintain their loyalty to the Constitution and the Union. I do oppose the extension of slavery, because my judgment and feeling so prompt me, and I am under no obligations to the contrary. If for this you and I must differ, differ we must. You say if you were President, you would send an army and hang the leaders of the Missouri outrages upon the Kansas elections; still, if Kansas fairly votes herself a slave State she must be admitted, or the Union must be dissolved. But how if she votes herself a slave State unfairly; that is, by the very means for which you say you would hang men? Must she still be admitted, or the Union dissolved? That will be the phase of the question when it first becomes a practical one. In your assumption that there may be a fair decision of the slavery question in Kansas, I plainly see that you and I would differ about the Nebraska law. I look upon that enactment, not as a law, but as a violence from the beginning. It was conceived in violence, is maintained in violence, and is being executed in violence. I say it was conceived in violence, because the destruction of the Missouri Compromise, under the circumstances, was nothing less than violence. It was passed in violence, because it could not have passed at all but for the votes of many members in violence of the known will of their constituents. It is maintained in violence, because the elections since clearly demand its repeal, and the demand is openly disregarded.

You say men ought to be hung for the way they are executing the law; I say that the way it is being executed is quite as good as any of its antecedents. It is being executed in the precise way which was intended from the first, else why does no Nebraska man express astonishment or condemnation? Poor Reeder is the only public man who has been silly enough to believe that anything like fairness was ever intended, and he has been bravely undeceived.

That Kansas will form a slave constitution, and with it ask to be admitted into the Union, I take to be already a settled question, and so settled by the very means you so pointedly condemn. By every principle of law ever held by any court North or South, every negro taken to Kansas is free; yet in utter disregard of this—in the spirit of violence merely—that beautiful Legislature gravely passes a law to hang any man who shall venture to inform a negro of his legal rights. This is the subject and real object of the law. If, like Haman, they should hang upon the gallows of their own building, I shall not be among the mourners for their fate. In my humble sphere, I shall advocate the restoration of the Missouri Compromise so long as Kansas remains a Territory; and when, by all these foul means, it seeks to come into the Union as a slave State, I shall oppose it. I am very loath in any case to withhold my assent to the enjoyment of property acquired or located in good faith; but I do not admit that good faith in taking a negro to Kansas to be held in slavery is a probability with any man. Any man who has sense enough to be the controller of his own property has too much sense to misunderstand the outrageous character of the whole Nebraska business. But I digress. In my opposition to the admission of Kansas, I shall have some company, but we may be beaten, If we are, I shall not, on that account, attempt to dissolve the Union. I think it probable, however, we shall be beaten. Standing as a unit among yourselves, you can, directly and indirectly, bribe enough of our men to carry the day, as you could on the open proposition to establish a monarchy. Get hold of some man in the North whose position and ability are such that he can make the support of your measure, whatever it may be, a Democratic party necessity, and the thing is done. Apropos of this, let me tell you an anecdote. Douglas introduced the Nebraska Bill in January. In February afterward, there was a called session of the Illinois Legislature. Of the one hundred members composing the two branches of that body, about seventy were Democrats. These latter held a caucus, in which the Nebraska Bill was talked of, if not formally discussed. It was thereby discovered that just three, and no more, were in favour of the measure. In a day or two Douglas's orders came on to have resolutions passed approving the bill; and they were passed by large majorities! The truth of this is vouched for by a bolting Democratic member. The masses too, Democratic as well as Whig, were even nearer unanimous against it; but as soon as the party necessity of supporting it became apparent, the way the Democrats began to see the wisdom and justice of it was perfectly astonishing.

You say that if Kansas fairly votes herself a free State, as a Christian you will rejoice at it. All decent slaveholders talk that way, and I do not doubt their candour; but they never vote that way. Although in a private letter or conversation you will express your preference that Kansas should be free, you would vote for no man for Congress who would say the same thing publicly. No such man could be elected from any district in a slave State. You think Stringfellow and company ought to be hung . . . The slave breeders and slave traders are a small, odious, and detested class among you; and yet in politics they dictate the course of all of you, and are as completely your masters as you are the master of your own negroes. You inquire where I now stand. That is a disputed point. I think I am a Whig; but others say there are no Whigs, and that I am an Abolitionist. When I was at Washington, I voted for the Wilmot Proviso as good as forty times; and I never heard of any one attempting to unwhig me for that. I now do no more that oppose the extension of slavery. I am not a know nothing; that is certain. How could I be? How can any one who abhors the oppression of negroes be in favour of degrading classes of white people? Our progress in degeneracy appears to me to be pretty rapid. As a nation, we began by declaring that *all men are created equal*. We now practically read it, *all men are created equal except negroes*. When the know nothings get control, it will read, *all men are created equal except negroes* and foreigners and Catholics. When it comes to this, I shall prefer emigrating to some country where they make no pretence of loving liberty—to Russia, for instance, where despotism can be taken pure, and without the base alloy of hypocrisy . . . My kindest regards to Mrs Speed. On the leading subject of this letter I have more of her sympathy than I have of yours; and yet let me say I am your friend for ever.

A. LINCOLN

MR LINCOLN'S SPEECH.

MAY 19, 1856

Mr Chairman and Gentlemen, I was over at [cries of 'Platform!' 'Take the platform!']—I say, that while I was at Danville Court, some of our friends of anti-Nebraska got together in Springfield and elected me as one delegate to represent old Sangamon with them in this convention, and I am here certainly as a sympathizer in this movement and by virtue of that meeting and selection. But we can hardly be called delegates strictly, inasmuch as, properly speaking, we represent nobody but ourselves. I think it altogether fair to say that we have no anti-Nebraska party in Sangamon, although there is a good deal of anti-Nebraska feeling there; but I say for myself, and I think I may speak also for my colleagues, that we who are here fully approve of the platform and of all that has been done [A voice: 'Yes!']; and even if we are not regularly delegates, it will be right for me to answer your call to speak. I suppose we truly stand for the public sentiment of Sangamon on the great question of the repeal, although we do not yet represent many numbers who have taken a distinct position on the question.

We are in a trying time—it ranges above mere party— and this movement to call a halt and turn our steps backward needs all the help and good counsels it can get; for unless popular opinion makes itself very strongly felt, and a change is made in our present course, *blood will flow on account of Nebraska, and brother's hand will be raised against brother!* [The last sentence was uttered in such an earnest, impressive, if not, indeed, tragic, manner, as to make a cold chill creep over me. Others gave a similar experience.]

I have listened with great interest to the earnest appeal made to Illinois men by the gentleman from Lawrence [James S. Emery] who has just addressed us so eloquently and forcibly. I was deeply moved by his statement of the wrongs done to free State men out there. I think it just to say that all true men North should sympathize with them, and ought to be willing to do any possible and needful thing to right their wrongs. But we must not promise what we ought not, lest we be called on to perform what we cannot; we must be calm and moderate, and consider the whole difficulty, and determine what is possible and just. We must not be led by excitement and passion to do that which our sober judgments would not approve in our cooler moments. We have higher aims; we will have more serious business than to dally with temporary measures.

We are here to stand firmly for a principle—to stand firmly for a right. We know that great political and moral wrongs are done, and outrages committed, and we denounce those wrongs and outrages, although we cannot, at present, do much more. But we desire to reach out beyond those personal outrages and establish a rule that will apply to all, and so prevent any future outrages.

We have seen today that every shade of popular opinion is represented here, with *Freedom* or rather *Free Soil* as the basis. We have come together as in some sort representatives of popular opinion against the extension of slavery into territory now free in fact as well as by law, and the pledged word of the statesmen of the nation who are now no more. We come—we are here assembled together—to protest as well as we can against a great wrong, and to take measures, as well as we now can, to make that wrong right; to place the nation, as far as it may be possible now, as it was before the repeal of the Missouri Compromise;

and the plain way to do this is to restore the Compromise, and to demand and determine that *Kansas shall be free!* [Immense applause.] While we affirm, and reaffirm, if necessary, our devotion to the principles of the Declaration of Independence, let our practical work here be limited to the above. We know that there is not a perfect agreement of sentiment here on the public questions which might be rightfully considered in this convention, and that the indignation which we all must feel cannot be helped; but all of us must give up something for the good of the cause. There is one desire which is uppermost in the mind, one wish common to us all—to which no dissent will be made; and I counsel you earnestly to bury all resentment, to sink all personal feeling, make all things work to a common purpose in which we are united and agreed about, and which all present will agree is absolutely necessary—which *must* be done by any rightful mode if there be such: *Slavery must be kept out of Kansas!* [Applause.] The test—the pinch—is right there. If we lose Kansas to freedom, an example will be set which will prove fatal to freedom in the end. We, therefore, in the language of the *Bible*, must 'lay the axe to the root of the tree.' Temporizing will not do longer; now is the time for decision—for firm, persistent, resolute action. [Applause.]

The Nebraska bill, or rather Nebraska law, is not one of wholesome legislation, but was and is an act of legislative usurpation, whose result, if not indeed intention, is to make slavery national; and unless headed off in some effective way, we are in a fair way to see this land of boasted freedom converted into a land of slavery in fact. [Sensation.] Just open your two eyes, and see if this be not so. I need do no more than state, to command universal approval, that almost the entire North, as well as a large following in the border States, is radically opposed to the planting of slavery in free territory. Probably in a popular vote through-out the nation nine tenths of the voters in the free States, and at least one half in the border States, if they could express their sentiments freely, would vote NO on such an issue; and it is safe to say that two-thirds of the votes of the entire nation would be opposed to it. And yet, in spite of this overbalancing of sentiment in this free country, we are in a fair way to see Kansas present itself for admission as a slave State. Indeed, it is a felony, by the local law of Kansas, to deny that slavery exists there even now. By every principle of law, a negro in Kansas is free; yet the *bogus* legislature makes it an infamous crime to tell him that he is free!

The party lash and the fear of ridicule will overawe justice and liberty; for it is a singular fact, but none the less a fact, and well known by the most common experience, that men will do things under the terror of the party lash that they would not on any account or for any consideration do otherwise; while men who will march up to the mouth of a loaded cannon without shrinking, will run from the terrible name of 'Abolitionist' even when pronounced by a worthless creature whom they, with good reason, despise. For instance—to press this point a little—Judge Douglas introduced his anti-Nebraska bill in January; and we had an extra session of our legislature in the succeeding February, in which were seventy-five Democrats; and at a party caucus, fully attended, there were just three votes out of the whole seventy five, for the measure. But in a few days orders came on from Washington, commanding them to approve the measure; the party lash was applied, and it was brought up again in caucus, and passed by a large majority. The masses were against it, but party necessity carried it; and it was passed through the lower house of Congress against the will of the people, for the same reasons. Here is where the greatest danger lies—that, while we profess to be a government of law and reason, law will give way to violence on demand of this awful and crushing power. Like the great Juggernaut—I think that is the name—the great idol, it crushes everything that comes in its way, and makes a—or as I read once, in a black letter law book, 'a slave is a human being who is legally not a *person*, but a *thing*.' And if the safeguards to liberty are broken down, as is now attempted, when they have made *things* of all the free negroes, how long, think you, before they will begin to make *things* of poor white men? [Applause.] Be not deceived. Revolutions do not go backward. The founder of the Democratic party declared that *all* men were created equal. His successor in the leadership has written the word 'white' before men, making it read 'all *white* men are created equal.' Pray, will or may not the Know nothings, if they should get in power, add the word 'protestant' making it read *'all protestant white men'*?

Meanwhile the hapless negro is the fruitful subject of reprisals in other quarters. John Pettit, whom Tom Benton paid his respects to, you will recollect, calls the immortal Declaration 'a self-evident lie;' while at the birthplace of freedom—in the shadow of Bunker Hill and of the 'cradle of liberty' at the home of the Adamses and Warren and Otis—Choate, from our side of the house, dares to fritter away the birthday promise of liberty by proclaiming the Declaration to be 'a string of glittering generalities;' and the Southern Whigs, working hand in hand with pro-slavery Democrats, are making Choate's theories practical. Thomas Jefferson, a slaveholder, mindful of the moral element in slavery, solemnly declared that he 'trembled for his country when he remembered that God is just;' while Judge Douglas, with an insignificant wave of the hand, 'don't care whether slavery is voted up or voted down.' Now, if slavery is right, or even negative, he has a right to treat it in this trifling manner. But if it is a moral and political wrong, as all Christendom considers it to be, how can he answer to God for this attempt to spread and fortify it? [Applause.]

But no man, and Judge Douglas no more than any other, can maintain a negative, or merely neutral, position on this question; and, accordingly, he avows that the Union was made *by* white men and *for* white men and their descendants. As a matter of fact, the first branch of the proposition is historically true; the government was made by white men. and they were and are the superior race. This I admit. But the corner stone of the government, so to speak, was the declaration that '*all* men are crated equal' and all entitled to 'life, liberty, and the pursuit of happiness' [Applause.]

And not only so, but the framers of the Constitution were particular to keep out of that instrument the word 'slave' the reason being that slavery would ultimately come to an end, and they did not wish to have any reminder that in this free country human beings were ever prostituted to slavery. [Applause.] Nor is it any argument that we are superior and the negro inferior—that he has but one talent while we have ten. Let the negro possess the little he has in independence; if he has but one talent, he should be permitted to keep the little he has. [Applause.] But slavery will endure no test of reason or logic; and yet its advocates, like Douglas, use a sort of bastard logic, or noisy assumption, it might better be termed, like the above, in order to prepare the mind for the gradual, but none the less certain, encroachments of the Moloch of slavery upon the fair domain of freedom. But however much you may argue upon it, or smother it in soft phrases, slavery can only be maintained by force—by violence. The repeal of the Missouri Compromise was by violence. It was a violation of both law and the sacred obligations of honour, to overthrow and trample underfoot a solemn compromise, obtained by the fearful loss to freedom of one of the fairest of our Western domains. Congress violated the will and confidence of its constituents in voting for the bill; and while public sentiment, as shown by the elections of 1854, demanded the restoration of this compromise, Congress violated its trust by refusing, simply because it had the force of numbers to hold on to it. And murderous violence is being used now, in order to force slavery on to Kansas; for it cannot be done in any other way. [Sensation.]

The necessary result was to establish the rule of violence—force, instead of the rule of law and reason; to perpetuate and spread slavery, and, in time, to make it general. We see it at both ends of the line. In Washington, on the very spot where the outrage was started, the fearless Sumner is beaten to insensibility, and is now slowly dying; while senators who claim to be gentlemen and Christians stood by, countenancing the act, and even applauding it afterwards in their places in the Senate. Even Douglas, our man, saw it all and was within helping distance, yet let the murderous blows fall unopposed. Then, at the other end of the line, at the very time Sumner was being murdered, Lawrence was being destroyed for the crime of Freedom. It was the most prominent stronghold of liberty in Kansas, and must give way to the all-dominating power of slavery. Only two days ago, Judge Trumbull found it necessary to propose a bill in the Senate to prevent a general civil war and to restore peace in Kansas.

We live in the midst of alarms; anxiety beclouds the future; we expect some new disaster with each newspaper we read. Are we in a healthful political state? Are not the tendencies plain? Do not the signs of the times point plainly the way in which we are going? [Sensation.]

In the early days of the Constitution slavery was recognized, by South and North alike, as an evil, and the division of sentiment about it was not controlled by geographical lines or considerations of climate, but by moral and philanthropic views. Petitions for the abolition of slavery were presented to the very first Congress by Virginia and Massachusetts alike. To show the harmony which prevailed, I will state that a fugitive slave law was passed in 1793, with no dissenting voice in the Senate, and but seven dissenting votes in the House. It was, however, a wise law, moderate, and, under the Constitution, a just one. Twenty-five years later, a more stringent law was proposed and defeated; and thirty-five years after that, the present law, drafted by Mason of Virginia, was passed by Northern votes. I am not, just now, complaining of this law, but I am trying to show how the current sets; for the proposed law of 1817 was far less offensive than the present one. In 1774 the Continental Congress pledged itself, without a dissenting vote, to wholly discontinue the slave trade, and to neither purchase nor import any slave: and less than three months before thepassage of the Declaration of Independence, the same Congress which adopted that declaration unanimously resolved 'that *no slave be imported into any of the thirteen United Colonies.'* [Great applause.]

On the second day of July, 1776, the draft of a Declaration of Independence was reported to Congress by the committee, and in it the slave trade was characterized as 'an execrable commerce' as 'a piratical warfare' as the 'opprobrium of infidel powers' and as 'a cruel war against human nature.' [Applause.] All agreed on this except South Carolina and Georgia, and in order to preserve harmony, and from the necessity of the case, these expressions were omitted. Indeed, abolition societies existed as far south as Virginia; and it is a well-known fact that Washington, Jefferson, Madison, Lee, Henry, Mason, and Pendleton were qualified abolitionists, and much more radical on that subject than we of the Whig and Democratic parties claim to be today. On March 1, 1784, Virginia ceded to the confederation all its lands lying northwest of the Ohio River. Jefferson, Chase of Maryland, and Howell of Rhode Island, as a committee on that and territory thereafter *to be ceded*, reported that no slavery should exist after the year 1800. Had this report been adopted, not only the Northwest, but Kentucky, Tennessee, Alabama, and Mississippi also would have been free; but it required the assent of nine States to ratify it. North Carolina was divided, and thus its vote was lost; and Delaware, Georgia, and New Jersey refused to vote. In point of fact, as it was, it was assented to by six States. Three years later, on a square vote to exclude slavery from the Northwest, only one vote, and that from New York, was against it. And yet, thirty-seven years later, five thousand citizens of Illinois out of a voting mass of less than twelve thousand, deliberately, after a long and heated contest, voted to introduce slavery in Illinois; and, today, a large party in the free State of Illinois are willing to vote to fasten the shackles of slavery on the fair domain of Kansas, notwithstanding it received the dowry of freedom long before its birth as a political community. I repeat, therefore, the question, Is it not plain in what direction we are tending? [Sensation.] In the colonial time, Mason, Pendleton, and Jefferson were as hostile to slavery in Virginia as Otis, Ames, and the Adamses were in Massachusetts; and Virginia made as earnest an effort to get rid of it as old Massachusetts did. But circumstances were against them and they failed; but not that the goodwill of its leading men was lacking.

Yet within less than fifty years Virginia changed its tune, and made negro breeding for the cotton and sugar States one of its leading industries. [Laughter and applause.]

In the Constitutional Convention, George Mason of Virginia made a more violent abolition speech than my friends Lovejoy or Codding would desire to make here today—a speech which could not be safely repeated anywhere on Southern soil in this enlightened year. But while there were some differences of opinion on this subject even then, discussion was allowed; but as you see by the Kansas slave code, which, as you know, is the Missouri slave code, merely ferried across the river, it is a felony to even express an opinion hostile to that foul blot in the land of Washington and the Declaration of Independence. [Sensation.]

In Kentucky—my State—in 1849, on a test vote, the mighty influence of Henry Clay and many other good men there could not get a symptom of expression in favour of gradual emancipation on a plain issue of marching toward the light of civilization with Ohio and Illinois; but the State of Boone and Hardin and Henry Clay, with a *nigger* under each arm, took the black trail toward the deadly swamps of barbarism. Is there—can there be—any doubt about this thing? And is there any doubt that we must all lay aside our prejudices and march, shoulder to shoulder, in the great army of Freedom? [Applause.]

Every Fourth of July our young orators all proclaim this to be 'the land of the *free* and the home of the brave!' Well, now, when you orators get that off next year, and, may be, this very year, how would you like some old grizzled farmer to get up in the grove and deny it? [Laughter.] How would you like that? But suppose Kansas comes in as a slave State, and all the 'border ruffians' have barbecues about it, and free State men come trailing back to the dishonoured North, like whipped dogs with their tails between their legs, it is—ain't it?—evident that this is no more the 'land of the free;' and if we let it go so, we won't dare to say 'home of the brave' out loud. [Sensation and confusion.]

Can any man doubt that, even in spite of the people's will, slavery will triumph through violence, unless that will be made manifest and enforced? Even Governor Reeder claimed at the outset that the contest in Kansas was to be fair, but he got his eyes open at last; and I believe that, as a result of this moral and physical violence, Kansas will soon apply for admission as a slave State. And yet we can't mistake that the people don't want it so, and that it is a land which is free both by natural and political law. *No law is free law!* Such is the understanding of all Christendom. In the Somerset case, decided nearly a century ago, the great Lord Mansfield held that slavery was of such a nature that it must take its rise in *positive* (as distinguished from *natural*) law; and that in no country or age could it be traced back to any other source. Will some one please tell me where is the *positive* law that establishes slavery in Kansas? [A voice: 'The *bogus* laws.'] Aye, the *bogus* laws! And, on the same principle, a gang of Missouri horse-thieves could come into Illinois and declare horse-stealing to be legal [Laughter], and it would be just as legal as slavery is in Kansas. But by express statute, in the land of Washington and Jefferson, we may soon be brought face to face with the discreditable fact of showing to the world by our acts that we prefer slavery to freedom—darkness to light! [Sensation.]

It is, I believe, a principle in law that when one party to a contract violates it so grossly as to chiefly destroy the object for which it is made, the other party may rescind it. I will ask Browning if that ain't good law. [Voices: 'Yes!'] Well, now if that be right, I go for rescinding the whole, entire Missouri Compromise and thus turning Missouri into a free State; and I should like to know the difference—should like for any one to point out the difference—between *our* making a free State of Missouri and *their* making a slave State of Kansas. [Great applause.] There ain't one bit of difference, except that our way would be a great mercy to humanity. But I have never said—and the Whig party has never said— and those who oppose the Nebraska bill do not as a body say, that they have any intention of interfering with slavery in the slave States. Our platform says just the contrary. We allow slavery to exist in the slave States—not because slavery is right or good, but from the necessities of our Union. We grant a fugitive slave law because it is so 'nominated in the bond;' because our fathers so stipulated—had to— and we are bound to carry out this agreement. But they did not agree to introduce slavery in regions where it did not previously exist. On the contrary, they said by their example and teachings that they did not deem it expedient—did not consider it right—to do so; and it is wise and right to do just as they did about it [Voices: 'Good!'], and that is what we propose—not to interfere with slavery where it exists (we have never tried to do it), and to give them a reasonable and efficient fugitive slave law. [A voice: 'No!'] I say YES! [Applause.] It was part of the bargain, and I'm for living up to it; but I go no further; I'm not bound to do more, and I won't agree any further. [Great applause.]

We, here in Illinois, should feel especially proud of the provision of the Missouri Compromise excluding slavery from what is now Kansas; for an Illinois man, Jesse B. Thomas, was its father. Henry Clay, who is credited with the authorship of the Compromise in general terms, did not even vote for that provision, but only advocated the ultimate admission by a second compromise; and, Thomas was, beyond all controversy, the real author of the 'slavery restriction' branch of the Compromise. To show the generosity of the Northern members toward the Southern side; on a test vote to exclude slavery from Missouri, ninety voted not to exclude, and eighty-seven to exclude, every vote from the slave States being ranged with the former and fourteen votes from the free States, of whom seven were from New England alone; while on a vote to exclude slavery from what is now Kansas, the vote was one hundred and thirty-four *for* to forty-two *against*. The scheme, as a whole, was, of course, a Southern triumph. It is idle to contend otherwise,, as is now being done by the Nebraskaites; it was so shown by the votes and quite as emphatically by the expressions of representative men. Mr Lowndes of South Carolina was never known to commit a political mistake; his was the great judgment of that section; and he declared that this measure 'would restore tranquillity to the country—a result demanded by every consideration of discretion, of moderation, of wisdom, and of virtue.' When the measure came before President Monroe for his approval, he put to each member of his cabinet this question: 'Has Congress the constitutional power to prohibit slavery in a territory?' And John C. Calhoun and William H. Crawford from the South, equally with John Quincy Adams, Benjamin Rush, and Smith Thompson from the North, alike answered, '*Yes!*' without qualification or equivocation; and this measure, of so great consequence to the South, was passed; and Missouri was, by means of it, finally enabled to knock at the door of the Republic for an open passage to its brood of slaves. And, in spite of this, Freedom's share is about to be taken by violence—by the force of misrepresentative votes, not called for by the popular will. What name can I, in common decency, give to this wicked transaction? [Sensation.]

But even then the contest was not over; for when the Missouri constitution came before Congress for its approval, it forbade any free negro or mulatto from entering the State. In short, our Illinois 'black laws' were hidden away in their constitution [Laughter], and the controversy was thus revived. Then it was that Mr Clay's talents shone out conspicuously, and the controversy that shook the Union to its foundation was finally settled to the satisfaction of the conservative parties on both sides of the line, though not to the extremists on either, and Missouri was admitted by the small majority of six in the lower House. How great a majority, do you think, would have been given had Kansas also been secured for slavery? [A voice: 'A majority the other way.'] 'A majority the other way' is answered. Do you think it would have been safe for a Northern man to have confronted his constituents after having voted to consign both Missouri and Kansas to hopeless slavery? And yet this man Douglas, who misrepresents his constituents, and who has exerted his highest talents in that direction, will be carried in triumph through the State, and hailed with honour while applauding that act. [Three groans for '*Dug!*'] And this shows whither we are tending. This thing of slavery is more powerful than its supporters—even than the high priests that minister at its altar. It debauches even our greatest men. It gathers strength, like a rolling snowball, by its own infamy. Monstrous crimes are committed in its name by persons collectively which they would not dare to commit as individuals. Its aggressions and encroachments almost surpass belief. In a despotism, one might not wonder to see slavery advance steadily and remorselessly into new dominions; but is it not wonderful, is it not even alarming, to see its steady advance in a land dedicated to the proposition that 'all men are created equal'? [Sensation.]

It yields nothing itself; it keeps all it has, and gets all it can besides. It really came dangerously near securing Illinois in 1824; it did get Missouri in 1821. The first proposition was to admit what is now Arkansas *and* Missouri as one slave State. But the territory was divided, and Arkansas came in, without serious question, as a slave State; and afterward Missouri, not as a sort of equality, *free*, but also as a slave State. Then we had Florida and Texas; and now Kansas is about to be forced into the dismal procession. [Sensation.] And so it is wherever you look. We have not forgotten—it is but six years since—how dangerously near California came to being a slave State. Texas is a slave State, and four other slave States may be carved from its vast domain. And yet, in the year 1829, slavery was abolished throughout that vast region by a royal decree of the then sovereign of Mexico. Will you please tell me by what *right* slavery exists in Texas today? By the same right as, and no higher or greater than, slavery is seeking dominion in Kansas; by political force— peaceful, if that will suffice; by the torch (as in Kansas) and the bludgeon (as in the Senate chamber), if required. And so history repeats itself;

and even as slavery has kept its course by craft, intimidation, and violence in the past, so it will persist, in my judgment, until met and dominated by the will of a people bent on its restriction.

We have, this very afternoon, heard bitter denunciations of Brooks in Washington, and Titus, Stringfellow, Atchison, Jones, and Shannon in Kansas—the battle ground of slavery. I certainly am not going to advocate or shield them; but they and their acts are but the necessary outcome of the Nebraska law. We should reserve our highest censure for the authors of the mischief, and not for the catspaws which they use. I believe it was Shakespeare who said, 'Where the offence lies, there let the axe fall;' and, in my opinion, this man Douglas and the Northern men in Congress who advocate 'Nebraska' are more guilty than a thousand Joneses and Stringfellows, with all their murderous practices, can be. [Applause.]

We have made a good beginning here today. As our Methodist friends would say, 'I feel it is good to be here.' While extremists may find some fault with the moderation of our platform, they should recollect that 'the battle is not always to the strong, nor the race to the swift.' In grave emergencies, moderation is generally safer than radicalism; and as this struggle is likely to be long and earnest, we must not, by our action, repel any who are in sympathy with us in the main, but rather win all that we can to our standard. We must not belittle nor overlook the facts of our condition—that we are new and comparatively weak, while our enemies are entrenched and relatively strong. They have the administration and the political power; and, right or wrong, at present they have the numbers. Our friends who urge an appeal to arms with so much force and eloquence, should recollect that the government is arrayed against us, and that the numbers are now arrayed against us as well; or, to state it near to the truth, they are not yet expressly and affirmatively for us; and we should repel friends rather than gain them by anything savouring of revolutionary methods. As it now stands, we must appeal to the sober sense and patriotism of the people. We will make converts day by day; we will grow strong by calmness and moderation; we will grow strong by the violence and injustice of our adversaries. And, unless truth be a mockery and justice a hollow lie, we will be in the majority after a while, and then the revolution which we will accomplish will be none the less radical from being the result of pacific measures. The battle of freedom is to be fought out on principle. Slavery is a violation of the eternal right. We have temporized with it from the necessities of our condition; but *as sure as God reigns and school children read*, THAT BLACK FOUL LIE CAN NEVER BE CONSECRATED INTO GOD'S HALLOWED TRUTH! [Immense applause lasting some time.] One of our greatest difficulties is, that men who *know* that slavery is a detestable crime and ruinous to the nation, are compelled, by our peculiar condition and other circumstances, to advocate it concretely, though damning it in the raw. Henry Clay was a brilliant example of this tendency; others of our purest statesmen are compelled to do so; and thus slavery secures actual support from those who detest it at heart. Yet Henry Clay perfected and forced through the Compromise which secured to slavery a great State as well as a political advantage. Not that he hated slavery less, but that he loved the whole Union more. As long as slavery profited by his great Compromise, the hosts of pro-slavery could not sufficiently cover him with praise; but now that his Compromise stands in their way—

> '. . . they never mention him,
> His name is never heard:
> Their lips are now forbid to speak
> That once familiar word.'

They have slaughtered one of his most cherished measures, and his ghost would arise to rebuke them. [Great applause.]

Now, let us harmonize, my friends, and appeal to the moderation and patriotism of the people: to the sober second thought; to the awakened public conscience. The repeal of the sacred Missouri Compromise has installed the weapons of violence: the bludgeon, the incendiary torch, the death-dealing rifle, the bristling cannon—the weapons of kingcraft, of the inquisition, of ignorance, of barbarism, of oppression. We see its fruits in the dying bed of the heroic Sumner; in the ruins of the 'Free State' hotel; in the smoking embers of the *Herald of Freedom*; in the free State Governor of Kansas chained to a stake on freedom's soil like a horse-thief, for the crime of freedom. [Applause.] We see it in Christian statesmen, and Christian newspapers, and Christian pulpits, applauding *the cowardly act of a low bully,* WHO CRAWLED UPON HIS VICTIM BEHIND HIS BACK AND DEALT THE DEADLY BLOW. [Sensation and applause.] We note our political demoralization in the catchwords that are coming into such common use; on the one hand, 'freedom shriekers' and sometimes 'freedom screechers' [Laughter]; and, on the other hand, 'border ruffians' and that fully deserved. And the significance of catch-words cannot pass unheeded, for they constitute a sign of the times. Everything in this world 'jibes' in with everything else, and all the fruits of this Nebraska bill are like the poisoned source from which they come. I will not say that we may not sooner or later be compelled to meet force by force; but the time has not yet come, and if we are true to ourselves, may never come. Do not mistake that the ballot is stronger than the bullet. Therefore let the legions of slavery use bullets; but let us wait patiently till November, and fire ballots at them in return; and by that peaceful policy, I believe we shall ultimately win. [Applause.]

It was by that policy that here in Illinois the early fathers fought the good fight and gained the victory. In 1824 the free men of our State, led by Governor Coles (who was a native of Maryland and President Madison's private secretary), determined that those beautiful groves should never re-echo the dirge of one who has no title to himself. By their resolute determination, the winds that sweep across our broad prairies shall never cool the parched brow, nor shall the unfettered streams that bring joy and gladness to our free soil water the tired feet, of a *slave*; but so long as those heavenly breezes and sparkling streams bless the land, or the groves and their fragrance or their memory remain, the humanity to which they minister SHALL BE FOR EVER FREE! [Great applause.] Palmer, Yates, Williams, Browning, and some more in this convention came from Kentucky to Illinois (instead of going to Missouri), not only to better their conditions, but also to get away from slavery. They have said so to me, and it is understood among us Kentuckians that we don't like it one bit. Now, can we, mindful of the blessings of liberty which the early men of Illinois left to us, refuse a like privilege to the free men who seek to plant Freedom's banner on our Western outposts? ['No! No!'] Should we not stand by our neighbours who seek to better their conditions in Kansas and Nebraska? ['Yes! Yes!'] Can we as Christian men, and strong and free ourselves, wield the sledge or hold the iron which is to manacle anew an already oppressed race? ['No! No!'] 'Woe unto them' it is written, 'that decree unrighteous decrees and that write grievousness which they have prescribed.' Can we afford to sin any more deeply against human liberty? ['No! No!']

One great trouble in the matter is, that slavery is an insidious and crafty power, and gains equally by open violence of the brutal as well as by sly management of the peaceful. Even after the ordinance of 1787, the settlers in Indiana and Illinois (it was all one government then) tried to get Congress to allow slavery temporarily, and petitions to that end were sent from Kaskaskia, and General Harrison, the Governor, urged it from Vincennes the capital. If that had succeeded, goodbye to liberty here. But John Randolph of Virginia made a vigorous report against it; and although they persevered so well as to get three favourable reports for it, yet the United States Senate, with the aid of some slave States, finally *squelched* it for good. [Applause.] And that is why this hall is today a temple for free men instead of a negro livery stable. [Great applause and laughter.] Once let slavery get planted in a locality, by ever so weak or doubtful a title, and in ever so small numbers, and it is like the Canada thistle or Bermuda grass—you can't root it out. You yourself may detest slavery; but your neighbour has five or six slaves, and he is an excellent neighbour, or your son has married his daughter, and they beg you to help save their property, and you vote against your interest and principles to accommodate a neighbour, hoping that your vote will be on the losing side. And others do the same; and in those ways slavery gets a sure foothold. And when that is done the whole mighty Union—the force of the nation—is committed to its support. And that very process is working in Kansas today. And you must recollect that the slave property is worth a billion of dollars (£1,000,000,000); while free State men must work for sentiment alone. Then there are 'blue lodges'—as they call them—everywhere doing their secret and deadly work.

It is a very strange thing, and not solvable by any moral law that I know of, that if a man loses his horse, the whole country will turn out to help hang the thief; but if a man but a shade or two darker than I am is himself stolen, the same crowd will hang one who aids in restoring him to liberty. Such are the inconsistencies of slavery, where a horse is more sacred than a man; and the essence of *squatter* or popular sovereignty—I don't care how you call it—is that if one man chooses to make a slave of another, no third man shall be allowed to object. And if you can do this in free Kansas, and it is allowed to stand, the next thing you will see is shiploads of negroes from Africa at the wharf at Charleston; for one thing is as truly lawful as the other; and these are the bastard notions we have got to stamp out, else they will stamp us out. [Sensation and applause.]

Two years ago, at Springfield, Judge Douglas avowed that Illinois came into the Union as a slave State, and that slavery was weeded out by the operation of his great patent, everlasting principle of 'popular sovereignty.' [Laughter.] Well, now, that argument must be answered, for it has a little grain of truth at the bottom. I do not mean that it is true in essence, as he would have us believe. It could not be essentially true if the ordinance of '87 was valid. But, in point of fact, there were some degraded beings called slaves in Kaskaskia and the other French settlements when our first State constitution was adopted; that is a fact, and I don't deny it. Slaves were brought here as early as 1720, and were kept here in spite of the ordinance of 1787 against it. But slavery did not thrive here. On the contrary, under the influence of the ordinance, the number *decreased* fifty-one from 1810 to 1820; while under the influence of *squatter* sovereignty, right across the river in Missouri, they *increased* seven thousand two hundred and eleven in the same time; and slavery finally faded out in Illinois, under the influence of the law of freedom, while it grew stronger and stronger in Missouri, under the law or practice of 'popular sovereignty.' In point of fact there were but one hundred and seventeen slaves in Illinois one year after its admission, or one to every four hundred and seventy of its population; or, to state it in another way, if Illinois was a slave State in 1820, so were New York and New Jersey much greater slave States from having had greater numbers, slavery having been established there in very early times. But there is this vital difference between all these States and the judge's Kansas experiment: that they sought to disestablish freedom, which had been established there by the Missouri Compromise. [Voices: 'Good!']

The Union is undergoing a fearful strain; but it is a stout old ship, and has weathered many a hard blow, and 'the stars in their courses' aye, an invisible power, greater than the puny efforts of men, will fight for us. But we ourselves must not decline the burden of responsibility, nor take counsel of unworthy passions. Whatever duty urges us to do or to omit, must be done or omitted; and the recklessness with which our adversaries break the laws, or counsel their violation, should afford no example for us. Therefore, let us revere the Declaration of Independence; let us keep step to the music of the Union. Let us draw a cordon, so to speak, around the slave States, and the hateful institution, like a reptile poisoning itself, will perish by its own infamy. [Applause.]

But we cannot be free men if this is, by our national choice, to be a land of slavery. Those who deny freedom to others, deserve it not for themselves; and, under the rule of a just God, cannot long retain it. [Loud applause.]

Did you ever, my friends, seriously reflect upon the speed with which we are tending downward? Within the memory of men now present the leading statesmen of Virginia could make genuine, red-hot abolitionist speeches in old Virginia; and, as I have said, now even in 'free Kansas' it is a crime to declare that it is 'free Kansas.' The very sentiments that I and others have just uttered would entitle us, and each of us, to the ignominy and seclusion of a dungeon; and yet I suppose that, like Paul, we were 'free born.' But if this thing is allowed to continue, it will be but one step further to impress the same rule in Illinois. [Sensation.]

The conclusion of all is, that we must restore the Missouri Compromise. We must highly resolve that *Kansas must be free!* [Great applause.] We must reinstate the birthday promise of the Republic; we must reaffirm the Declaration of Independence; we must make good in essence as well as in form Madison's avowal that 'the word *slave* ought not to appear in the Constitution;' and we must even go further, and decree that only local law, and not that time-honoured instrument, shall shelter a slave holder. We must make this a land of liberty in fact, as it is in name. But in seeking to attain these results—so indispensable if the liberty which is our pride and boast shall endure—we will be loyal to the Constitution and to the 'flag of our Union' and no matter what our grievance—even though Kansas shall come in as a slave State; and no matter what theirs—even if we shall restore the Compromise—WE WILL SAY TO THE SOUTHERN DISUNIONISTS, WE WON'T GO OUT OF THE UNION, AND YOU SHAN'T!!! [This was the climax; the audience rose to its feet *en masse*, applauded, stamped, waved handkerchiefs, threw hats in the air, and ran riot for several minutes. The arch enchanter who wrought this transformation looked, meanwhile, like the personification of political justice.]

But let us, meanwhile, appeal to the sense and patriotism of the people, and not to their prejudices; let us spread the floods of enthusiasm here aroused all over these vast prairies, so suggestive of freedom. Let us commence by electing the gallant soldier Governor (Colonel) Bissell who stood for the honour of our State alike on the plains and amidst the chaparral of Mexico and on the floor of Congress, while he defied the Southern Hotspur; and that will have a greater moral effect than all the border ruffians can accomplish in all their raids on Kansas. There is both a power and a magic in popular opinion. To that let us now appeal; and while, in all probability, no resort to force will be needed, our moderation and forbearance will stand us in good stead when, if ever, WE MUST MAKE AN APPEAL TO BATTLE AND TO THE GOD OF HOSTS!! [Immense applause and a rush for the orator.]

FROM A LETTER TO J. W. FELL.

DECEMBER 20, 1859

I was born February 12, 1809, in Hardin County, Kentucky. My parents were both born in Virginia, of undistinguished families—second families, perhaps I should say. My mother, who died in my tenth year, was of a family of the name of Hanks, some of whom now reside in Adams, and others in Macon County, Illinois. My paternal grandfather, Abraham Lincoln, emigrated from Rockingham County, Virginia, to Kentucky about 1781 or 1782, where a year or two later he was killed by the Indians, not in battle, but by stealth, when he was labouring to open a farm in the forest. His ancestors, who were Quakers, went to Virginia from Berks County, Pennsylvania. An effort to identify them with the New England family of the same name ended in nothing more definite than a similarity of Christian names in both families, such as Enoch, Levi, Mordecai, Solomon, Abraham, and the like.

My father, at the death of his father, was but six years of age, and he grew up literally without education. He removed from Kentucky to what is now Spencer County, Indiana, in my eighth year. We reached our new home about the time the State came into the Union. It was a wild region, with many bears and other wild animals still in the woods. There I grew up. There were some schools, so called, but no qualification was ever required of a teacher beyond 'readin', writin', and cipherin' to the rule of three. If a straggler supposed to understand Latin happened to sojourn in the neighbourhood, he was looked upon as a wizard. There was absolutely nothing to excite ambition for education. Of course, when I came of age I did not know much. Still, somehow, I could read, write and cipher to the rule of three, but that was all. I have not been to school since. The little advance I now have upon this store of education I have picked up from time to time under the pressure of necessity.

I was raised to farm work, which I continued till I was twenty-two. At twenty-one I came to Illinois, Macon County. Then I got to New Salem, at that time in Sangamon, now in Menard County, where I remained a year as a sort of clerk in a store.

Then came the Black Hawk War; and I was elected a captain of volunteers, a success which gave me more pleasure than any I have had since.

I went the campaign, was elated, ran for the legislature the same year (1832), and was beaten—the only time I ever have been beaten by the people. The next and three succeeding biennial elections I was elected to the legislature. I was not a candidate afterward. During this legislative period I had studied law, and removed to Springfield to practice it. In 1846 I was once elected to the lower House of Congress. Was not a candidate for re-election. From 1849 to 1854, both inclusive, practiced law more assiduously than ever before. Always a Whig in politics; and generally on the Whig electoral tickets, making active canvasses. I was losing interest in politics when the repeal of the Missouri Compromise aroused me again. What I have done since then is pretty well known.

If any personal description of me is thought desirable, it may be said I am, in height, six feet four inches, nearly; lean in flesh, weighing on an average one hundred and eighty pounds; dark complexion, with coarse black hair and gray eyes. No other marks or brands recollected.

Margaret Fuller

1810–1850

Margaret Fuller was an important inspiration for and intellectual influence on the New England transcendentalists. After her untimely death, her Memoirs *(1852) were compiled and part written by such admirers as Emerson, W.H. Channing and J.F. Clarke. The following extract is her own work, an unfinished sketch of youth, found among her papers.*

PARENTS.

'MY FATHER WAS a lawyer and a politican. He was a man largely endowed with that sagacious energy, which the state of New England society, for the last half century, has been so well fitted to develop. His father was a clergyman, settled as pastor in Princeton, Massachusetts, within the bounds of whose parish-farm was Wachuset. His means were small, and the great object of his ambition was to send his sons to college. As a boy, my father was taught to think only of preparing himself for Harvard University, and when there of preparing himself for the profession of law. As a lawyer, again, the ends constantly presented were to work for distinction in the community, and for the means of supporting a family. To be an honoured citizen, and to have a home on earth, were made the great aims of existence. To open the deeper fountains of the soul, to regard life here as the prophetic entrance to immortality, to develop this spirit to perfection,—motives like these had never been suggested to him, either by fellow beings or by outward circumstances. The result was a character, in its social aspect, of quite the common sort. A good son and brother, a kind neighbour, an active man of business—in all these outward relations he was but one of a class, which surrounding conditions have made the majority among us. In the more delicate and individual relations, he never approached but two mortals, my mother and myself.

'His love for my mother was the green spot on which he stood apart from the common places of a mere bread-winning, bread-bestowing existence. She was one of those fair and flower-like natures, which sometimes spring up even beside the most dusty highways of life—a creature not to be shaped into a merely useful instrument, but bound by one law with the blue sky, the dew, and the frolic birds. Of all persons whom I have known, she had in her most of the angelic,—of that spontaneous love for every living thing, for man, and beast, and tree, which restores the golden age.'

DEATH IN THE HOUSE

'My earliest recollection is of a death,—the death of a sister, two years younger than myself. Probably there is a sense of childish endearments, such as belong to this tie, mingled with that of loss, of wonder, and mystery; but these last are prominent in memory. I remember coming home and meeting our nursery maid, her face streaming with tears.

That strange sight of tears made an indelible impression. I realize how little I was of stature, in that I looked up to this weeping face;—and it has often seemed since, that full-grown for the life of this earth, I have looked up just so, at times of threatening, of doubt, and distress, and that just so has some being of the next higher order of existence looked down, aware of a law unknown to me, and tenderly commiserating the pain I must endure in emerging from my ignorance.

'She took me by the hand and led me into a still and dark chamber, then drew aside the curtain and showed me my sister. I see yet that beauty of death! The highest achievements of sculpture are only the reminder of its severe sweetness. Then I remember the house all still and dark,—the people in their black clothes and dreary faces,—the scent of the newly-made coffin,—my being set up in a chair and detained by a gentle hand to hear the clergyman,—the carriages slowly going, the procession slowly doling out their steps to the grave. But I have no remembrance of what I have since been told I did,—insisting, with loud cries, that they should not put the body in the ground. I suppose that my emotion was spent at the time, and so there was nothing to fix that moment in my memory.

'I did not then, nor do I now, find any beauty in these ceremonies. What had they to do with the sweet playful child? Her life and death were alike beautiful, but all this sad parade was not. Thus my first experience of life was one of death. She who would have been the companion of my life was severed from me, and I was left alone. This had made a vast difference in my lot. Her character, if that fair face promised right, would have been soft, graceful, and lively; it would have tempered mine to a gentler and more gradual course.

OVER-WORK.

'My father—all whose feelings were now concentrated on me—instructed me himself. The effect of this was so far good that, not passing through the hands of many ignorant and weak persons, as so many do at preparatory schools, I was put at once under discipline of considerable severity, and, at the same time, had a more than ordinarily high standard presented to me. My father was a man of business, even in literature; he had been a high scholar at college, and was warmly attached to all he had learned there, both from the pleasure he had derived in the exercise of his faculties and the associated memories of success and good repute. He was, beside, well read in French literature, and in English, a Queen Anne's man. He hoped to make me the heir of all he knew, and of as much more as the income of his profession enabled him to give me means of acquiring. At the very beginning, he made one great mistake, more common, it is to be hoped, in the last generation, than the warnings of physiologists will permit it to be with the next. He thought to gain time, by bringing forward the intellect as early as possible. Thus I had tasks given me, as many and various as the hours would allow, and on subjects beyond my age; with the additional disadvantage of reciting to him in the evening, after he returned from his office. As he was subject to many interruptions, I was often kept up till very late; and as he was a severe teacher, both from his habits of mind and his ambition for me, my feelings were kept on the stretch till the recitations were over. Thus frequently, I was sent to bed several hours too late, with nerves unnaturally stimulated. The consequence was a premature development of the brain, that made me a 'youthful prodigy' by day, and by night a victim of spectral illusions, nightmare, and somnambulism, which at the time prevented and checked my growth, while, later, they induced continual headache, weakness, and nervous affections of all kinds. As these again reacted on the brain, giving undue force to every thought and every feeling, there was finally produced a state of being both too active and too intense, which wasted my constitution, and will bring me,—even although I have learned to understand and regulate my morbid temperament,—to a premature grave.

'No one understood this subject of health then. No one knew why this child, already kept up so late, was still unwilling to retire. My aunts cried out upon the 'spoiled child, the most unreasonable child that ever was,—if brother could but open his eyes to see it,—who was never willing to go to bed.' They did not know that, so soon as the light was taken away, she seemed to see colossal faces advancing slowly towards her, the eyes dilating, and each feature swelling loathsomely as they came, till at last, when they were about to close upon her, she started up with a shriek which drove them away, but only to return when she lay down again. They did not know that, when at last she went to sleep, it was to dream of horses trampling over her, and to awake once more in fright; or, as she had just read in her Virgil, of being among trees that dripped with blood, where she walked and walked and could not get out, while the blood became a pool and splashed over her feet, and rose higher and higher, till soon she dreamed it would reach her lips. No wonder the child arose and walked in her sleep, moaning all over the house, till once, when they heard her, and came and waked her, and she told what she had dreamed, her father sharply bid her 'leave off thinking of such nonsense, or she would be crazy'—never knowing that he was himself the cause of all these horrors of the night. Often she dreamed of following to the grave the body of her mother, as she had done that of her sister, and woke to find the pillow drenched in tears. These dreams softened her heart too much, and cast a deep shadow over her young days; for then, and later, the life of dreams,— probably because there was in it less to distract the mind from its own earnestness,—has often seemed to her more real, and been remembered with more interest, than that of waking hours.

'Poor child! Far remote in time, in thought, from that period, I look back on these glooms and terrors, wherein I was enveloped, and perceive that I had no natural childhood.'

BOOKS.

'Thus passed my first years. My mother was in delicate health, and much absorbed in the care of her younger children. In the house was neither dog nor bird, nor any graceful animated form of existence. I saw no persons who took my fancy, and real life offered no attraction. Thus my already over-excited mind found no relief from without, and was driven for refuge from itself to the world of books. I was taught Latin and English grammar at the same time, and began to read Latin at six years old, after which, for some years, I read it daily. In this branch of study, first by my father, and afterwards by a tutor, I was trained to quite a high degree of precision. I was expected to understand the mechanism of the language thoroughly, and in translating to give the thoughts in as few well-arranged words as possible, and without breaks or hesitation,—for with these my father had absolutely no patience.

'Indeed, he demanded accuracy and clearness in everything: you must not speak, unless you can make your meaning perfectly intelligible to the person addressed; must not express a thought, unless you can give a reason for it, if required; must not make a statement, unless sure of all particulars—such were his rules. ''But,'' ''if,'' ''unless I am mistaken,'' and ''it may be so,'' were words and phrases excluded from the province where he held sway. Trained to great dexterity in artificial methods, accurate, ready, with entire command of his resources, he had no belief in minds that listen, wait, and receive. He had no conception of the subtle and indirect motions of imagination and feeling. His influence on me was great, and opposed to the natural unfolding of my character, which was fervent, of strong grasp, and disposed to infatuation and self-forgetfulness. He made the common prose world so present to me, that my natural bias was controlled. I did not go mad, as many would do, at being continually roused from my dreams. I had too much strength to be crushed,— and since I must put on the fetters, could not submit to let them impede my motions. My own world sank deep without, away from the surface of my life; in what I did and said I learned to have reference to other minds. But my true life was only the dearer that it was secluded and veiled over by a thick curtain of available intellect, and that coarse, but wearable stuff woven by the ages,—Common Sense.

'In accordance with this discipline in heroic common sense, was the influence of those great Romans, whose thoughts and lives were my daily food during those plastic years. The genius of Rome displayed itself in character, and scarcely needed an occasional wave of the torch of thought to show its lineaments, so marble strong they gleamed in every light. Who, that has lived with those men, but admires the plain force of fact, of thought passed into action? They take up things with their naked hands. There is just the man, and the block he casts before you,—no divinity, no demon, no unfulfilled aim, but just the man, and Rome, and what he did for Rome. Everything turns your attention to what a man can become, not by yielding himself freely to impressions, not by letting nature play freely through him, but by a single thought, an earnest purpose, unindomitable will, by hardihood, self command, and force of expression. Architecture was the art in which Rome excelled,

and this corresponds with the feeling these men of Rome excite. They
did not grow,—they built themselves up, or were built up by the fate
of Rome, as a temple for Jupiter Stator. The ruined Roman sits among
the ruins; he flies to no green garden; he does not look to heaven;
if his intent is defeated, if he is less than he meant to be, he lives no
more. The names which end in "*us,*" seem to speak with lyric cadenced.
That measured cadence,—that tramp and march,—which are not stilted,
because they indicate real force, yet which seem so when compared
with any other language,—make Latin a study in itself of mighty
influence. The language alone, without the literature, would give one
the *thought* of Rome. Man present in nature, commanding nature too
sternly to be inspired by it, standing like the rock amid the sea, or moving
like the fire over the land, either impassive, or irresistible: knowing
not the soft mediums or fine flights of life, but by the force which he
expresses, piercing to the centre.

'We are never better understood than when we speak of a "Roman
virtue," a "Roman outline." There is somewhat indefinite, somewhat
yet unfulfilled in the thought of Greece, of Spain, of modern Italy; but
ROME! it stands by itself, a clear word. The power of will, the dignity
of a fixed purpose is what it utters. Every Roman was an emperor.
It is well that the infallible Church should have been founded on this
rock, that the presumptuous Peter should hold the keys, as the conquering Jove did before his thunderbolts, to be seen of all the world. The
Apollo tends flocks with Admetus; Christ teaches by the lonely lake,
or plucks wheat as he wanders through the fields some Sabbath morning.
They never come to this stronghold; they could not have breathed freely
where all became stone as soon as spoken, where divine youth found
no horizon for its all-promising glance, but every thought put on, before
it dared issue to the day in action, its *toga virilis*.

'Suckled by this wolf, man gains a different complexion from that
which is fed by the Greek honey. He takes a noble bronze in camps
and battlefields; the wrinkles of council well beseem his brow, and the
eye cuts its way like the sword. The Eagle should never have been used
as a symbol by any other nation: it belonged to Rome.

'The history of Rome abides in mind, of course, more than the literature. It was degeneracy for a Roman to use the pen; his life was in
the day. The "vaunting" of Rome, like that of the North American
Indians, is her proper literature. A man rises; he tells who he is, and
what he has done, he speaks of his country and her brave men; he

knows that a conquering god is there, whose agent is his own right hand: and he should end like the Indian, ''I have no more to say.''

'It never shocks us that the Roman is self conscious. One wants no universal truths from him, no philosophy, no creation, but only his life, his Roman life felt in every pulse, realized in every gesture. The universal heaven takes in the Roman only to make us feel his individuality the more. The Will, the Resolve of Man!—it has been expressed,—fully expressed!

'I steadily loved this ideal in my childhood, and this is the cause, probably, why I have always felt that man must know how to stand firm on the ground, before he can fly. In vain for me are men more, if they are less, than Romans. Dante was far greater than any Roman, yet I feel he was right to take the Mantuan as his guide through hell, and to heaven.

'Horace was a great deal to me then, and is so still. Though his words do not abide in memory, his presence does: serene, courtly, of darting hazel eye, a self-sufficient grace, and an appreciation of the world of stern realities, sometimes pathetic, never tragic. He is the natural man of the world; he is what he ought to be, and his darts never fail of their aim. There is a perfume and raciness, too, which make life a banquet, where the wit sparkles no less that the viands were bought with blood.

'Ovid gave me not Rome, nor himself, but a view into the enchanted gardens of the Greek mythology. This path I followed, have been following ever since; and now, life half over, it seems to me, as in my childhood, that every thought of which man is susceptible, is intimated there. In those young years, indeed, I did not see what I now see, but loved to creep from amid the Roman pikes to lie beneath this great vine, and see the smiling and serene shapes go by, woven from the finest fibres of all the elements. I knew not why, at that time,—but I loved to get away from the hum of the forum, and the mailed clang of Roman speech, to these shifting shows of nature, these Gods and Nymphs born of the sunbeam, the wave, the shadows on the hill.

'As with Rome I antedated the world of deeds, so I lived in those Greek forms the true faith of a refined and intense childhood. So great was the force of a reality with which these forms impressed me, that I prayed earnestly for a sign,—that it would lighten in some particular region of the heavens, or that I might find a bunch of grapes in the path, when I went forth in the morning. But no sign was given, and

I was left a waif stranded upon the shores of modern life!

'Of the Greek language, I knew only enough to feel that the sounds told the same story as the mythology;—that the law of life in that land was beauty, as in Rome it was a stern composure. I wish I had learned as much of Greece as of Rome,—so freely does the mind play in her sunny waters, where there is no chill, and the restraint is from within out; for these Greeks, in an atmosphere of ample grace, could not be impetuous, or stern, but loved moderation, as equable life always must, for it is the law of beauty.

'With these books I passed my days. The great amount of study exacted of me soon ceased to be a burden, and reading became a habit and a passion. The force of feeling, which, under other circumstances, might have ripened thought, was turned to learn the thoughts of others. This was not a tame state, for the energies brought out by rapid acquisition gave glow enough. I thought with rapture of the all-accomplished man, him of the many talents, wide resources, clear sight, and omnipotent will. A Caesar seemed great enough. I did not then know that such men impoverish the treasury to build the palace. I kept their statues as belonging to the hall of my ancestors, and loved to conquer obstacles, and fed my youth and strength for their sake.

'Still, though this bias was so great that in earliest years I learned, in these ways, how the world takes hold of a powerful nature, I had yet other experiences. None of these were deeper than what I found in the happiest haunt of my childish years,—our little garden. Our house, though comfortable, was very ugly, and in a neighbourhood which I detested,—every dwelling and its appurtenances having a *mesquin* and huddled look. I liked nothing about us except the tall graceful elms before the house, and the dear little garden behind. Our back door opened on a high flight of steps, by which I went down to a green plot, much injured in my ambitious eyes by the presence of the pump and tool house. This opened into a little garden, full of choice flowers and fruit trees, which was my mother's delight and was carefully kept. Here I felt at home. A gate opened thence into the fields,—a wooden gate made of boards, in a high, unpainted board wall, and embowered in the clematis creeper. This gate I used to open to see the sunset heaven; beyond this black frame I did not step, for I liked to look at the deep gold behind it. How exquisitely happy I was in its beauty, and how I loved the silvery wreaths of my protecting vine! I never would pluck one of its flowers at that time, I was so jealous of its beauty, but often since I carry off wreaths of it from the wild wood, and it stands in nature to my mind as the emblem of domestic love.

'Of late I have thankfully felt what I owe to that garden, where the best hours of my lonely childhood were spent. Within the house everything was socially utilitarian; my books told of a proud world, but in another temper were the teachings of the little garden. There my thoughts could lie callow in the nest, and only be fed and kept warm, not called to fly or sing before the time. I loved to gaze on the roses, the violets, the lilies, the pinks; my mother's hand had planted them, and they bloomed for me. I culled the most beautiful. I looked at them on every side. I kissed them, I pressed them to my bosom with passionate emotions, such as I have never dared express to any human being. An ambition swelled my heart to be as beautiful, as perfect as they. I have not kept my vow. Yet, forgive, ye wild asters, which gleam so sadly amid the fading grass; forgive me, ye golden autumn flowers, which so strive to reflect the glories of the departing distant sun; and ye silvery flowers, whose moonlight eyes I knew so well, forgive! Living and blooming in your unchecked law, ye know nothing of the blights, the distortions, which beset the human being; and which at such hours it would seem that no glories of free agency could ever repay!

'There was, in the house, no apartment appropriated to the purpose of a library, but there was in my father's room a large closet filled with books, and to these I had free access when the task-work of the day was done. Its window overlooked wide fields, gentle slopes, a rich and smiling country, whose aspect pleased without much occupying the eye, while a range of blue hills, rising at about twelve miles distance, allured to reverie. ''Distant mountains'' says Tieck ''excite the fancy, for beyond them we place the scene of our Paradise.'' Thus, in the poems of fairy adventure, we climb the rocky barrier, pass fearless its dragon caves and dark pine forests, and find the scene of enchantment in the vale behind. My hopes were never so definite, but my eye was constantly allured to that distant blue range, and I would sit, lost in fancies, till tears fell on my cheek. I loved this sadness; but only in later years, when the realities of life had taught me moderation, did the passionate emotions excited by seeing them again teach how glorious were the hopes that swelled my heart while gazing on them in those early days.

Horace Greeley

1811–1872

*Horace Greeley was one of the first great American
newspaper men. A formidable anti-slavery campaigner and
supporter of Lincoln, he is now however best remembered
for the famous exhortation 'Go West, Young Man!'. The
following extract from* Recollections of a Busy Life
*describes his first newspaper enterprise, a critical weekly
entitled* The New Yorker.

HAVING BEEN FAIRLY driven to New York two or three years earlier than
I deemed desirable, I was in like manner impelled to undertake the
responsibilities of business while still in my twenty-second year. My
friend Story, barely older than myself, but far better acquainted with
city ways, having been for many years the only son of a poor widow,
and accustomed to struggling with difficulties, had already conceived

the idea of starting a printery, and offering me a partnership in the enterprise. His position in Wall Street, on The Spirit of the Times, made him acquainted with Mr S. J. Sylvester, then a leading broker and seller of lottery tickets, who issued a weekly 'Bank-Note Reporter' largely devoted to the advertising of his own business, and who offered my friend the job of printing that paper. Story was also intimate with Dr W. Beach, who, in addition to his medical practice, dabbled considerably in ink, and at whose office my friend made the acquaintance of a young graduate, Dr H. D. Shepard, who was understood to have money, and who was intent on bringing out a cheap daily paper, to be sold about the streets,—then a novel idea,—daily papers being presumed desirable only for mercantile men, and addressed exclusively to their wants and tastes. Dr Shepard had won over my friend to a belief in the practicability of his project; and the latter visited me at my work and my lodging, urging me to unite with him in starting a printery on the strength of Mr Sylvester's and Dr Shepard's proffered work. I hesitated, having very little means,—for I had sent a good part of my past year's scanty savings to aid my father in his struggle with the stubborn wilderness; but Story's enthusiastic confidence at length triumphed over my distrust; we formed a partnership, hired part of two rooms already devoted to printing, on the southwest corner of Nassau and Liberty Streets (opposite our city's present post office), spending our little all (less than $200), and stretching our credit to the utmost, for the requisite materials. I tried Mr James Conner, the extensive type-founder in Ann Street,— having a very slight acquaintance with him, formed in the course of frequent visits to his foundry in quest of 'sorts' (type found deficient in the several offices for which I had worked at one time or another),—but he, after hearing me patiently, decided not to credit me six months for the $40 worth of type I wanted of him; and he did right,—my exhibit did not justify my request. I went directly thence to Mr George Bruce, the older and wealthier founder, in Chambers Street,—made the same exhibit, and was allowed by him the credit I asked; and that purchase has since secured to his concern the sale of not less than £50,000 worth of type. I think he must have noted something in my awkward, bashful ways, that impelled him to take the risk.

The Morning Post—Dr Shepard's two-cent daily, which he wished to sell for one cent—was issued on the 1st of January, 1833. Nobody in New York reads much (except visitor's cards) on New Year's Day; and that one happened to be very cold, with the streets much obstructed by a fall of snow throughout the preceding night. Projectors of newspapers in those days, though expecting other people to advertise in their columns, did not comprehend that *they* also must advertise, or the public will never know that their bantling has been ushered into existence; and Dr Shepard was too poor to give his sheet the requisite publicity, had he understood that matter. He was neither a writer nor a man of affairs; had no editors, no reporters worth naming, no correspondents, and no exchanges even; he fancied that a paper would sell, if remarkable for cheapness, though remarkable also for the absence of every other desirable quality. He was said to have migrated, while a youth, from New Jersey to New York, with $1,500 in cash; if he did, his capital must have nearly all melted away before he had issued his first number. Though his enterprise involved no outlay of capital by him, and his weekly outgoes were less than $200, he was able to meet them for single week only, while his journal obtained a circulation of but two or three hundred copies. Finally, he reduced its price to one cent; but the public would not buy it even at that, and we printers, already considerably in debt for materials, were utterly unable to go on beyond the second or third week after the publisher had stopped paying. Thus the first cheap for cash daily in New York—perhaps in the world—died when scarcely yet a month old; and we printers were hard aground on a lee shore, with little prospect of getting off.

We were saved from sudden bankruptcy by the address of my partner, who had formed the acquaintance of a wealthy, eccentric Briton, named Schols, who had a taste for editorial life, and who was somehow induced to buy the wreck of The Morning Post, remove it to an office of his own, and employ Story as foreman. He soon tired of his thriftless, profitless speculation, and threw it up; but we had meantime surmounted our embarrassments by the help of the little money he paid for a portion of our materials and for my partner'sservices. Meantime, the managers of the New York lotteries, then regularly drawn under State auspices, had allowed a portion of their letter-press printing to follow Mr Sylvester's into our concern, and were paying us very fairly for it; I doing most of the composition. For two or three months after Dr Shepard's collapse, I was frequently sent for to work as a substitute in the composing-room of The Commercial Advertiser, not far from our shop; And I was at length offered a regular situation there; but our business had by this time so improved that I was constrained to decline. Working early and late, and looking sharply on every side for jobs, we were beginning to make decided headway, when my partner was drowned (July 9, 1833) while bathing in the East River near his mother's residence in Brooklyn, and I bitterly mourned the loss of my nearest and dearest friend. His place in the concern was promptly taken by another young printer, a friend of the bereaved family, Mr Jonas Winchester, who soon married Story's oldest sister; and we thus went on, with moderate but steady prosperity, until the ensuing Spring, when we issued (March 22, 1834), without premonitory sound of trumpet, THE NEW YORKER, a large, fair, and cheap weekly folio (afterward changed to a double quarto), devoted mainly to current literature, but giving regularly a digest of all important news, including a careful exhibit and summary of election returns and other political intelligence. I edited and made up this paper, while my partner took charge of our more profitable jobbing business.

The New Yorker was issued under my supervision, its editorials written, its selections made, for the most part, by me, for seven years and a half from the date just given. Though not calculated to enlist partisanship or excite enthusiasm, it was at length extensively liked and read. It began with scarcely a dozen subscribers; these steadily increased to nine thousand; and it might, under better business management, (perhaps I should add, at a more favorable time,) have proved profitable and permanent. That it did not was mainly owing to these circumstances: 1. It was not extensively advertised at the start, and at least annually thereafter, as it should have been. 2. It was never really published, though it had half a dozen nominal publishers in succession. 3. It was sent to subscribers on credit, and a large share of them never paid for it, and never will, while the cost of collecting from others ate up the proceeds. 4. The machinery of railroads, expresses, news companies, news offices, &c., whereby literary periodicals are now mainly disseminated, did not then exist. I believe that just such a paper, issued today, properly published and advertised, would obtain a circulation of one hundred thousand in less time that was required to give The New Yorker scarcely a tithe of that aggregate, and would make money for its owners, instead of nearly starving them ,as mine did. I was worth at least $1,500 when it was started; I worked hard and lived frugally throughout its existence; it subsisted for the first two years on the profits of our job work; when I, deeming it established, dissolved with my partner, he taking the jobbing business and I The New Yorker, which held its own pretty fairly thenceforth till the Commercial Revulsion of 1837 swept over the land, whelming it and me in the general ruin. I had married in

1836 (July 5th), deeming myself worth $5,000, and the master of a business which would thenceforth yield me for my labor at least $1,000 per annum; but, instead of that, or of any income at all, I found myself obliged, throughout 1837, to confront a net loss of about $100 per week—my income averaging $100, and my inevitable expenses $200. It was in vain that I appealed to delinquents to pay up; many of them migrated; some died; others were so considerate as to order the paper stopped, but very few of these paid; and I struggled on against a steadily rising tide of adversity that might have appalled a stouter heart. Often did I call on this or that friend with intent to solicit a small loan to meet some demand that could no longer be postponed nor evaded, and, after wasting a precious hour, leave him, utterly unable to broach the loathsome topic. I have borrowed $500 of a broker late on Saturday, and paid him $5 for the use of it till Monday morning, when I somehow contrived to return it. Most gladly would I have terminated the struggle by a surrender; but, if I had failed to pay my notes continually falling due, I must have paid money for my weekly supply of paper,—so that would have availed nothing. To have stopped my journal (for I could not give it away) would have left me in debt, beside my notes for paper, from fifty cents to two dollars each, to at least three thousand subscribers who had paid in advance; and that is the worst kind of bankruptcy. If any one would have taken my business and debts off my hands, upon my giving him my note for $2,000, I would have jumped at the chance, and tried to work out the debt by setting type, if nothing better offered. If it be suggested that my whole indebtedness was at no time more than $5,000 to $7,000, I have only to say that even $1,000 of debt is ruin to him who keenly feels his obligation to fulfil every engagement, yet is utterly without the means of so doing, and who finds himself dragged each week a little deeper into hopeless insolvency. To be hungry, ragged, and penniless is not pleasant; but this is nothing to the horrors of bankruptcy. All the wealth of the Rothschilds would be a poor recompense for a five years' struggle with the consciousness that you had taken the money or property of trusting friends,—promising to return or pay for it when required,— and had betrayed their confidence through insolvency.

I dwell on this point, for I would deter others from entering that place of torment. Half the young men in the country , with many old enough to know better, would 'go into business'—that is, into debt—tomorrow, if they could. Most poor men are so ignorant as to envy the merchant

or manufacturer whose life is an incessant struggle with pecuniary difficulties, who is driven to constant 'shinning' and who, from month to
month, barely evades that insolvency which sooner or later overtakes
most men in business; so that it has been computed that but one in
twenty of them achieve a pecuniary success. For my own part,—and
I speak from sad experience,—I would rather be a convict in a State
prison, a slave in a rice swamp, than to pass through life under the
harrow of debt. Let no young man misjudge himself unfortunate, or
truly poor, so long as he has the full use of his limbs and faculties,
and is substantially free from debt. Hunger, cold, rags, hard work, contempt, suspicion, unjust reproach, are disagreeable; but debt is infinitely
worse than them all. And, if it had pleased God to spare either or all
of my sons to be the support and solace of my declining years, the
lesson which I should have most earnestly sought to impress upon them
is,—'Never run into debt! Avoid pecuniary obligation as you would pestilence or famine. If you have but fifty cents, and can get no more for
a week, buy a peck of corn, parch it, and live on it, rather than owe
any man a dollar!' Of course, I know that some men must do business
that involves risks, and must often give notes and other obligations,
and I do not consider him really in debt who can lay his hands directly
on the means of paying, at some little sacrifice, all he owes; I speak
of *real* debt,—that which involves risk or sacrifice on the one side, obligation and dependence on the other,—and I say, From all such, let every
youth humbly pray God to preserve him evermore!

When I at length stopped The New Yorker (September 20, 1841), though
poor enough, I provided for making good all I owed to its subscribers
who had paid in advance and shut up its books whereon were inscribed
some $10,000 owed me in sums of $1 to $10 each, by men to whose
service I had faithfully devoted the best years of my life,—years that,
though full of labor and frugal care, might have been happy had they
not been made wretched by those men's dishonesty. They took my
journal, and probably read it; they promised to pay for it, and defaulted;
leaving me to pay my papermaker, typefounder, journeymen, &c., as
I could. My only requital was a sorely achieved but wholesome lesson.
I had been thoroughly burned out, only saving my books, in the great
Ann Street fire (August 12, 1835); I was burned out again in February,
1845; and, while the destruction was complete, and the insurance but
partial, I had the poor consolation, that the account books of The New

Yorker—which I had never opened since I first laid them away, but which had been an eyesore and a reminder of evil days whenever I stumbled upon them—were at length dissolved in smoke and flame, and lost to sight for ever.

Harriet Beecher Stowe

1811–1896

Harriet Beecher Stowe was a New England writer who remains celebrated for Uncle Tom's Cabin. *Inspired by her observation of slaves in Kentucky, it was the most popular novel of its time, one of the most powerful ever written. Harriet Beecher Stowe's son compiled her letters and journals in a biographical volume from which is taken this account of the publication and success of* Uncle Tom's Cabin.

THE WONDERFUL STORY that was begun in the 'National Era' June 5, 1851, and was announced to run for about three months, was not completed in that paper until April 1, 1852. It had been contemplated as a mere magazine tale of perhaps a dozen chapters, but once begun it could no more be controlled than the waters of the swollen Mississippi, bursting through a crevasse in its levees. The intense interest excited by the story, the demands made upon the author for more facts, the unmeasured words of encouragement to keep on in her good work that poured in from all sides, and above all the ever-growing conviction that she had been intrusted with a great and holy mission, compelled her to keep on until the humble tale had assumed the proportions of a volume prepared to stand among the most notable books in the world. As Mrs Stowe has since repeatedly said, 'I could not control the story; it wrote itself;' or 'I the author of "Uncle Tom's Cabin"? No, indeed. The Lord himself wrote it, and I was but the humblest of instruments in his hand. To Him alone should be given all the praise.'

Although the publication of the 'National Era' has been long since suspended, the journal was in those days one of decided literary merit and importance. On its title page, with the name of Dr Gamaliel Bailey as editor, appeared that of John Greenleaf Whittier as corresponding editor. In its columns Mrs Southworth made her first literary venture, while Alice and Phoebe Cary, Grace Greenwood, and a host of other well known names were published with that of Mrs Stowe, which appeared last of all in its prospectus for 1851.

Before the conclusion of 'Uncle Tom's Cabin' Mrs Stowe had so far outstripped her contemporaries that her work was pronounced by competent judges to be the most powerful production ever contributed to the magazine literature of this country, and she stood in the foremost rank of American writers.

After finishing her story Mrs Stowe penned the following appeal to its more youthful readers, and its serial publication was concluded:-

'The author of "Uncle Tom's Cabin" must now take leave of a wide circle of friends whose faces she has never seen, but whose sympathies coming to her from afar have stimulated and cheered her in her work.

'The thought of the pleasant family circles that she has been meeting in spirit week after week has been a constant refreshment to her, and she cannot leave them without a farewell.

'In particular the dear children who have followed her story have her warmest love. Dear children, you will soon be men and women, and I hope that you will learn from this story always to remember and pity the poor and oppressed. When you grow up, show your pity by doing all you can for them. Never, if you can help it, let a colored child be shut out from school or treated with neglect and contempt on account of his color. Remember the sweet example of little Eva, and try to feel the same regard for all that she did. Then, when you grow up, I hope the foolish and unchristian prejudice against people merely on account of their complexion will be done away with.

'Farewell, dear children, until we meet again.'

With the completion of the story the editor of the 'Era' wrote: 'Mrs Stowe has at last brought her great work to a close. We do not recollect any production of an American writer that has excited more general and profound interest.'

For the story as a serial the author received $300. In the mean time, however, it had attracted the attention of Mr John P. Jewett, a Boston publisher, who promptly made overtures for its publication in book form. He offered Mr and Mrs Stowe a half share in the profits, provided they would share with him the expense of publication. This was refused by Professor Stowe, who said he was altogether too poor to assume any such risk; and the agreement finally made was that the author should receive a ten per cent. royalty upon all sales.

Mrs Stowe had no reason to hope for any large pecuniary gain from this publication, for it was practically her first book. To be sure, she had, in 1832, prepared a small school geography for a Western publisher, and ten years later the Harpers had brought out her 'Mayflower.' Still, neither of these had been sufficiently remunerative to cause her to regard literary work as a money-making business, and in regard to this new contract she writes: 'I did not know until a week afterward precisely what terms Mr Stowe had made, and I did not care. I had the most perfect indifference to the bargain.'

The agreement was signed March 13, 1852, and, as by arrangement with the 'National Era' the book publication of the story was authorized before its completion as a serial, the first edition of five thousand copies was issued on the twentieth of the same month.

In looking over the first semi-annual statement presented by her publishers we find Mrs Stowe charged, a few days before the date of publication of her book, with 'one copy U.T.C. cloth $.56' and this was the first copy of 'Uncle Tom's Cabin' ever sold in book form. Five days earlier we find her charged with one copy of Horace Mann's speeches. In writing of this critical period of her life Mrs Stowe says:-

'After sending the last proof sheet to the office I sat alone reading Horace Mann's eloquent plea for these young men and women, then about to be consigned to the slave warehouse of Bruin & Hill in Alexandria, Va.,—a plea impassioned, eloquent, but vain, as all other pleas on that side had ever proved in all courts hitherto. It seemed that there was no hope, that nobody would hear, nobody would read, nobody pity; that this frightful system, that had already pursued its victims into the free States, might at last even threaten them in Canada.'—

Filled with this fear, she determined to do all that one woman might to enlist the sympathies of England for the cause, and to avert, even as a remote contingency, the closing of Canada as a haven of refuge for the oppressed. To this end she at once wrote letters to Prince Albert, to the Duke of Argyll, to the Earls of Carlisle and Shaftesbury, to Macauley, Dickens, and others whom she knew to be interested in the cause of anti-slavery. These she ordered to be sent to their several addresses, accompanied by the very earliest copies of her book that should be printed.

Then, having done what she could, and committed the result to God, she calmly turned her attention to other affairs.

In the mean time the fears of the author as to whether or not her book would be read were quickly dispelled. Three thousand copies were sold the very first day, a second edition was issued the following week, a third on the 1st of April, and within a year one hundred thousand copies of the book, had been issued and sold in this country. Almost in a day the poor professor's wife had become the most talked-of woman in the world, her influence for good was spreading to its remotest corners, and henceforth she was to be a public character, whose every movement would be watched with interest, and whose every word would be quoted. The long, weary struggle with poverty was to be hers no longer; for, in seeking to aid the oppressed, she had also so aided herself that within four months from the time her book was published it had yielded her $10,000 in royalties.

Now letters regarding the wonderful book, and expressing all shades of opinion concerning it, began to pour in upon the author. Her lifelong friend, whose words we have already so often quoted, wrote:—

'I sat up last night until long after one o'clock reading and finishing "Uncle Tom's Cabin." I could not leave it any more than I could have left a dying child, nor could I restrain an almost hysterical sobbing for an hour after I laid my head upon my pillow. I thought I was a thoroughgoing abolitionist before, but your book has awakened so strong a feeling of indignation and of compassion that I never seem to have had any feeling on this subject until now.'

The poet Longfellow wrote:-

I congratulate you most cordially upon the immense success and influence of 'Uncle Tom's Cabin.' It is one of the greatest triumphs recorded in literary history, to say nothing of the higher triumph of its moral effect.

With great regard, and friendly remembrance to Mr Stowe, I remain,

Yours most truly

HENRY W. LONGFELLOW

Whittier wrote to Garrison:—

'What a glorious work Harriet Beecher Stowe has wrought. Thanks for the Fugitive Slave Law! Better would it be for slavery if that law had never been enacted; for it gave occasion for "Uncle Tom's Cabin."'

Garrison wrote to Mrs Stowe:—

'I estimate the value of anti-slavery writing by the abuse it brings. Now all the defenders of slavery have let me alone and are abusing you.'

To Mrs Stowe, Whittier wrote:—

Ten thousand thanks for thy immortal book. My young friend Mary Irving (of the 'Era') writes me that she has been reading it to some twenty young ladies, daughters of Louisiana slaveholders, near New Orleans, and amid the scenes described in it, and that they, with one accord, pronounce it true.

Truly thy friend,

JOHN G. WHITTIER

From Thomas Wentworth Higginson came the following:—

To have written at once the most powerful of contemporary fiction and the most efficient of anti-slavery tracts is a double triumph in literature and philanthropy, to which this country has heretofore seen no parallel.

Yours respectfully and gratefully

T. W. HIGGINSON

A few days after the publication of the book, Mrs Stowe, writing from Boston to her husband in Brunswick, says: 'I have been in such a whirl ever since I have been here. I found business prosperous. Jewett animated. He has been to Washington and conversed with all the leading senators, Northern and Southern. Seward told him it was the greatest book of the times, or something of that sort, and he and Sumner went around with him to recommend it to Southern men and get them to read it.'

It is true that with these congratulatory and commendatory letters came hosts of others, threatening and insulting, from the Haleys and Legrees of the country.

Of them Mrs Stowe said: 'They were so curiously compounded of blasphemy, cruelty, and obscenity, that their like could only be expressed by John Bunyan's account of the speech of Apollyon: ''He spake as a dragon.''

A correspondent of the 'National Era' wrote: ''Uncle Tom's Cabin'' is denounced by time-serving preachers as a meretricious work. Will you not come out in defense of it and roll back the tide of vituperation?'

To this the editor answered: 'We should as soon think of coming out in defense of Shakespeare.'

Several attempts were made in the South to write books controverting 'Uncle Tom's Cabin' and showing a much brighter side of the slavery question, but they all fell flat and were left unread. Of one of them, a clergyman of Charleston, S. C., wrote in a private letter:—

'I have read two columns in the ''Southern Press'' of Mrs Eastman's ''Aunt Phillis' Cabin'', or ''Southern Life as it is'' with the remarks of the editor. I have no comment to make on it, as that is done by itself. The editor might have saved himself being writ down an ass by the public if he had withheld his nonsense. If the two columns are a fair specimen of Mrs Eastman's book, I pity her attempt and her name as an author.'

In due time Mrs Stowe began to receive answers to the letters she had forwarded with copies of her book to prominent men in England, and these were without exception flattering and encouraging. Through his private secretary Prince Albert acknowledged with thanks the receipt of his copy, and promised to read it. Succeeding mails brought scores of letters from English men of letters and statesmen. Lord Carlisle wrote:—

'I return my deep and solemn thanks to Almighty God who has led and enabled you to write such a book. I do feel indeed the most thorough assurance that in his good Providence such a book cannot have been written in vain. I have long felt that slavery is by far the *topping* question of the world and age we live in, including all that is most thrilling in heroism and most touching in distress; in short, the real epic of the universe. The self interest of the parties most nearly concerned on the one hand, the apathy and ignorance of unconcerned observers on the other, have left these august pretensions to drop very much out of sight. Hence my rejoicing that a writer has appeared who will be read and must be felt, and that happen what may to the transactions of slavery they will no longer be suppressed.'

To this letter, of which but an extract has been given, Mrs Stowe sent the following reply:—

MY LORD,

It is not with the common pleasure of gratified authorship that I say how much I am gratified by the receipt of your very kind communication with regard to my humble efforts in the cause of humanity. The subject is one so grave, so awful—the success of what I have written has been so singular and so unexpected—that I can scarce retain a self-conscious-ness and am constrained to look upon it all as the work of a Higher Power, who, when He pleases, can accomplish his results by the feeblest instruments. I am glad of anything which gives notoriety to the book, because it is a plea for the dumb and the helpless! I am glad particularly of notoriety in England because I see with what daily increasing power England's opinion is to act on this country. No one can tell but a *native* born here by what an infinite complexity of ties, nerves, and ligaments this terrible evil is bound in one body politic; how the slightest touch upon it causes even the free States to thrill and shiver, what a terribly corrupting and tempting power it has upon the conscience and moral sentiment even of a free community. Nobody can tell the thousand ways in which by trade, by family affinity, or by political expediency, the free part of our country is constantly tempted to complicity with the slaveholding part. It is a terrible thing to become used to hearing the enormities of slavery, to hear of things day after day that one would think the sun should hide his face from, and yet, to *get used to them*, to discuss them coolly, to dismiss them coolly. For example, the sale of intelligent, handsome colored females for vile purposes, facts of the most public nature, have made this a perfectly understood matter in our Northern States. I have now, myself, under charge and educating, two girls of whose character any mother might be proud, who have actually been rescued from this sale in the New Orleans market.

I desire to include a tract in which I sketched down a few incidents in the history of the family to which these girls belong; it will show more than words can the kind of incident to which I allude. The tract is not a published document, only *printed* to assist me in raising money, and it would not, at present, be for the good of the parties to have it published even in England.

But though these things are known in the free States, and other things, if possible, worse, yet there is a terrible deadness of moral sense. They are known by clergymen who yet would not on any account so far commit themselves as to preach on the evils of slavery, or pray for the slaves in their pulpits. They are known by politicians who yet give their votes for slavery extension and perpetuation.

This year both our great leading parties voted to suppress all agitation of the subject, and in both those parties were men who knew personally facts of slavery and the internal slave trade that one would think no man could ever forget. Men *united* in pledging themselves to the Fugitive Slave Law, who yet would tell you in private conversation that it was an abomination, and who do not hesitate to say, that as a matter of practice they always help the fugitive because they *can't* do otherwise.

The moral effect of this constant insincerity, the moral effect of witnessing and becoming accustomed to the most appalling forms of crime and oppression, is to me the most awful and distressing part of the subject. Nothing makes me feel it so painfully as to see with how much more keenness the English feel the disclosures of my book than the Americans. I myself am blunted by use—by seeing, touching, handling the details. In dealing even for the ransom of slaves, in learning market prices of men, women, and children, I feel that I acquire a horrible familiarity with evil.

Here, then, the great, wise, and powerful mind of England, if she will but fully master the subject, may greatly help us. Hers is the same kind of mind as our own, but disembarrassed from our temptations and unnerved by the thousands of influences that blind and deaden us. There is a healthful vivacity of moral feeling on this subject that must electrify our paralysed vitality. For this reason, therefore, I rejoice when I see minds like your lordship's turning to this subject; and I feel an intensity of emotion, as if I could say, Do not for Christ's sake let go; you know not what you may do.

Your lordship will permit me to send you two of the most characteristic documents of the present struggle, written by two men who are, in their way, as eloquent for the slave as Chatham was for us in our hour of need.

I am now preparing some additional notes to my book, in which I shall further confirm what I have said by facts and statistics, and in particular by extracts from the *codes of slaveholding States,* and the *records of their courts*. These are documents that cannot be disputed, and I pray your lordship to give them your attention. No disconnected facts can be so terrible as these legal decisions. They will soon appear in England.

It is so far from being irrelevant for England to notice slavery that I already see indications that this subject, on *both sides*, is yet to be presented there, and the battle fought on *English ground*. I see that my friend the South Carolinian gentleman has sent to 'Fraser's Magazine' an article, before published in this country, on 'Uncle Tom's Cabin.' The article in the London *Times* was eagerly reprinted in this country, was issued as a tract and sold by the hundred, headed, 'What they think of ''Uncle Tom'' in England.' If I mistake not, a strong effort will be made to pervert the public mind of England, and to do away the impression which the book has left.

For a time after it was issued it seemed to go by acclamation. From quarters the most unexpected, from all political parties, came an almost unbroken chorus of approbation. I was very much surprised, knowing the explosive nature of the subject. It was not till the sale had run to over a hundred thousand copies that reaction began, and the reaction was led off by the London *Times*. Instantly, as by a preconcerted signal, all papers of a certain class began to abuse; and some who had at first issued articles entirely commendatory, now issued others equally depreciatory. Religious papers, notably the *New York Observer*, came out and denounced the book as *anti-Christian*, anti-evangelical, resorting even to personal slander on the author as a means of diverting attention from the work.

All this has a meaning, but I think it comes too late. I can think of no reason why it was not tried sooner, excepting that God had intended that the cause should have a hearing. It is strange that they should have waited so long for the political effect of a book which they might have foreseen at first; but not strange that they should, now they *do* see what it is doing, attempt to root it up.

The effects of the book so far have been, I think, these: 1st. To soften and moderate the bitterness of feeling in *extreme abolitionists*. 2d. To convert to abolitionist views many whom this same bitterness had repelled. 3d. To inspire the free colored people with self-respect, hope, and confidence. 4th. To inspire universally through the country a kindlier feeling toward the negro race.

It was unfortunate for the cause of freedom that the first agitators of this subject were of that class which your lordship describes in your note as 'well-meaning men.' I speak sadly of their faults, for they were men of *noble* hearts. 'But oppression maketh a wise man *mad*' and they spoke and did many things in the frenzy of outraged humanity that repelled sympathy and threw multitudes off to a hopeless distance. It is mournful to think of all the absurdities that have been said and done in the name and for the sake of this holy cause, that have so long and so fatally retarded it.

I confess that I expected for myself nothing but abuse from extreme abolitionists, especially as I dared to name a forbidden shibboleth, 'Liberia' and the fact that the wildest and extremist abolitionists united with the coldest conservatives, at first, to welcome and advance the book is a thing that I have never ceased to wonder at.

I have written this long letter because I am extremely desirous that some leading minds in England should know how *we* stand. The subject is now on trial at the bar of a civilized world—a Christian world! and I feel sure that God has not ordered this without a design.

Yours for the cause,
HARRIET BEECHER STOWE

In December the Earl of Shaftesbury wrote to Mrs Stowe:—

MADAM,
It is very possible that the writer of this letter may be wholly unknown to you. But whether my name be familiar to your ears, or whether you now read it for the first time, I cannot refrain from expressing to you the deep gratitude that I feel to Almighty God who has inspired both your heart and your head in the composition of 'Uncle Tom's Cabin.' None but a Christian believer could have produced such a book as yours, which has absolutely startled the whole world, and impressed many thousands by revelations of cruelty and sin that give us an idea of what would be the uncontrolled dominion of Satan on this fallen earth.

To this letter Mrs Stowe replied as follows:—

ANDOVER, JANUARY 6, 1853.

TO THE EARL OF SHAFTESBURY:

MY LORD,

The few lines I have received from you are a comfort and an encouragement to me, feeble as I now am in health, and pressed oftentimes with sorrowful thoughts.

It is a comfort to know that in other lands there are those who feel as we feel, and who are looking with simplicity to the gospel of Jesus, and prayerfully hoping his final coming.

My lord, before you wrote me I read with deep emotion your letter to the ladies of England, and subsequently the noble address of the Duchess of Sutherland, and I could not but feel that such movements, originating in such a quarter, prompted by a spirit so devout and benevolent, were truly of God, and must result in a blessing to the world.

I grieve to see that both in England and this country there are those who are entirely incapable of appreciating the Christian and truly friendly feeling that prompted this movement, and that there are even those who meet it with coarse personalities such as I had not thought possible in an English or American paper.

When I wrote my work it was in simplicity and in the love of Christ, and if I felt anything that seemed to me like a call to undertake it, it was this, that I had a true heart of love for the Southern people, a feeling appreciation of their trials, and a sincere admiration of their many excellent traits, and that I thus felt, I think, must appear to every impartial reader of the work.

It was my hope that a book so kindly intended, so favorable in many respects, might be permitted free circulation among them, and that the gentle voice of Eva and the manly generosity of St Clare might be allowed to say those things of the system which would be invidious in any other form.

At first the book seemed to go by acclamation; the South did not condemn, and the North was loud and unanimous in praise; not a dissenting voice was raised; to my astonishment everybody praised. But when the book circulated so widely and began to penetrate the Southern States, when it began to be perceived how powerfully it affected every mind that read it, there came on a reaction.

Answers, pamphlets, newspaper attacks came thick and fast, and certain Northern papers, religious,—so called,—turned and began to denounce the work as unchristian, heretical, etc. The reason of all this is that it has been seen that the book has a direct tendency to do what it was written for,—to awaken conscience in the slaveholding States and lead to emancipation.

Now there is nothing that Southern political leaders and capitalists so dread as anti-slavery feeling among themselves. All the force of lynch law is employed to smother discussion and blind conscience on this question. The question is not allowed to be discussed, and he who sells a book or publishes a tract makes himself liable to fine and imprisonment.

My book is, therefore, as much under an interdict in some parts of the South as the Bible is in Italy. It is not allowed in the bookstores, and the greater part of the people hear of it and me only through grossly caricatured representations in the papers, with garbled extracts from the book.

A cousin residing in Georgia this winter says that the prejudice against my name is so strong that she dares not have it appear on the outside of her letters, and that very amiable and excellent people have asked her if such as I could be received into reputable society at the North.

Under these circumstances, it is a matter of particular regret that the *New York Observer*, an old and long established religious paper in the United States, extensively read at the South, should have come out in such a bitter and unscrupulous style of attack as even to induce some Southern papers, with a generosity one often finds at the South, to protest against it.

That they should use their Christian character and the sacred name of Christ still further to blind the minds and strengthen the prejudices of their Southern brethren is to me a matter of deepest sorrow. All those things, of course, cannot touch me in my private capacity, sheltered as I am by a happy home and very warm friends. I only grieve for it as a dishonor to Christ and a real injustice to many noble-minded people at the South, who, if they were allowed quietly and dispassionately to hear and judge, might be led to the best results.

But, my lord, all this only shows us how strong is the interest we touch. *All the wealth of America* may be said to be interested in it. And, if I may judge from the furious and bitter tone of some English papers, they also have some sensitive connection with the evil.

I trust that those noble and gentle ladies of England who have in so good a spirit expressed their views of the question will not be discouraged by the strong abuse that will follow. England is doing us good. We need the vitality of a disinterested country to warm our torpid and benumbed public sentiment.

Nay, the storm of feeling which the book raises in Italy, Germany, and France is all good, though truly 'tis painful for us Americans to bear. The fact is, we have become used to this frightful evil, and we need the public sentiment of the world to help us.

I am now writing a work to be called 'Key to Uncle Tom's Cabin.' It contains, in an undeniable form, the facts which corroborate all that I have said. One third of it is taken up with judicial records of trials and decisions, and with statute law. It is a most fearful story, my lord,—I can truly say that I write with lifeblood, but as called of God. I give in my evidence, and I hope that England may so fix the attention of the world on the facts of which I am the unwilling publisher, that the Southern States may be compelled to notice what hitherto they have denied and ignored. If they call the fiction dreadful, what will they say of the fact, where I cannot deny, suppress, or color? But it is God's will that it must be told, and I am the unwilling agent.

This coming month of April, my husband and myself expect to sail for England on the invitation of the Anti-slavery Society of the Ladies and Gentlemen of Glasgow, to confer with friends there.

There are points where English people can do much good; there are also points where what they seek to do may be made more efficient by a little communion with those who know the feelings and habits of our countrymen : but I am persuaded that England can do much for us.

My lord, they greatly mistake who see, in this movement of English Christians for the abolition of slavery, signs of disunion between the nations. It is the purest and best proof of friendship England has ever shown us, and will, I am confident, be so received. I earnestly trust that all who have begun to take in hand the cause will be in nothing daunted, but persevere to the end; for though everything else be against us, *Christ* is certainly on our side and He *must at last prevail*, and it will be done, 'not by might, nor by power, but by His Spirit.'

Yours in Christian sincerity,
H. B. STOWE

Mrs Stowe also received a letter from Arthur Helps accompanying a review of her work written by himself and published in *Fraser's*

Magazine.' In his letter Mr Helps took exception to the comparison insti-
tuted in 'Uncle Tom's Cabin' between the working classes of England
and the slaves of America. In her answer to this criticism and complaint
Mrs Stowe says:—

MR ARTHUR HELPS:
MY DEAR SIR,
I cannot but say I am greatly obliged to you for the kind opinions
expressed in your letter. On one point, however, it appears that my
book has not faithfully represented to you the feelings of my heart.
I mean in relation to the English nation as a nation. You will notice
that the remarks on the subject occur in the *dramatic* part of the book,
in the mouth of an intelligent Southerner. As a fair-minded person,
bound to state for both sides all that could be said in the person of
St Clare, the best that could be said on that point, and what I know
is in fact constantly reiterated, namely, that the laboring class of the
South are in many respects, as to physical comfort, in a better condition
than the poor of England.

This is the slaveholder's stereotyped apology,—a defense it cannot
be, unless two wrongs make one right.

It is generally supposed among us that this estimate of the relative
condition of the slaves and the poor of England is correct, and we base
our ideas on reports made in Parliament and various documentary evidence; also such sketches as more 'London Labor and London Poor'
which have been widely circulated among us. The inference, however,
which *we* of the freedom party draw from it, is *not* that the slave is,
on the whole, in the best condition because of this striking difference;
that in America the slave has not a recognized *human* character *in law,
has not even an existence*, whereas in England the law recognizes and
protects the meanest subject, in theory *always*, and in *fact* to a certain
extent. A prince of the blood could not strike the meanest laborer without
a liability to prosecution, in *theory* at least, and that is something. In
America any man may strike any slave he meets, and if the master
does not choose to notice it, he has no redress.

I do not suppose *human nature* to be widely different in England and
America. In both countries, when any class holds power and wealth
by institutions which in the long run bring misery on lower classes,
they are very unwilling still to part with that wealth and power. They
are unwilling to be convinced that it is their duty, and unwilling to

do it if they are. It is always so everywhere; it is not English nature or American nature, but human nature. We have seen in England the battle for popular rights fought step by step with as determined a resistance from parties in possession as the slaveholder offers in America.

There was the same kind of resistance in certain quarters there to the laws restricting the employing of young children eighteen hours a day in factories, as there is here to the anti-slavery effort.

Again, in England as in America, there are, in those very classes whose interests are most invaded by what are called popular rights, some of the most determined supporters of them, and here I think that the balance preponderates in favor of England. I think there are more of the high nobility of England who are friends of the common people and willing to help the cause of human progress, irrespective of its influence on their own interests, than there are those of a similar class among slaveholding aristocracy, though even that class is not without such men. But I am far from having any of that senseless prejudice against the English nation as a nation which, greatly to my regret, I observe sometimes in America. It is a relic of barbarism for two such nations as England and America to cherish any such unworthy prejudice.

For my own part, I am proud to be of English blood; and though I do not think England's national course faultless, and though I think many of her institutions and arrangements capable of much revision and improvement, yet my heart warms to her as, *on the whole*, the strongest, greatest, and best nation on earth. Have not England and America one blood, one language, one literature, and a glorious literature it is! Are not Milton and Shakespeare, and all the wise and brave and good of old, common to us both, and should there be anything but cordiality between countries that have so glorious an inheritance in common? If there is, it will be elsewhere than in hearts like mine.

Sincerely yours,

H. B. STOWE

Louisa May Alcott

1832–1888

Louisa May Alcott was the successful and prolific author of Little Women *(1868–1869) and its many sequels. She was also a spirited and effective supporter of many reform movements including temperance and female suffrage. The following small selection of Louisa May Alcott's letters portrays a writer at the peak of her fame yet responsive to an enthusiastic reader and still working for worthwhile causes.*

TO LUCY STONE

CONCORD, MASS., OCT. 1, 1873.

DEAR MRS STONE

I am so busy just now proving 'Woman's Right to Labor' that I have no time to help prove 'Woman's Right to Vote.' When I read your note aloud to the family, asking 'What shall I say to Mrs Stone?' my honored father instantly replied: 'Tell her you are ready to follow your leader, sure that you could not have a better one.' My brave old mother, with the ardor of many unquenchable Mays shining in her face, cried out: 'Tell her I am seventy-three, but I mean to go to the polls before I die, even if my three daughters have to carry me.' And two little men already mustered in added the cheering words: 'Go ahead, Aunt Weedy, we will let you vote as much as you like.' Such being the temper of the small convention of which I am now President, I can not hesitate to say that though I may not be with you in the body I shall be in spirit, and I am, as ever, hopefully and heartily yours, LOUISA MAY ALCOTT

TO MARIA S. PORTER

[1874]

I rejoice greatly thereat, and hope that the first thing that you and Mrs Sewall propose in your first meeting will be to reduce the salary of the head master of the High School, and increase the salary of the first woman assistant, whose work is quite as good as his, and even harder, to make the pay equal. I believe in the same pay for the same good work. Don't you? In future let woman do whatever she can do; let men place no more impediments in the way; above all things let's have fair play,—let *simple justice* be done, say I. Let us hear no more of 'woman's sphere' either from our wise (?) legislators beneath the State House dome, or from our clergymen in their pulpits. I am tired, year after year, of hearing such twaddle about sturdy oaks and clinging vines and man's chivalric protection of woman. Let woman find out her own limitations, and if as is so confidently asserted, nature has defined her sphere, she will be guided accordingly, but in heaven's name give her a chance! Let the professions be open to her; let fifty years of college education be hers, and then we shall see what we shall see. Then, and not until then, shall we be able to say what woman can and what she cannot do, and coming generations will know and be able to define more clearly what is a 'woman's sphere' than these benighted men who now try to do it.

TO MRS H. KOORDERS-BOEKE

CONCORD, 7 AUGUST 1875

DEAR MADAME.

It gave me much pleasure to receive the letters from you and other friends and then to realize that people far away in Holland know me through my little books.

If you want to know something about me, even though there is not much to tell, I would like very much to mention a few little things.

I live with my worthy parents out in the country, just above Boston; they are both old; my father is a minister, my mother is frail. Two sisters still live with me, May ('Amy') a skilful artist, and Anna ('Meg') now a widow with two children, 'Daisy and Demi'; and I am the second daughter, an old spinster of 42 years. 'Beth' the fourth daughter died a few years past, as in the book.

Many things in my story truly happened; and much of *Little Women* is a reflection of the life led by us four sisters. I am 'Jo' in the principal characteristics, not the good ones. I have written, have taught, have worked as a housekeeper, have edited a magazine, and have followed the army in war as a nurse. I went to the hospital in Washington and took care of at least forty 'colored men' until I became sick myself, and almost lost my life in the affair. Since then I have never again felt completely well, but I have no regret about the experience that cost me so dearly; that is one of the lessons that makes one's life rich and precious, and measures one's powers.

Now I am at home again, taking care of my mother, and doing that which I can which is beneficial to show what is good in the world.

Since then I have been in Europe, and plan to go there yet again. The last time I was in Antwerp, and would have gladly gone on to Haarlem, had I known that I had such good friends there. When I cross the ocean again I shall try to extend my trip as far as there, but unfortunately I speak no language well other than my own.

I shall receive my books in their Dutch dress with pleasure, as I already have them in their French and German attire. My next book comes out in October, and is called Eight Cousins. I wrote it for a children's magazine, but it did not turn out so well as I had certainly wished, because I had to shorten it. There is to be a sequel in which the cousins are adults.

Young girls in America do not get a good education in various respects, even though much is taught to them. They know nothing of health care, or of housekeeping, and are presented into society too early. My story is intended to encourage a better plan of child rearing, and my heroine shows that such a plan is feasible.

I could not read the addresses of the other ladies who wrote me, and thus cannot answer them. Be so kind as to convey my gratitude and greetings, and I remain Yours

very gratefully,
L. M. ALCOTT

TO LUCY STONE

DEAR MRS STONE:

One should be especially inspired this Centennial year before venturing to speak or write. I am not so blest, and find myself so busy trying to get ready for the good time that is surely coming, I can only in a very humble way, help on the cause all women should have at heart.

As reports are in order, I should like to say a word for the girls, on whom in a great measure, depends the success of the next generation.

My lines fell in pleasant places last year, and I looked well about me as I went among the young people, who unconsciously gave me some very cheering facts in return for very poor fictions.

I was both surprised and delighted with the nerve and courage, the high aims and patient persistence which appeared, not only among the laborious young women whose teacher is necessity, but among tenderly nurtured girls who cherished the noblest ambitions and had learned to earn the happiness no wealth could buy them.

Having great faith in young America, it gave me infinite satisfaction to find such eager interest in all good things, and to see how irresistibly the spirit of our new revolution, stirring in the hearts of sisters and daughters, was converting the fathers and brothers who loved them. One shrewd, business man said, when talking of Woman Suffrage, 'How *can* I help believing in it, when I've got a wife and six girls who are *bound* to have it?'

And many a grateful brother declared he could not be mean enough to shut any door in the face of the sister who had made him what he was.

So I close this hasty note by proposing three cheers for the girls of 1876—and the hope that they will prove themselves worthy descendants of the mothers of this Revolution, remembering that

> 'Earth's fanatics make
> Too often Heaven's saints.'

L. M. ALCOTT

CONCORD, JUNE 29 [1876]

TO JOHN PRESTON TRUE

CONCORD, OCTOBER 24 [1878]

J. P. TRUE

DEAR SIR,

I never copy or 'polish' so I have no old manuscripts to send you; and if I had it would be of little use, for one person's method is no rule for another. Each must work in his own way; and the only drill needed is to keep writing and profit by criticism. Mind grammar, spelling, and punctuation, use short words, and express as briefly as you can your meaning. Young people use too many adjectives to try to 'write fine.' The strongest, simplest words are best, and no *foreign* ones if it can be helped.

Write, and print if you can; if not, still write, and improve as you go on. Read the best books, and they will improve your style. See and hear good speakers and wise people, and learn of them. Work for twenty years, and then you may some day find that you have a style and place of your own, and can command good pay for the same things no one would take when you were unknown.

I know little of poetry, as I never read modern attempts, but advise any young person to keep to prose, as only once in a century is there a true poet; and verses are so easy to do that it is not much help to write them. I have so many letters like your own that I can say no more, but wish you success, and give you for a motto Michael Angelo's wise words: 'Genius is infinite patience.'

Your friend,

L. M. ALCOTT

P.S.—The lines you send me are better than many I see, but boys of nineteen cannot know much about hearts, and had better write of things they understand. Sentiment is apt to become sentimentality; and sense is always safer, as well as better drill, for young fancies and feelings.

Read Ralph Waldo Emerson, and see what good prose is, and some of the best poetry we have. I much prefer him to Longfellow.

TO THE WOMAN'S JOURNAL

EDITORS JOURNAL

As other towns report their first experience of women at the polls, Concord should be heard from, especially as she has distinguished herself by an unusually well conducted and successful town meeting.

Twenty eight women intended to vote, but owing to the omission of some formality several names could not be put upon the lists. Three or four were detained at home by family cares and did not neglect their domestic duties to rush to the polls as has been predicted. Twenty, however, were there, some few coming alone, but mostly with husbands, fathers or brothers as they should; all in good spirits and not in the least daunted by the awful deed about to be done.

Our town meetings I am told are always orderly and decent, this one certainly was; and we found it very like a lyceum lecture only rather more tedious than most, except when gentlemen disagreed and enlivened the scene with occasional lapses into bad temper or manners, which amused but did not dismay the womenfolk, while it initiated them into the forms and courtesies of parliamentary debate.

Voting for school committee did not come till about three, and as the meeting began at one, we had ample time to learn how the mystic rite was performed, so, when at last our tickets were passed to us we were quite prepared to follow our leader without fear.

Mr Alcott with a fatherly desire to make the new step as easy as possible for us, privately asked the moderator when the women were to vote, and on being told that they could take their chance with the men or come later, proposed that they should come first as a proper token of respect and for the credit of the town. One of the selectmen said 'By all means' and proved himself a tower of strength by seconding the philosopher on this momentous occasion.

The moderator (who is also the registrar and has most kindly and faithfully done his duty to the women in spite of his own difference of opinion) then announced that the ladies would prepare their votes and deposit them before the men did. No one objected, we were ready, and filed out in good order, dropping our votes and passing back to our seats as quickly and quietly as possible, while the assembled gentlemen watched us in solemn silence.

No bolt fell on our audacious heads, no earthquake shook the town, but a pleasing surprise created a general outbreak of laughter and applause, for, scarcely were we seated when Judge Hoare rose and proposed that the polls be closed. The motion was carried before the laugh subsided, and the polls were closed without a man's voting; a perfectly fair proceeding we thought since we were allowed no voice on any other question.

The superintendent of schools expressed a hope that the whole town would vote, but was gracefully informed that it made no difference as the women had all voted as the men would.

Not quite a correct statement by the way, as many men would probably have voted for other candidates, as tickets were prepared and some persons looked disturbed at being deprived of their rights. It was too late, however, for the joke became sober earnest, and the women elected the school committee for the coming year, feeling satisfied, with one or two exceptions, that they had secured persons whose past services proved their fitness for the office.

The business of the meeting went on, and the women remained to hear the discussion of ways and means, and see officers elected with neatness and dispatch by the few who appeared to run the town pretty much as they pleased.

At five the housewives retired to get tea for the exhausted gentlemen, some of whom certainly looked as if they would need refreshment of some sort after their labors. It was curious to observe as the women went out how the faces which had regarded them with disapproval, derision or doubt when they went in now smiled affably, while several men hoped the ladies would come again, asked how they liked it, and assured them that there had not been so orderly a meeting for years.

One of the pleasant sights to my eyes was a flock of schoolboys watching with great interest their mothers, aunts and sisters, who were showing them how to vote when their own emancipation day came. Another was the spectacle of women sitting beside their husbands, who greatly enjoyed the affair though many of them differed in opinion and had their doubts about the Suffrage question.

Among the new voters were descendants of Major Buttrick of Concord fight renown, two of Hancock and Quincy, and others whose grandfathers or great grandfathers had been among the first settlers of the town. A goodly array of dignified and earnest women, though some of the 'first families' of the historic town were conspicuous by their absence.

But the ice is broken, and I predict that next year our ranks will be fuller, for it is the first step that counts, and when the timid or indifferent, several of whom came to look on, see that we still live, they will venture to express publicly the opinions they held or have lately learned to respect and believe.

L. M. A.

CONCORD, MARCH 30, 1880.

TO HORACE P. CHANDLER

[CA. 7 DECEMBER 1881]

DEAR MR CHANDLER

The corrections are certainly rather peculiar, & I fear my struggles to set them right have only produced greater confusions.

Fortunately punctuation is a free institution, & all can pepper to suit the taste. I don't care much, & always leave proof readers to quiddle if they like.

Thanks for the tickets. I fear I cannot come till Thursday, but will try; & won't forget the Office since I am not that much-tried soul the Editor.

Yrs truly
L. M. A.

TO THE WOMAN'S JOURNAL

EDITOR JOURNAL:

You ask what we are going to do about Municipal Suffrage for women in Concord? and I regret to be obliged to answer, as before—'Nothing but make a motion asking for it at town meeting, and see it promptly laid upon the table again.'

It is always humiliating to have to confess this to outsiders, who look upon Concord as a representative town, and are amazed to learn that it takes no active part in any of the great reforms of the day, but seems to be content with the reflected glory of dead forefathers and imported geniuses, and falls far behind smaller but more wide awake towns with no pretensions to unusual intelligence, culture, or renown.

I know of few places where Municipal Suffrage might more safely be granted to our sex than this, for there is an unusually large proportion of tax paying, well to do and intelligent women, who only need a little training, courage, and good leadership to take a helpful and proper share in town affairs. They would not ask or accept town offices, but would be glad to work in their own efficient and womanly way, as they have proved they could work by the success of their church, charity and social labors for years past.

To those who see what brave and noble parts women elsewhere are taking in the larger and more vital questions of the time, the thought very naturally comes: 'What a pity that so much good sense, energy, time, and money could not be used for more pressing needs than church fairs, tea parties, or clubs for the study of pottery, Faust and philosophy!'

While a bar room door stands open between two churches, and men drink themselves to death before our eyes, it seems as if Christian men and women should bestir themselves to try at least to stop it; else the commandment 'Thou shalt love they neighbor as thyself' is written over the altars in vain, and the daily prayer 'Lead us not into temptation' is but empty breath.

If the women could vote on the license question I think the bar room would be closed; but while those who own the place say, 'It would lessen the value of the property to make a temperance house of it' and the license matter is left to the decision of those men who always grant it, the women can only wait and hope and pray for the good time when souls are counted of more value than dollars, and law and gospel can go hand in hand.

A forty years acquaintance with the town leads me to believe that as the conservative elders pass away, the new generation will care less for the traditions of the past, more for the work of the present, and taking a brave part in it, will add fresh honors to the fine old town, which should be marching abreast with the foremost, not degenerating into a museum for revolutionary relics, or a happy hunting ground for celebrity seekers.

A rumor has just reached me that some of the husbands of our few Suffrage women intend to settle the license question in the right way, and perhaps say a good word for our petition before it is shelved. This is encouraging, for it shows that the power behind the throne is gently working, and though the good women have little to say in public, they do know how to plead, advise, and convince in private. So, even if fewer should vote this year than last, and if nothing seems to come of our effort to secure Municipal Suffrage this time, we shall not be disheartened, but keep stirring our bit of leaven, and wait, as housewives know how to do, for the fermentation which slowly but surely will take place, if our faith hope and charity are only strong, bright and broad enough.

L. M. ALCOTT

CONCORD, MASS., FEB 4, 1882.

Mark Twain

1835–1910

Mark Twain, born Samuel Langhorne Clemens, holds a special place in American literature as the first uniquely American man of letters. His masterpiece The Adventures of Huckleberry Finn *sums up a whole tradition of Western humor and realism. The following speeches, given to mark his 67th and 70th birthdays, celebrate a rich and varied life.*

SIXTY-SEVENTH BIRTHDAY

AT THE METROPOLITAN CLUB, NEW YORK, NOVEMBER 28, 1902.

Address at a dinner given in honor of Mr Clemens by Colonel Harvey, President of Harper & Brothers.

I THINK I ought to be allowed to talk as long as I want to, for the reason that I have cancelled all my winter's engagements of every kind, for good and efficient reasons, and am making no new engagements for this winter, and, therefore, this is the only chance I shall have to disembowel my skull for a year—close the mouth in that portrait for a year. I want to offer thanks and homage to the chairman for this innovation which he has introduced here, which is an improvement, as I consider it, on the old-fashioned style of conducting occasions like these. That was bad—that was a bad, bad, bad arrangement. Under that old custom the chairman got up and made a speech, he introduced the prisoner at the bar, and covered him all over with compliments, nothing but compliments, not a thing but compliments, never a slur, and sat down and left that man to get up and talk without a text. You cannot talk on compliments; that is not a text. No modest person, and I was born one, can talk on compliments. A man gets up and is filled to the eyes with happy emotions, but his tongue is tied; he has nothing to say; he is in the condition of Doctor Rice's friend who came home drunk and explained it to his wife, and his wife said to him, 'John, when you have drunk all the whiskey you want, you ought to ask for sarsaparilla.' He said, 'Yes, but when I have drunk all the whiskey I want I can't say sarsaparilla.' And so I think it is much better to leave a man unmolested until the testimony and pleadings are all in. Otherwise he is dumb—he is at the sarsaparilla stage.

Before I get to the higgledy-piggledy point, as Mr Howells suggested I do, I want to thank you, gentlemen, for this very high honor you are doing me, and I am quite competent to estimate it at its value. I see around me captains of all the illustrious industries, most distinguished men; there are more than fifty here, and I believe I know thirty-nine of them well. I could probably borrow money from—from the others anyway. It is a proud thing to me, indeed, to see such a distinguished company gather here on such an occasion as this, when there is no foreign prince to be feted—when you have come here not to do honor to hereditary privilege and ancient lineage, but to do reverence to mere mortal excellence and elemental veracity—and, dear me, how old it seems to make me! I look around me and I see three or four persons I have known so many, many years. I have known Mr Secretary Hay—John Hay, as the nation and the rest of his friends love to call him—I have known John Hay and Tom Reed and the Reverend Twitchell close upon thirty-six years. Close upon thirty-six years I have known those venerable men. I have known Mr Howells nearly thirty-four years, and I knew Chauncey Depew before he could walk straight, and before he learned to tell the truth. Twenty-seven years ago I heard him make the most noble and eloquent and beautiful speech that has ever fallen from even his capable lips. Tom Reed said that my principal defect was inaccuracy of statement. Well, suppose that that is true. What's the use of telling the truth all the time? I never tell the truth about Tom Reed—but that is his defect, truth; he speaks the truth always. Tom Reed has a good heart, and he has a good intellect, but he hasn't any judgment. Why, when Tom Reed wa invited to lecture to the Ladies Society for the Procreation or Procrastination, or something, of morals, I don't know what it was—advancement I suppose, of pure morals—he had the immortal indiscretion to begin by saying that some of us can't be optimists, but by judiciously utilizing the opportunities that Providence puts in our way we can all be bigamists. You perceive his limitations. Anything he has in his mind he states, if he thinks it is true. Well, that was true, but that was no place to say it—so they fired him out.

A lot of accounts have been settled here tonight for me; I have held grudges against some of these people; but they have all been wiped out by the very handsome compliments that have been paid me. Even Wayne MacVeagh—I have had a grudge against him for many years. The first time I saw Wayne MacVeagh was at a private dinner-party at Charles A. Dana's, and when I got there he was clattering along, and I tried to get a word in here and there; but you know what Wayne MacVeagh is when he is started, and I could not get in five words to his one—or one to his five. I struggled along and struggled along, and—well, I wanted to tell and I was trying to tell a dream I had had the night before, and it was a remarkable dream worth people's while to listen to, a dream recounting Sam Jones the revivalist's reception in heaven. I was on a train, and was approaching the celestial station—I had a through ticket—and I noticed a man sitting alongside of me asleep, and he had his ticket in his hat. He was the remains of the Archbishop of Canterbury; I recognized him by his photograph. I had nothing against him, so I took his ticket and let him have mine. He didn't object—he wasn't in a condition to object—and presently when the train stopped at the heavenly station—well, I got off, and he went on by request—but there they all were, the angels, you know, millions of them, every one with a torch; they had arranged for a torch-light procession; they were expecting the Archbishop, and when I got off they started to raise a shout, but it didn't materialize. I don't know whether they were disappointed. I suppose they had a lot of superstitious ideas about the Archbishop and what he should look like, and I didn't fill the bill, and I was trying to explain to Saint Peter, and was doing it in the German tongue, because I didn't want to be too explicit. Well, I found it was no use, I couldn't get along, for Wayne MacVeagh was occupying the whole place, and I said to Mr Dana, 'What is the matter with that man? Who is that man with the long tongue? What's the trouble with him, that long, lank cadaver, old oil-derrick out of a job—who is that?' 'Well now' Mr Dana said, 'you don't want to meddle with him; you had better keep quiet; just keep quiet, because that's a bad man. Talk! He was born to talk. Don't let him get out with you; he'll skin you.' I said, 'I have been skinned, skinned and skinned for years, there is nothing left.' He said, 'Oh you'll find there is; that man is the very seed and inspiration of that proverb which says, ''No matter how close you skin an onion, a clever man can always peel it again.'' Well I reflected and I quieted down. That would never occur to Tom Reed. He's got no discretion. Well, MacVeagh is just the same man; he hasn't changed a bit in all those years; he has been peeling Mr Mitchell lately. That's the kind of man he is.

Mr Howells—that poem of his is admirable; that's the way to treat a person. Howells has a peculiar gift for seeing the merits of people, and he has always exhibited them in my favor. Howells has never written anything about me that I couldn't read six or seven times a day; he is always just and always fair; he has written more appreciatively of me than any one in this world, and published it in the *North American Review*. He did me the justice to say that my intentions—he italicized that—that my intentions were always good, that I wounded people's conventions rather than their convictions. Now, I wouldn't want anything handsomer than that said of me. I would rather wait, with anything harsh I might have to say, till the convictions become conventions. Bangs has traced me all the way down. He can't find that honest man, but I will look for him in the looking-glass when I get home. It was intimated by the Colonel that it is New England that makes New York and builds up this country and makes it great, overlooking the fact that there's a lot of people here who came from elsewhere, like John Hay from away out West, and Howells from Ohio, and St Clair McKelway and me from Missouri, and we are doing what we can to build up New

York a little—elevate it. Why, when I was living in that village of Hannibal, Missouri, on the banks of the Mississippi, and Hay up in the town
of Warsaw, also on the banks of the Mississippi River—it is an emotional
bit of the Mississippi, and when it is low water you have to climb up
to it on a ladder, and when it floods you have to hunt for it with a
deep-sea lead—but it is a great and beautiful country. In that old time
it was a paradise for simplicity—it was a simple, simple life, cheap but
comfortable, and full of sweetness, and there was nothing of this rage
of modern civilization there at all. It was a delectable land. I went out
there last June, and I met in that town of Hannibal a schoolmate of
mine, John Briggs, whom I had not seen for more than fifty years. I
tell you, that was a meeting! That pal whom I had known as a little
boy long ago, and knew now as a stately man three or four inches over
six feet and browned by exposure to many climes, he was back there
to see that old place again. We spent a whole afternoon going about
here and there and yonder, and hunting up the scenes and talking of
the crimes which we had committed so long ago. It was a heartbreaking
delight, full of pathos, laughter, and tears, all mixed together; and we
called the roll of the boys and girls that we picnicked and sweethearted
with so many years ago, and there were hardly half a dozen of them
left; the rest were in their graves; and we went up there on the summit
of that hill, a treasured place in my memory, the summit of Holiday's
Hill, and looked out again over that magnificent panorama of the Mississippi River, sweeping along league after league, a level green paradise
on one side, and retreating capes and promontories as far as you could
see on the other, fading away in the soft, rich lights of the remote distance. I recognized then that I was seeing now the most enchanting
river view the planet could furnish. I never knew it when I was a boy;
it took an educated eye that had travelled over the globe to know and
appreciate it; and John said, 'Can you point out the place where Bear
Creek used to be before the railroad came?' I said, 'Yes, it ran along
yonder.' 'And can you point out the swimming-hole?' 'Yes, out there.'
And he said, 'Can you point out the place where we stole the skiff?'
Well, I didn't know which one he meant. Such a wilderness of events
had intervened since that day, more than fifty years ago, it took me
more than five minutes to call back that little incident, and then I did
call it back; it was a white skiff, and we painted it red to allay suspicion.
And the saddest, saddest man came along—a stranger he was—and he
looked that red skiff over so pathetically and he said: 'Well if it weren't

for the complexion I'd know whose skiff that was.' He said it in that pleading way, you know, that appeals for sympathy and suggestion; we were full of sympathy for him, but we weren't in any condition to offer suggestions. I can see him yet as he turned away with that same sad look on his face and vanished out of history forever. I wonder what became of that man. I know what became of the skiff. Well, it was a beautiful life, a lovely life. There was no crime. Merely little things like pillaging orchards and watermelon-patches and breaking the Sabbath—we didn't break the Sabbath often enough to signify—once a week perhaps. But we were good boys, good Presbyterian boys, all Presbyterian boys, and loyal and all that; anyway, we were good Presbyterian boys when the weather was doubtful; when it was fair, we did wander a little from the fold.

Look at John Hay and me. There we were in obscurity, and look where we are now. Consider the ladder which he has climbed, the illustrious vocations he has served—and vocations is the right word; he has in all those vocations acquitted himself with high credit and honor to his country and to the mother that bore him. Scholar, soldier, diplomat, poet, historian—now, see where we are. He is Secretary of State and I am a gentleman. It could not happen in any other country. Our institutions give men the positions that of right belong to them through merit; all you men have won your places, not by heredities, and not by family influence or extraneous help, but only by the natural gifts God gave you at your birth, made effective by your own energies; this is the country to live in.

Now, there is one invisible guest here. A part of me is present; the larger part, the better part, is yonder at her home; that is my wife, and she has a good many personal friends here, and I think it won't distress any of them to know that, although she is going to be confined to that bed for many months to come from that nervous prostration, there is not any danger and she is coming along very well—and I think it quite appropriate that I should speak of her. I knew her for the first time just in the same year that I first knew John Hay and Tom Reed and Mr Twichell—thirty-six years ago—and she has been the best friend I have ever had, and that is saying a good deal; she has reared me—she and Twichell together—and what I am I owe to them. Twichell—why, it is such a pleasure to look upon Twichell's face! For five and twenty years I was under the Rev. Mr Twichell's tuition, I was in his pastorate, occupying a pew in his church, and held him in due reverence. That man is full of all the graces that go to make a person companionable and beloved; and wherever Twichell goes to start a church the people flock there to buy the land; they find real estate goes up all around the spot, and the envious and the thoughtful always try to get Twichell to move to their neighborhood and start a church; and wherever you see him go you can go and buy land there with confidence, feeling sure that there will be a double price for you before very long. I am not saying this to flatter Mr Twichell; it is the fact. Many and many a time I have attended the annual sale in his church, and bought up all the pews on a margin—and it would have been better for me spiritually and financially if I had stayed under his wing.

I have tried to do good in this world, and it is marvellous in how many different ways I have done good, and it is comfortable to reflect—now, there's Mr Rogers—just out of the affection I bear that man many a time I have given him points in finance that he had never thought of—and if he could lay aside envy, prejudice, and superstition, and utilize those ideas in his business, it would make a difference in his bank account.

Well, I like the poetry. I like all the speeches and the poetry, too. I liked Dr Van Dyke's poem. I wish I could return thanks in proper measure to you, gentlemen, who have spoken and violated your feelings to pay me compliments; some were merited and some you overlooked, it is true; and Colonel Harvey did slander every one of you, and put things into my mouth that I never said, never thought of at all.

And now, my wife and I, out of our single heart, return you our deepest and most grateful thanks, and—yesterday was her birthday.

SEVENTIETH BIRTHDAY

ADDRESS AT A DINNER GIVEN BY COLONEL GEORGE HARVEY AT DELMONICO'S, DECEMBER 5, 1905, TO CELEBRATE THE SEVENTIETH ANNIVERSARY OF MR CLEMENS' BIRTH.

Mr Howells introduced Mr Clemens:

'Now, ladies and gentlemen, and Colonel Harvey, I will try not
to be greedy on your behalf in wishing the health of our honored
and, in view of his great age, our revered guest. I will not say,
''Oh King, live forever!'' but ''Oh King, live as long as you like!'''
[Amid great applause and waving of napkins all rise and drink to
Mark Twain.]

Well, if I made that joke, it is the best one I ever made, and it is in
the prettiest language too. I never can get quite to that height. But I
appreciate that joke, and I shall remember it—and I shall use it when
occasion requires.

I have had a great many birthdays in my time. I remember the first
one very well, and I always think of it with indignation; everything
was so crude, unaesthetic, primeval. Nothing like this at all. No proper
appreciative preparation made; nothing really ready. Now, a person
born with high and delicate instinct—why, even the cradle wasn't white-
washed—nothing ready at all. I hadn't any hair, I hadn't any teeth,
I hadn't any clothes, I had to go to my first banquet just like that. Well,
everybody came swarming in. It was the merest little bit of a village—
hardly that, just a little hamlet in the backwoods of Missouri, where
nothing ever happened, and the people were all interested, and they
all came; they looked me over to see if there was anything fresh in
my line. Why, nothing ever happened in that village—I—why, I was
the only thing that had really happened there for months and months
and months; and although I say it myself that shouldn't, I came the
nearest to being a real event that had happened in that village in more
than two years. Well, those people came, they came with that curiosity
which is so provincial, with that frankness which also is so provincial,
and they examined me all around and gave their opinion. Nobody asked
them, and I shouldn't have minded if anybody had paid me a compli-
ment, but nobody did. Their opinions were all just green with prejudice,
and I feel those opinions to this day. Well, I stood that as long as—well,
you know I was born courteous, and I stood it to the limit. I stood
it an hour, and then the worm turned. I was the worm; it was my
turn to turn, and I turned. I knew very well the strength of my position;
I knew that I was the only spotlessly pure and innocent person in that
whole town, and I came out and said so. And they could not say a
word. It was so true. They blushed; they were embarrassed. Well, that
was the first after-dinner speech I ever made. I think it was after dinner.

It's a long stretch between that first birthday speech and this one. That was my cradle-song; and this is my swan-song, I suppose. I am used to swan-songs; I have sung them several times.

This is my seventieth birthday, and I wonder if you all rise to the size of that proposition, realizing all the significance of that phrase, seventieth birthday.

The seventieth birthday! It is the time of life when you arrive at a new and awful dignity; when you may throw aside the decent reserves which have oppressed you for a generation and stand unafraid and unabashed upon your seven-terraced summit and look down and teach—unrebuked. You can tell the world how you got there. It is what they all do. You shall never get tired of telling by what delicate arts and deep moralities you climbed up to that great place. You will explain the process and dwell on the particulars with senile rapture. I have been anxious to explain my own system this long time, and now at last I have the right.

I have achieved my seventy years in the usual way; by sticking strictly to a scheme of life which would kill anybody else. It sounds like an exaggeration, but that is really the common rule for attaining to old age. When we examine the programme of any of these garrulous old people we always find that the habits which have preserved them would have decayed us; that the way of life which enabled them to live upon the property of their heirs so long, as Mr Choate says, would have put us out of commission ahead of time. I will offer here, as a sound maxim, this: That we can't reach old age by another man's road.

I will now teach, offering my way of life to whomsoever desires to commit suicide by the scheme which has enabled me to beat the doctor and the hangman for seventy years. Some of the details may sound untrue, but they are not. I am not here to deceive; I am here to teach.

We have no permanent habits until we are forty. Then they begin to harden, presently they petrify, then business begins. Since forty I have been regular about going to bed and getting up—and that is one of the main things. I have made it a rule to go to bed when there wasn't anybody left to sit up with; and I have made it a rule to get up when I had to. This has resulted in an unswerving regularity of irregularity. It has saved me sound, but it would injure another person.

In the matter of diet—which is another main thing—I have been persistently strict in sticking to the things which didn't agree with me until one or the other of us got the best of it. Until lately I got the best of it myself. But last spring I stopped frolicking with mince-pie after mid-night; up to then I had always believed it wasn't loaded. For thirty years I have taken coffee and bread at eight in the morning, and no bite nor sup until seven-thirty in the evening. Eleven hours. That is all right for me, and is wholesome, because I have never had a headache in my life, but headachy people would not reach seventy comfortably by that road and they would be foolish to try it. And I wish to urge upon you this—which I think is wisdom— that if you find you can't make seventy by any but an uncomfortable road, don't you go. When they take off the Pullman and retire you to the rancid smoker, put on your things, count your checks, and get out at the first way station where there's a cemetery.

I have made it a rule never to smoke more than one cigar at a time. I have no other restriction as regards smoking. I do not know just when I began to smoke, I only know that it was in my father's lifetime, and that I was discreet. He passed from this life early in 1847, when I was a shade past eleven; ever since then I have smoked publicly. As an example to others, and not that I care for moderation myself, it has always been my rule never to smoke when asleep, and never to refrain when awake. It is a good rule. I mean, for me; but some of you know quite well that it wouldn't answer for everybody that's trying to get to be seventy.

I smoke in bed until I have to go to sleep; I wake up in the night, sometimes once, sometimes twice, sometimes three times, and I never waste any of these opportunities to smoke. This habit is so old and dear and precious to me that I would feel as you, sir, would feel if you should lose the only moral you've got—meaning the chairman—if you've got one: I am making no charges. I will grant, here, that I have stopped smoking now and then, for a few months at a time, but it was not on principle, it was only to show off; it was to pulverize those critics who said I was a slave to my habits and couldn't break my bonds.

To-day it is all of sixty years since I began to smoke the limit. I have never bought cigars with life-belts around them. I early found that those were too expensive for me. I have always bought cheap cigars—reasona-bly cheap, at any rate. Sixty years ago they cost me four dollars a barrel, but my taste has improved, latterly, and I pay seven now. Six or seven. Seven, I think. Yes, it's seven. But that includes the barrel. I often have smoking-parties at my house; but the people that come have always just taken the pledge. I wonder why that is?

As for drinking, I have no rule about that. When the others drink I like to help; otherwise I remain dry, by habit and preference. This dryness, does not hurt me, but it could easily hurt you, because you are different. You let it alone.

Since I was seven years old I have seldom taken a dose of medicine, and have still seldomer needed one. But up to seven I lived exclusively on allopathic medicines. Not that I needed them, for I don't think I did; it was an economy; my father took a drug-store for a debt, and it made cod-liver oil cheaper than the other breakfast foods. We had nine barrels of it, and it lasted me seven years. Then I was weaned. The rest of the family had to get along with rhubarb and ipecac and such things, because I was the pet. I was the first Standard Oil Trust. I had it all. By the time the drug-store was exhausted my health was established, and there has never been much the matter with me since. But you know very well it would be foolish for the average child to start for seventy on that basis. It happened to be just the thing for me, but that was merely an accident; it couldn't happen again in this century.

I have never taken any exercise, except sleeping and resting, and I never intend to take any. Exercise is loathsome. And it cannot be any benefit when you are tired; and I was always tired. But let another person try my way, and see where he will come out.

I desire now to repeat and emphasize that maxim: We can't reach old age by another man's road. My habits protect my life, but they would assassinate you.

I have lived a severely moral life. But it would be a mistake for other people to try that, or for me to recommend it. Very few would succeed: you have to have a perfectly colossal stock of morals; and you can't get them on a margin; you have to have the whole thing, and put them in your box. Morals are an acquirement—like music, like a foreign language, like piety, poker, paralysis—no man is born with them. I wasn't myself, I started poor. I hadn't a single moral. There is hardly a man in this house that is poorer than I was then. Yes, I started like that—the world before me, not a moral in the slot. Not even an insurance moral. I can remember the first one I ever got. I can remember the landscape, the weather, the—I can remember how everything looked. It was an old moral, an old second-hand moral, all out of repair, and didn't fit, anyway. But if you are careful with a thing like that, and keep it in a dry place, and save it for processions, and Chautauquas, and World's Fairs, and so on, and disinfect it now and then, and give it a fresh

coat of whitewash once in a while, you will be surprised to see how
well she will last and how long she will keep sweet, or at least inoffensive.
When I got that mouldy old moral, she had stopped growing, because
she hadn't any exercise; but I worked her hard, I worked her Sundays
and all. Under this cultivation she waxed in might and stature beyond
belief and served me well and was my pride and joy for sixty-three
years; then she got to associating with insurance presidents, and lost
flesh and character, and was a sorrow to look at and no longer competent
for business. She was a great loss to me. Yet not all loss. I sold her—ah,
pathetic skeleton, as she was—I sold her to Leopold, the pirate King
of Belgium; he sold her to our Metropolitan Museum, and it was very
glad to get her, for without a rag on, she stands 57 feet long and 16
feet high, and they think she's a brontosaur. Well, she looks it. They
believe it will take nineteen geological periods to breed her match.

Morals are of inestimable value, for every man is born crammed with
sin microbes, and the only thing that can extirpate these sin microbes
is morals. Now you take a sterilized Christian—I mean, you take *the*
sterilized Christian, for there's only one. Dear sir, I wish you wouldn't
look at me like that.

Threescore years and ten!

It is the Scriptural statue of limitations. After that, you owe no active
duties; for you the strenuous life is over. You are a time-expired man,
to use Kipling's military phrase: You have served your term, well or
less well, and you are mustered out. You are become an honorary member of the republic, you are emancipated, compulsions are not for you,
not any bugle-call but 'lights out.' You pay the time-worn duty bills
if you choose, or decline if you prefer—and without prejudice—for they
are not legally collectable.

The previous-engagements plea, which in forty years has cost you
so many twinges, you can lay aside forever; on this side of the grave
you will never need it again. If you shrink at the thought of night,
and winter, and the late home-coming from the banquet and the lights
and the laughter through the deserted streets—a desolation which would
not remind you now, as for a generation it did, that your friends are
sleeping, and you must creep in a-tiptoe and not disturb them, but
would only remind you that you need not tiptoe, you can never disturb
them more—if you shrink at the thought of these things, you need only
reply, 'Your invitation honors me, and pleases me because you still
keep me in your remembrance, but I am seventy; seventy, and would

nestle in the chimney-corner, and smoke my pipe, and read my book, and take my rest, wishing you well in all affection, and that when you in your return shall arrive at pier No. 70 you may step aboard your waiting ship with a reconciled spirit, and lay your course toward the sinking sun with a contented heart.

Frances E. Willard

1839 – 1898

Frances Elizabeth Willard was a leading force in women's education and the temperance movement and from 1879 was President of the Women's Christian Temperance Union. The following extract from her autobiography My Happy Half Century *describes her early commitment to the temperance movement.*

IN JUNE OF that year (1874) I resigned my position as Dean in the Woman's College and Professor of Aesthetics in the North-western University. It has been often said in my praise that I did this for the explicit purpose of enlisting in the temperance army, but it is my painful duty in this plain, unvarnished tale to admit that the reasons upon which I based that act, so revolutionary of all my most cherished plans and purposes, related wholly to the local situation in the University itself. However, having resigned, my strongest impulses were towards the Crusade movement, as is sufficiently proved by the fact that, going East immediately, I sought the leaders of the newly formed societies of temperance women, and these were the first persons who befriended and advised me in the unknown field of 'Gospel temperance.' With them I saw the great unwashed, unkempt, ungospelled, and sin-scarred multitude for the first time in my life, as they gathered in a dingy down-town square of New York city to hear Dr Boole preach on Sabbath afternoon.

With several of these new friends I went to Old Orchard Beach, Me, where Francis Murphy, a drinking man and saloon-keeper, recently reformed, had called the first 'Gospel Temperance Camp Meeting' known to our annals. Here I met General Neal Dow, and heard the story of Prohibitory Law, and here in a Portland hotel, where I stayed and wondered 'where the money was to come from', as I had none, and had mother's expenses and my own to meet, I opened the Bible lying on a hotel table, and lighted on this memorable verse: *'Trust in the Lord, and do good; so shalt thou dwell in the land, and verily thou shalt be fed'* (Psalm xxxvii.3).

That was a turning point in life with me. Great spiritual illumination, unequalled in all my history before, had been vouchsafed me in the sorrowful last days at Evanston, but here came clinching faith for what was to me a most difficult emergency.

Convinced that I must make my own experience and determine my own destiny, I now bent all my forces to find what Archimedes wanted 'where to stand' within the charmed circle of the temperance reform. Chicago must be my field, for home was there, and the sacred past with its graves of the living and dead. But nobody had asked me to work there, and I was specially in mood to wait and watch for providential intimations. Meanwhile many and varied offers came from the educational field, tempting in respect of their wide outlook and large promise of financial relief. In this dilemma I consulted my friends as to their sense of my duty, every one of them, including my dear mother and my revered counsellor, Bishop Simpson, uniting in the decision that he thus expressed: 'If you were not dependent on your own exertions for the supply of current needs, I would say, be a philanthropist; but of all work, the temperance work pays least, and you cannot afford to take it up. I therefore counsel you to remain in your chosen and successful field of the higher education.'

No one stood by me in the preference I freely expressed to join the

Crusade women except Mrs Mary A. Livermore, who sent me a letter full of enthusiasm for the new line of work, and predicted success for me therein. It is said that Napoleon was wont to consult his marshals and then do as he pleased, but I have found this method equally characteristic of ordinary mortals, and certainly it was the one I followed in the greatest decision of my life. When I went east I first met Mr Henry F. Durant, founder of Wellesley College, at Old Orchard, and he said to me, 'I have built a college as perfect and beautiful as any palace, and I have dedicated it to the girls of the nation. It is my firm resolve to have only women in the faculty. You are a believer in the emancipation of women. I ask you to become a member of my faculty when I have searched this country as with a lighted candle to find the women whom I can trust, but you deliberately decline. Come and see the college, and it will give you everlasting regrets, to say the least of it.' So I went out to Wellesley and saw its beauty, comparing favourably with the finest buildings that one finds abroad. We lingered longest in the library, which was Mr Durant's delight, a perfect gem, as everybody truly said; and he asked me again if this college were not my fitting place. But I had turned my face for ever from the only educational institution in all the world to which I was devotedly attached, and nothing that I could see anywhere after that could ever give me either regret or hope. While visiting in Cambridge, Mass., I received two letters on the same day. The first was from Rev. Dr Van Norman, of New York, inviting me to become 'Lady Principal' of his fashionable school for young women, adjoining Central Park, where I was to have just what and just as few classes as I chose, and a salary of twenty-four hundred dollars a year. The other was from Mrs Louise S Rounds, of Centenary M.E. Church, Chicago, one of the women who had gone to the City Council on that memorable night of March 1874, and she wrote in substance as follows:-

'I was sitting at my sewing-work to-day, pondering the future of our young temperance association. Mrs O. B. Wilson, our president, does all she can, and has shown a really heroic spirit, coming to Lower Farwell Hall for a prayer-meeting every day in the week, though she lives a long distance from there, and is old and feeble, and the heat has been intense. She cannot go on much longer, and it has come to me, as I believe from the Lord, that you ought to be our President. We are a little band without money or experience, but with strong faith. I went right out to see some of our leading women, and they all say that if you will agree to come, there will be no trouble about your election. Please let me hear at once.

I cannot express the delight with which I greeted this announcement. Here was my 'open door' all unknown and unsought—a place prepared for me in one true temperance woman's heart, and a chance to work for the cause that had in so short a time become so dear to me. I at once declined the New York offer, and very soon after started for the West.

The first saloon I ever entered was Sheffner's on Market Street, Pittsburgh, on my way home. In fact, that was the only glimpse I ever personally had of the Crusade. It had lingered in this dun-colored city well-nigh a year and when I visited my old friends at the Pittsburgh Female College I spoke with enthusiasm of the Crusade, and of the women who were, as I judged from a morning paper, still engaged in it here. They looked upon me with astonishment when I proposed to seek out those women and go with them to the saloons, for in the two years that I had taught in Pittsburgh these friends associated me with the recitation room, the Shakespeare club, the lecture course, the opera—indeed, all the haunts open to me that a literary-minded woman would care to enter. However, they were too polite to desire to disappoint me, and so they had me piloted by some of the factotums of the place to the headquarters of the Crusade, where I was warmly welcomed and soon found myself walking down street arm-in-arm with a young teacher from the public school, who said she had a habit of coming in to add to the procession when her day's duties were over. We paused in front of the saloon that I have mentioned. The women ranged themselves along the curbstone, for they had been forbidden in anywise to incommode the passersby, being dealt with much more strictly than a drunken man or a heap of dry-goods boxes would be. At a signal from our grey-haired leader, a sweet-voiced woman began to sing 'Jesus the water of life will give,' all our voices soon blending in sweet song. I think it was the most novel spectacle that I recall. There stood women of undoubted religious devotion and the highest character, most of them crowned with the glory of grey hairs. Along the stony pavement of that stoniest of cities rumbled a procession of heavy waggons, many of them carriers of beer; between us and the saloon in front of which were drawn up in line passed the motley throng, almost every man lifting his hat, and even the little newsboys doing the same. It was American manhood's tribute to Christianity and to womanhood and it was significant and full of pathos. The leader had already asked the saloon-keeper if we might enter, and he had declined, else the prayer-meeting would have occurred inside his door. A sorrowful old lady, whose only son had gone to ruin through that very death-trap knelt on the cold, moist pavement and offered a broken-hearted prayer, while all our heads were bowed. At a signal we moved on, and the next saloon-keeper permitted us to enter. I had no more idea of the inward appearance of a saloon than if there had been no such place on earth. I knew nothing of its high, heavily corniced bar, its barrels with the ends all pointed towards the looker-on, each barrel being furnished with a faucet; its shelves glittering with decanters and cut glass, its floors thickly strewn with sawdust, and here and there a round table with chairs—nor of its abundant fumes, sickening to healthful nostrils. The tall, stately lady who led us placed her Bible on the bar and read a psalm, whether hortatory or imprecatory, I do not remember; but the spirit of these crusaders was so gentle, I think it must have been the former. Then we sang 'Rock of Ages' as I thought I had never heard it sung before, with a tender confidence to the height of which one does not rise in the easy-going regulation prayer-meeting, and then one of the older women whispered to me softly that the leader wished to know if I would pray. It was strange, perhaps, but I felt not the least reluctance, and kneeling on that sawdust floor, with a group of earnest hearts around me, and behind them, filling every corner and extending out into the street, a crowd of unwashed, unkempt, hard-looking drinking men, I was conscious that perhaps never in my life, save beside my sister Mary's dying bed, had I prayed as truly as I did then. This was my Crusade baptism. Shortly after this I was made president of the Chicago W.C.T.U.

Henry James

1843–1916

Henry James was a member of a distinguished and intellectual family. His father, Henry James, Sr, was a lecturer on religious, social and literary topics; his brother, William James, was a philosopher and psychologist and he himself was the eminent author of many subtle masterpieces including The Portrait of a Lady, The Turn of the Screw *and* The Golden Bowl. *The following extract from his autobiographical narrative* Notes of a Son and Brother *(1913) explores one of his favourite themes—the Europeanized American returning to his homeland.*

IT HAD BEEN, however, neither at Newport nor at Cambridge—the Cambridge at least of that single year—that the plot began most to thicken for me: I figure it as a sudden stride into conditions of a sort to minister

and inspire much more, all round, that we early in 1864 migrated, as
a family, to Boston, and that I now seem to see the scene of our existence
there for a couple of years packed with drama of a finer consistency
than any I had yet tasted. We settled for the interesting time in Ashburton
Place—the 'sympathetic' old house we occupied, one of a pair of tallish
brick fronts based, as to its ground floor, upon the dignity of time-
darkened granite, was lately swept away in the interest of I know not
what grander cause; and when I wish to think of such intercourse as
I have enjoyed with the good city at its closest and, as who should
say, its kindest, though this comes doubtless but to saying at its freshest,
I live over again the story of that sojourn, a period bristling, while I
recover my sense of it, with an unprecedented number of simultaneous
particulars. To stick, as I can only do, to the point from which my own
young outlook worked, the things going on for me so tremendously
all at once were in the first place the last impressions of the War, a
whole social relation to it crowding upon us there as for many reasons,
all the best, it couldn't have done elsewhere; and then, more personally
speaking, the prodigious little assurance I found myself gathering as
from one day to another that fortune had in store some response to
my deeply reserved but quite unabashed design of becoming as 'literary'
as might be. It was as if, our whole new medium of existence aiding,
I had begun to see much further into the question of how that end
was gained. The vision, quickened by a wealth, a great mixture, of new
appearances, became such a throbbing affair that my memory of the
time from the spring of '64 to the autumn of '66 moves as through
an apartment hung with garlands and lights—where I have but to breathe
for an instant on the flowers again to see them flush with colour, and
but tenderly to snuff the candles to see them twinkle afresh. Things
happened, and happened repeatedly, the mere brush or side-wind of
which was the stir of life; and the fact that I see, when I consider, how
it was mostly the mere side-wind I got, doesn't draw from the picture
a shade of its virtue. I literally, and under whatever felt restriction of
my power to knock about, formed independent relations—several; and
two or three of them, as I then thought, of the very most momentous.
I may not attempt just here to go far into these, save for the exception
of the easiest to treat, which I also, by good fortune, win back as by
no means the least absorbing—the beautiful, the entrancing presumption
that I should have but to write with sufficient difficulty and sufficient
felicity to get once for all (that was the point) into the incredibility of

print. I see before me, in the rich, the many-hued light of my room that overhung dear Ashburton Place from our third floor, the very greenbacks, to the total of twelve dollars, into which I had changed the cheque representing my first earned wage. I had earned it, I couldn't but feel, with fabulous felicity: a circumstance so strangely mixed with the fact that literary composition of a high order had, at that very table where the greenbacks were spread out, quite viciously declined, and with the air of its being also once for all, to 'come' on any save its own essential terms, which it seemed to distinguish in the most invidious manner conceivable from mine. It was to insist through all my course on this distinction, and sordid gain thereby never again to seem so easy as in that prime handling of my fee. Other guerdons, of the same queer, the same often rather greasy, complexion followed; for what had I done, to the accompaniment of a thrill the most ineffable, an agitation that, as I recapture it, affects me as never exceeded in all my life for fineness, but go one beautiful morning out to Shady Hill at Cambridge and there drink to the lees the offered cup of editorial sweetness?—none ever again to be more delicately mixed. I had addressed in trembling hope my first fond attempt at literary criticism to Charles Eliot Norton, who had lately, and with the highest, brightest competence, come to the rescue of the North American Review, submerged in a stale tradition and gasping for life, and he had not only published it in his very next number—the interval for me of breathless brevity—but had expressed the liveliest further hospitality, the gage of which was thus at once his welcome to me at home. I was to grow fond of regarding as a positive consecration to letters that half-hour in the long library at Shady Hill, where the winter sunshine touched serene bookshelves and arrayed pictures, the whole embrowned composition of objects in my view, with I knew not what golden light of promise, what assurance of things to come: there was to be nothing exactly like it later on—the conditions of perfect rightness for a certain fresh felicity, certain decisive pressures of the spring, *can* occur, it would seem, but once. This was on the other hand the beginning of so many intentions that it mattered little if the particular occasion was not repeated; for what did I do again and again, through all the years, but handle in plenty what I might have called the small change of it?

I despair, however, as I look back, of rendering the *fusions* in that much mixed little time, every feature of which had something of the quality and interest of every other, and the more salient, the more 'epoch-

making'—I apply with complacency the portentous term—to drape themselves romantically in the purple folds of the whole. I think it must
have been the sense of the various climaxes, the enjoyed, because so
long postponed, revenges of the War, that lifted the moment in the
largest embrace: the general consciousness was of such big things at
last in sight, the huge national emergence, the widening assurance, however overdarkened, it is true, by the vast black cost of what General
Grant (no light-handed artist he!) was doing for us. He was at all events
working to an end, and something strange and immense, even like the
light of a new day rising above a definite rim, shot its rays through
the chinks of the immediate, the high-piled screen of sacrifice behind
which he wrought. I fail to seize again, to my wonder, the particular
scene of our acclamation of Lee's surrender, but I feel in the air the
exhalation of our relief, mingled, near and far, with the breath of the
springtime itself and positively seemed to become over the land, over
the world at large in fact, an element of reviving Nature. Sensible again
are certain other sharpest vibrations then communicated from the public
consciousness: Ashburton Place resounds for me with a wild cry, rocks
as from a convulsed breast, on that early morning of our news of Lincoln's death by murder; and, in a different order, but also darkening
the early day, there associates itself with my cherished chamber of application the fact that of a sudden, and while we were always and as much
as ever awaiting him, Hawthorne was dead. What I have called the
fusion strikes me as indeed beyond any rendering when I think of the
peculiar assault on my private consciousness of *that* news: I sit once
more, half-dressed, late of a summer morning and in a bedimmed light
which is somehow at once that of dear old green American shutters
drawn to against openest windows and that of a moral shadow projected
as with violence—I sit on my belated bed, I say, and yield to the pang
that made me positively and loyally cry. I didn't rise early in those
days of scant ease—I now even ask myself how sometimes I rose at
all; which ungrudged license withal, I thus make out, was not less bles-
sedly effective in the harmony I glance at than several showier facts.
To tell at all adequately why the pang was fine would nevertheless too
closely involve my going back, as we have learned to say, on the whole
rich interpenetration. I fondly felt it in those days invaluable that I had
during certain last and otherwise rather blank months at Newport taken
in for the first time and at one straight draught the full sweet sense
of our one fine romancer's work—for sweet it then above all seemed

to me; and I remember well how, while the process day after day drew itself admirably out, I found the actual exquisite taste of it, the strain of the revelation, justify up to the notch whatever had been weak in my delay. This prolonged hanging off from true knowledge had been the more odd, so that I couldn't have explained it, I felt, through the fact that The Wonder-Book and Twice-Told Tales had helped to enchant our childhood; the consequence at any rate seemed happy, since without it, very measurably, the sudden sense of recognition would have been less uplifting a wave. The joy of the recognition was to know at the time no lapse—was in fact through the years never to know one, and this by some rare action of a principle or a sentiment, I scarce know whether to call it a clinging consistency or a singular silliness, that placed the Seven Gables, the Blithedale Romance and the story of Donatello and Miriam (the accepted title of which I dislike to use, not the 'marble' but very particularly the human Faun being throughout in question) somewhere on a shelf unvisited by harsh inquiry. The feeling had perhaps at the time been marked by presumption, by a touch of the fatuity of patronage; yet wasn't well-nigh the best charm of a relation with the works just named in the impulse, known from the first, somehow to stand in *between* them and harsh inquiry? If I had asked myself what I meant by that term, at which freedom of appreciation, in fact of intelligence, might have looked askance, I hope I should have found a sufficient answer in the mere plea of a sort of *bêtise* of tenderness. I recall how once, in the air of Rome at a time ever so long subsequent, a friend and countryman now no more, who had spent most of his life in Italy and who remains for me, with his accomplishment, his distinction, his extraordinary play of mind and his too early and too tragic death, the clearest case of 'cosmopolitan culture' I was to have known, exclaimed with surprise on my happening to speak as from an ancient fondness for Hawthorne's treatment of the Roman scene: 'Why, can you read *that* thing, and *here*?—to me it means nothing at all!' I remember well that under the breath of this disallowance of any possibility of association, and quite most of such a one as I had from far back positively cultivated, the gentle perforated book tumbled before me from its shelf very much as old Polonius, at the thrust of Hamlet's sword, must have collapsed behind the pictured arras. Of course I might have picked it up and brushed it off, but I seem to feel again that I didn't so much as want to, lost as I could only have been in the sense that the note of harsh inquiry, or in other words of the very stroke I had anciently wished to avert, *there* fell straight upon my ear. It represented everything I had so early known we must have none of; though there was interest galore at the same time (as there almost always is in lively oppositions of sensibility, with the sharpness of each, its special exclusions, well exhibited), in an 'American' measure that could so reject our beautiful genius and in a Roman, as it were, that could so little see he had done anything for Rome. H. B. Brewster in truth, literary master of three tongues at least, was scarce American at all; homely superstitions had no hold on him; he was French, Italian, above all perhaps German; and there would have been small use, even had there been any importance, in my trying to tell him for instance why it had particularly been, in the gentle time, that I had settled once for all to take our author's case as simply exquisite and not budge from that taking. Which indeed scarce bears telling now, with matters of relative (if *but* of relative!) urgence on hand—consisting as it mainly did in the fact that his work was all charged with a *tone*, a full and rare tone of prose, and that this made for it an extraordinary value in an air in which absolutely nobody's else was or has shown since any aptitude for being. And the tone had been, in its beauty—for me at least—ever so appreciably American; which proved to what a use American matter could be put by an American hand: a consummation involving, it appeared, the happiest moral. For the moral was that an American could be an artist, one of the finest, without 'going outside' about it, as I liked to say; quite in fact as if Hawthorne had become one just by being American *enough*, by the felicity of how the artist in him missed nothing, suspected nothing, that the ambient air didn't affect him as containing. Thus he was at once so clear and so entire—clear without thinness, for he might have seemed underfed, it was his danger; and entire without heterogeneity, which might, with less luck and to the discredit of our sufficing manners, have had to be his help. These remarks, as I say, were those I couldn't, or at any rate didn't, make to my Roman critic; if only because I was so held by the other case he offered me—that of a culture for which, in the dense medium around us, Miriam and Donatello and their friends hadn't the virtue that shines or pushes through. I tried to feel that this *constatation* left me musing—and perhaps in truth it did; though doubtless if my attachment to the arranger of those images had involved, to repeat, my not budging, my meditation, whatever it was, respected that condition.

It has renewed itself, however, but too much on this spot, and the scene viewed from Ashburton Place claims at the best more filling in than I can give it. Any illustration of anything worth illustrating has beauty, to my vision, largely by its developments; and developments, alas, are the whole flowering of the plant, while what really meets such attention as one may hope to beguile is at the best but a plucked and tossed sprig or two. That my elder brother was during these months away with Professor Agassiz, a member of the party recruited by that great naturalist for a prolonged exploration of Brazil, is one of the few blooms, I see, that I must content myself with detaching—the main sense of it being for myself, no doubt, that his absence (and he had never been at anything like such a distance from us,) left me the more exposed, and thereby the more responsive, to contact with impressions that had to learn to suffice for me in their uncorrected, when not still more in their inspiringly emphasised state. The main sense for William himself is recorded in a series of letters from him addressed to us at home and for which, against my hope, these pages succeed in affording no space— they are to have ampler presentation; but the arrival of which at irregular intervals for the greater part of a year comes back to me as perhaps a fuller enrichment of my consciousness than it owed for the time to any other single source. We all still hung so together that this replete organ could yet go on helping itself, with whatever awkwardness, from the conception or projection of others of a like *general* strain, such as those of one's brothers might appear; thanks to which constant hum or borrowed experience, in addition to the quicker play of whatever could pass as more honestly earned, my stage of life knew no drop of the curtain. I literally came and went, I had never practised such coming and going; I went in particular, during summer weeks, and even if carrying my general difficulty with me, to the White Mountains of New Hampshire, with some repetition, and again and again back to Newport, on visits to John La Farge and to the Edmund Tweedys (*their* house almost a second summer home to us;) to say nothing of winter attempts, a little weak, but still more or less achieved, upon New York—which city was rapidly taking on the capital quality, the large worldly sense that dear old London and dear old Paris, with other matters in hand for them as time went on, the time they were 'biding' for me, indulgently didn't grudge it. The matters they had in hand wandered indeed as stray vague airs across to us—this I think I have noted; but Boston itself could easily rule, in default even of New York, when to 'go' in particular, was an act of such easy virtue. To go from

Ashburton Place was to go verily round the corner not less than further afield; to go the Athenaeum, to the Museum, to a certain door of importances, in fact of immensities, defiant of vulgar intonation, in Charles Street, at the opposite end from Beacon. The fruit of these mixed proceedings I found abundant at the time, and I think quite inveterately sweet, but to gather it in again now—by which I mean set it forth as a banquet for imaginations already provided—would be to presume too far; not least indeed even on my own cultivated art of exhibition. The fruit of golden youth is all and always golden—it touches to gold what it gathers; this was so the essence of the case that in the first place everything was in some degree an adventure, and in the second any differences of degree guiding my selection would be imperceptible at this end of time to the cold eye of criticism. Not least moreover in the third place the very terms would fail, under whatever ingenuity, for my really justifying so bland an account of the period at large. Do I speak of it as a thumping sum but to show it in the small change, the handful of separate copper and silver coin, the scattered occasions reduced to their individual cash value, that, spread upon the table as a treasure of reminiscence, might only excite derision? *Why* was 'staying at Newport' so absurdly, insistently romantic, romantic out of all proportion, as we say—why unless I can truly tell in proportion to what it became so? It consisted often in my 'sitting' to John La Farge, within his own precincts and in the open air of attenuated summer days, and lounging thereby just passive to the surge of culture that broke upon me in waves the most desultory and disjointed, it was true, but to an absolute effect of unceasingly scented spray. Particular hours and old (that is young!) ineffable reactions come back to me; it's like putting one's ear, doctor-fashion to the breast of time—or say as the subtle savage puts his to the ground—and catching at its start some vibratory hum that has been going on more or less for the fifty years since. Newport, the barren isle of our return from Europe, had thus become—and at no such great expense if the shock of public affairs, everywhere making interests start to their feet, be counted out of the process—a source of fifty suggestions to me; which it would have been much less, however, I hasten to add, if the call of La Farge hadn't worked in with our other most standing attraction, and this in turn hadn't practically been part of the positive affluence of certain elements of spectacle. Why again I should have been able to see the pictorial so freely suggested, that pictorial which was ever for me the dramatic, the social, the effectively human aspect, would be doubtless a baffling inquiry in presence of the queer and dear old phenomena themselves; those that, taken together, may be described at the best, I suppose, rather as a much-mixed grope or halting struggle, call it even a competitive scramble, toward the larger, the ideal elegance, the traditional forms of good society in possession, than as a presentation of great noble assurances.

Spectacle in any case broke out, spectacle accumulated by our then measure, many thicknesses deep, flushing in the sovereign light, as one felt it, of the waning Rhode Island afternoons of August and September with the most 'evolved' material civilisation our American world could then show; the vividest note of this in those years, unconscious, even to an artless innocence, of the wider wings still to spread, being the long daily *corso* or processional drive (with cavaliers and amazons not otherwise than conveniently intermixed,) which, with a different direction for different days, offered doubtless as good an example of that gregarious exercise at any cost distinguishing 'fashionable life' as was anywhere on the globe to be observed. The price paid for the sticking together was what emphasised, I mean, the wondrous resolve to stick, however scant and narrow and unadjusted for processional effect the various fields of evolution. The variety moreover was short, just as the incongruities of composition in the yearning array were marked; but the tender grace of old sunset hours, the happier breadth of old shining sands under favour of friendly tides, the glitter *quand même* of 'caparisoned' animals, appointed vehicles and approved charioteers, to say nothing of the other and more freely exchanged and interrelated brightnesses then at play (in the softer ease of women, the more moustachio'd swagger of men, the braver bonhomie of the social aspect at large), melted together for fond fancy into a tone, a rhythm, a representational virtue charged, as to the amenities, with authority. The amenities thus sought their occasion to multiply even to the sound of far cannonades, and I well remember at once reflecting, in such maturity as I could muster, that the luckier half of a nation able to carry a huge war-burden without sacrifice of amusement might well overcome the fraction that had to feed but on shrinkage and privation; at the same time that the so sad and handsome face of the most frequent of our hostesses, Mary Temple, the elder as she had been, now the apt image of a stern priestess of the public altar, was to leave with me for the years to come the grand expression and tragic irony of its revulsion from those who, offering us some high entertainment during days of particular tension, could fiddle, as she scathingly said, while Rome was burning. Blest again the state of youth which could appreciate that admirable look and preserve it for illustration of one of the forms of ancient piety lost to us, and yet at the same time stow away as part of the poetry of the general drama just the luxury and pride, overhanging summer seas and projecting into summer nights great shafts of light and sound, that prompted the noble scorn. The 'round of pleasure' all this with a grand good conscience of course—for it always in the like case has that, had it at least when arranging performances, dramatic and musical, at ever so much a ticket, under the advantage of rare amateur talent, in aid of the great Sanitary Commission that walked in the footsteps and renewed in various forms the excellence of Florence Nightingale; these exhibitions taking place indeed more particularly in the tributary cities, New York, Philadelphia, Boston (we were then shut up to those,) but with the shining stars marked for triumphant appearance announced in advance on the Newport scene and glittering there as beauties, as élégantes, as vocalists, as heroines of European legend. Hadn't there broken upon us, under public stress, a refluent wave from Paris, the mid-Empire Paris of the highest pitch, which was to raise our social water-mark to a point unprecedented and there strikingly leave it? We were learning new lessons in every branch—that was the sense of the so immensely quickened general pace; and though my examples may seem rather spectral I like to believe this bigger breathing of the freshness of the future to have been what the collective rumble and shimmer of the whole business most meant. It exhaled an artless confidence which yet momently increased; it had no great sense of a direction, but gratefully took any of which the least hint was given, gathering up by the way and after the fact whatever account of itself a vague voice might strike off. There were times when the account of itself as flooding Lawton's Valley for afternoon tea was doubtless what it would most comfortably have welcomed—Lawton's Valley, at a good drive's length from the seaward quarter, being the scene of villeggiatura of the Boston muse, as it were, and the Boston muse having in those after all battle-haunted seasons an authority and a finish of accent beyond any other Tyrtaean strain. The New York and perhaps still more the Philadelphia of the time fumbled more helplessly, even if aspiringly, with the Boston evidences in general, I think, than they were to be reduced to doing later on; and by the happy pretext, certainly, that these superior signs had then a bravery they were not perhaps on their own side indefinitely to keep up.

They rustled, with the other leafage of the umbrageous grove, in the summer airs that hung over the long tea-tables; afternoon tea was itself but a new and romantic possibility, with the lesson of it gratefully learnt at hands that dispensed, with the tea and sugar and in the charmingest voice perhaps then to be heard among us, a tone of talk that New York took for exotic and inimitable, yet all the more felt 'good' much better than it might if left *all* to itself, for thus flocking in every sort of conveyance to listen to. The Valley was deep, winding and pastoral—or at least looks so now to my attached vision; the infancy of a finer self-consciousness seemed cradled there; the inconsequent vehicles fraternised, the dim, the more dejected, with the burnished and upstanding; so that I may really perhaps take most for the note of the hour the first tremor of the sense on the part of fashion that, if it could, as it already more or less suspected, get its thinking and reading and writing, almost everything in fact but its arithmetic, a bit dingily, but just by that sign cleverly, done for it, so occasion seemed easy, after all, for a nearer view, without responsibility, of the odd performers of the service. When these last were not literally all Bostonians they were New Yorkers who might have been mistaken for such—never indeed by Bostonians themselves, but only by other New Yorkers, the rich and guileless; so the effect as of a vague tribute to culture the most authentic (if I speak not too portentously) was left over for the aftertaste of simple and subtle alike. Those were comparatively thin seasons, I recognise, in the so ample career of Mrs Howe, mistress of the Valley and wife of the eminent, the militant Phil-Hellene, Dr S. G. of the honoured name, who reached back to the Byronic time and had dedicated his own later to still more distinguished liberating work on behalf of deaf mutes; for if she was thus the most attuned of interlocutors, most urbane of disputants, most insidious of wits, even before her gathered fame as Julia Ward and the established fortune of her elegant Battle-Hymn, she was perhaps to have served the State scarce better through final organized activities and shining optimisms and great lucky lyric hits than by having in her vale of heterogeneous hospitality undermined the blank assurance of her thicker contingent—after all too but to an *amusing* vague unrest—and thereby scattered the first rare seed of new assimilations. I am moved to add that, by the old terminology, the Avenue might have been figured, in the connection, as descending into the glen to meet the Point—which, save for a very small number of the rarest representatives of the latter, it could meet nowhere else. The difficulty

was that of an encounter of birds and fishes; the two tribes were native
to elements as opposed as air and water, the Avenue essentially nothing
if not exalted on wheels or otherwise expertly mounted, and the Point
hopelessly pedestrian and unequipped with stables, so that the very
levels at which they materially moved were but upper and lower, dread-
fully lower, parallels. And indeed the way to see the Point—which,
without playing on the word, naturally became our highest law—was
at the Point, where it appeared to much higher advantage than in its
trudge through the purple haze or golden dust of supercilious parades.
Of the advantage to which it did so appear, off in its own more
languorous climate and on its own ground, we fairly cultivated a conviction, rejoicing by that aid very much as in certain old French towns
it was possible to distinguish invidiously the Ville from the Cité.
The Point was our *cité*, the primal aboriginal Newport—which, striking
us on a first acquaintance as not other than dilapidated, might well
have been restored quite as M. Viollet-le-Duc was even then restoring
Carcassonne; and this all the more because our elder Newport, the only
seat of history, had a dismantled grassy fort or archaic citadel that dozed
over the waterside and that might (though I do take the vision, at close
quarters, for horrible) be smartly waked up. The waterside, which was
that of the inner bay, the ample reach towards Providence, so much
more susceptible of quality than the extravagant open sea, the 'old
houses', the old elms, the old Quaker faces at the small-paned old windows, the appointedness of the scene for the literary and artistic people
who, by our fond constructive theory, lodged and boarded with the
Quakers, always thrifty these, for the sake of all the sweetness and
quaintness, for the sake above all somehow of *our* hungry felicity of
view, by which I mean mine and that of a trusty friend or two, T S
Perry in especial—those attributes, meeting a want, as the phrase is,
of the decent imagination, made us perhaps overdramatize the sphere
of the clever people, but made them at least also, when they unmistaka-
bly hovered, affect us as truly the finest touches in the picture. For
they were in their way ironic about the rest, and that was a tremendous
lift in face of an Avenue that not only, as one could see at a glance,
had no irony, but hadn't yet risen, the magazines and the Point aiding,
to so much as a suspicion of the effect, familiar to later generations,
with which the word can conversationally come in. Oh the old clever
people, with their difference of shade from that of the clever old ones—
some few of these to have been discerned, no doubt, as of Avenue

position: I read back into their various presences I know not what queer little functional value the exercise and privilege of which, uncontested, uncontrasted (save with the absence of everything but stables) represents a felicity for the individual that is lost to our age. It could count as functional then, it could count as felicitous, to have been reabsorbed into Boston, or to propose to absorb even, for the first time, New York, under cover of the old mantle, the old artistic draped cloak, that had almost in each case trailed round in Florence, in Rome, in Venice, in conversations with Landor, in pencilled commemoration, a little niggling possibly but withal so sincere, of the 'haunts' of Dante, in a general claim of having known the Brownings (ah 'the Brownings' of those days!) in a disposition to arrange readings of these and the most oddly associated other poets about the great bleak parlours of the hotels. I despair, however, of any really right register of the art with which the cité ingratiated itself with me in this character of a vivid missionary Bohemia; I met it of course more than half way, as I met everything in the faintest degree ingratiating, even suggesting to it with an art of my own that it should become so—though in this matter I rather missed, I fear, a happy conversion, as if the authenticity were there but my sort of personal dash too absent.

Booker T. Washington

1856–1915

Former slave Booker T. Washington was black America's leading spokesman for most of his life. Head of the Tuskegee Institute in Alabama and outstanding public speaker, he yet achieved his greatest impact with the publication of his autobiography Up from Slavery *in 1901. The following extract deals with his early life as a slave.*

I WAS BORN a slave on a plantation in Franklin County, Virginia. I am not quite sure of the exact place or exact date of my birth, but at any rate I suspect I must have been born somewhere at some time. As nearly as I have been able to learn, I was born near a cross-roads post-office called Hale's Ford, and the year was 1858 or 1859. I do not know the month or the day. The earliest impressions I can now recall are of the plantation and the slave quarters—the latter being the part of the plantation where the slaves had their cabins.

My life had its beginning in the midst of the most miserable, desolate, and discouraging surroundings. This was so, however, not because my owners were especially cruel, for they were not, as compared with many others. I was born in a typical log cabin, about fourteen by sixteen feet square. In this cabin I lived with my mother and a brother and sister till after the Civil War, when we were all declared free.

Of my ancestry I know almost nothing. In the slave quarters, and even later, I heard whispered conversations among the coloured people of the tortures which the slaves, including, no doubt, my ancestors on my mother's side, suffered in the middle passage of the slave ship while being conveyed from Africa to America. I have been unsuccessful in securing any information that would throw any accurate light upon the history of my family beyond my mother. She, I remember, had a half-brother and a half-sister. In the days of slavery not very much attention was given to family history and family records—that is, black family records. My mother, I suppose, attracted the attention of a purchaser who was afterward my owner and hers. Her addition to the slave family attracted about as much attention as the purchase of a new horse or cow. Of my father I know even less than of my mother. I do not even know his name. I have heard reports to the effect that he was a white man who lived on top of the near-by plantations. Whoever he was, I never heard of his taking the least interest in me or providing in any way for my rearing. But I do not find especial fault with him. He was simply another unfortunate victim of the institution which the Nation unhappily had engrafted upon it at that time.

The cabin was not only our living-place, but was also used as the kitchen for the plantation. My mother was the plantation cook. The cabin was without glass windows; it had only openings in the side which let in the light, and also the cold, chilly air of winter. There was a door to the cabin—that is, something that was called a door—but the uncertain hinges by which it was hung, and the large cracks in it, to say nothing of the fact that it was too small, made the room a very uncomfortable one. In addition to these openings there was, in the lower right-hand corner of the room, the 'cat-hole,'—a contrivance which almost every mansion or cabin in Virginia possessed during the ante-bellum period. The 'cat-hole' was a square opening, about seven by eight inches, provided for the purpose of letting the cat pass in and out of the house at will during the night. In the case of our particular cabin I could never understand the necessity for this convenience, since there were at least a half-dozen other places in the cabin that would have accommodated the cats. There was no wooden floor in our cabin, the naked earth being used as a floor. In the centre of the earthen floor there was a large, deep opening covered with boards, which was used as a place in which to store sweet potatoes during the winter. An impression of this potato-hole is very distinctly engraved upon my memory, because I recall that during the process of putting the potatoes in or taking them out I would often come into possession of one or two, which I roasted and thoroughly enjoyed. There was no cooking-stove on our plantation, and all the cooking for the whites and slaves my mother had to do over an open fireplace, mostly in pots and 'skillets'. While the poorly built cabin caused us to suffer with cold in the winter, the heat from the open fireplace in summer was equally trying.

The early years of my life, which were spent in the little cabin, were not very different from those of thousands of other slaves. My mother, of course, had little time in which to give attention to the training of her children during the day. She snatched a few moments for our care in the early morning before her work began, and at night after the day's work was done. One of my earliest recollections is that of my mother cooking a chicken late at night, and awakening her children for the purpose of feeding them. How or where she got it I do not know. I presume, however, it was procured from our owner's farm. Some people may call this theft. If such a thing should happen now, I should condemn it as theft myself. But taking place at the time it did, and for the reason that it did, no one could ever make me believe that my mother was guilty of thieving. She was simply a victim of the system of slavery. I cannot remember having slept in a bed until after our family was declared free by the Emancipation Proclamation. Three children—John, my older brother, Amanda, my sister, and myself—had a pallet on the dirt floor, or to be more correct, we slept in and on a bundle of filthy rags laid upon the dirt floor.

I was asked not long ago to tell something about the sports and pastimes that I engaged in during my youth. Until that question was asked it had never occurred to me that there was no period of my life that was devoted to play. From the time that I can remember anything, almost every day of my life has been occupied in some kind of labour; though

I think I would now be a more useful man if I had had time for sports. During the period that I spent in slavery I was not large enough to be of much service, still I was occupied most of the time in cleaning the yards, carrying water to the men in the fields, or going to the mill, to which I used to take the corn, once a week, to be ground. The mill was about three miles from the plantation. This work I always dreaded. The heavy bag of corn would be thrown across the back of the horse, and the corn divided evenly on each side; but in some way, almost without exception, on these trips, the corn would so shift as to become unbalanced and would fall off the horse, and often I would fall with it. As I was not strong enough to reload the corn upon the horse, I would have to wait, sometimes for many hours, till a chance passer-by came along who would help me out of my trouble. The hours while waiting for some one were usually spent in crying. The time consumed in this way made me late in reaching the mill, and by the time I got my corn ground and reached home it would be far into the night. The road was a lonely one, and often led through dense forests. I was always frightened. The woods were said to be full of soldiers who had deserted from the army, and I had been told that the first thing a deserter did to a Negro boy when he found him alone was to cut off his ears. Besides, when I was late in getting home I knew I would always get a severe scolding or a flogging.

I had no schooling whatever while I was a slave, though I remember on several occasions I went as far as the schoolhouse door with one of my young mistresses to carry her books. The picture of several dozen boys and girls in a schoolroom engaged in study made a deep impression upon me, and I had the feeling that to get into a schoolhouse and study in this way would be about the same as getting into paradise.

So far as I can now recall, the first knowledge that I got of the fact that we were slaves, and that freedom of the slaves was being discussed, was early one morning before day, when I was awakened by my mother kneeling over her children and fervently praying that Lincoln and his armies might be successful, and that one day she and her children might be free. In this connection I have never been able to understand how the slaves throughout the South, completely ignorant as were the masses so far as books or newspapers were concerned, were able to keep themselves so accurately and completely informed about the great National questions that were agitating the country. From the time that Garrison, Lovejoy, and others began to agitate for freedom, the slaves throughout the South kept in close touch with the progress of the movement. Though I was a mere child during the preparation for the Civil War and during the war itself, I now recall the many late-at-night whispered discussions that I heard my mother and the other slaves on the plantation indulge in. These discussions showed that they understood the situation, and that they kept themselves informed of events by what was termed the 'grape-vine' telegraph.

During the campaign when Lincoln was first a candidate for the Presidency, the slaves on our far-off plantation, miles from any railroad or large city or daily newspaper, knew what the issues involved were. When war was begun between the North and the South every slave on our plantation felt and knew that, though other issues were discussed, the primal one was that of slavery. Even the most ignorant members of my race on the remote plantations felt in their hearts, with a certainty that admitted of no doubt, that the freedom of the slaves would be the one great result of the war, if the Northern armies conquered. Every success of the Federal armies and every defeat of the Confederate forces was watched with the keenest and most intense interest. Often the slaves got knowledge of the results of great battles before the white people received it. This news was usually gotten from the coloured man who was sent to the post-office for the mail. In our case the post-office was about three miles from the plantation, and the mail came once or twice a week. The man who was sent to the office would linger about the place long enough to get the drift of the conversation from the group of white people who naturally congregated there, after receiving their mail, to discuss the latest news. The mail-carrier on his way back to our master's house would as naturally retail the news that he had secured among the slaves, and in this way they often heard of important events before the white people at the 'big house', as the master's house was called.

I cannot remember a single instance during my childhood or early boyhood when our entire family sat down to the table together, and God's blessing was asked, and the family ate a meal in a civilized manner. On the plantation in Virginia, and even later, meals were gotten by the children very much as dumb animals get theirs. It was a piece of bread here and a scrap of meat there. It was a cup of milk at one time and some potatoes at another. Sometimes a portion of our family would eat out of the skillet or pot, while some one else would eat from a tin plate held on the knees, and often using nothing but his hands with which to hold the food. When I had grown to a sufficient size, I was required to go to the 'big house' at meal-times to fan the flies from the table by means of a large set of paper fans operated by a pulley. Naturally much of the conversation of the white people turned upon the subject of freedom and the war, and I absorbed a good deal of it. I remember that at one time I saw two of my young lady mistresses and some lady visitors eating ginger-cakes in the yard. At that time those cakes seemed to me to be absolutely the most tempting and desirable things that I had ever seen; and I then and there resolved that, if I ever got free, the height of my ambition would be reached if I could get to the point where I could secure and eat ginger-cakes in the way that I saw those ladies doing.

Of course as the war was prolonged the white people, in many cases, often found it difficult to secure food for themselves. I think the slaves felt the deprivation less than the whites, because the usual diet for slaves was corn bread and pork, and these could be raised on the plantation; but coffee, tea, sugar, and other articles which the whites had been accustomed to use could not be raised on the plantation, and the conditions brought about by the war frequently made it impossible to secure these things. The whites were often in great straits. Parched corn was used for coffee, and a kind of black molasses was used instead of sugar. Many times nothing was used to sweeten the so-called tea and coffee.

The first pair of shoes that I recall wearing were wooden ones. They had rough leather on the top, but the bottoms, which were about an inch thick, were of wood. When I walked they made a fearful noise, and besides this they were very inconvenient, since there was no yielding to the natural pressure of the foot. In wearing them one presented an exceedingly awkward appearance. The most trying ordeal that I was forced to endure as a slave boy, however, was the wearing of a flax shirt. In the portion of Virginia where I lived it was common to use flax as part of the clothing for the slaves. That part of the flax from which our clothing was made was largely the refuse, which of course was the cheapest and roughest part. I can scarcely imagine any torture, except, perhaps, the pulling of a tooth, that is equal to that caused by putting on a new flax shirt for the first time. It is almost equal to the feeling that one would experience if he had a dozen or more chestnut burrs, or a hundred small pin-points in contact with his flesh. Even to this day I can recall accurately the tortures that I underwent when putting on one of these garments. The fact that my flesh was soft and tender added to the pain. But I had no choice. I had to wear the flax shirt or none; and had it been left to me to choose, I should have chosen to wear no covering. In connection with the flax shirt, my brother John, who is several years older than I am, performed one of the most generous acts that I ever heard of one slave relative doing for another. On several occasions when I was being forced to wear a new flax shirt, he generously agreed to put it on in my stead and wear it for several days, till it was 'broken in'. Until I had grown to be quite a youth this single garment was all that I wore.

One may get the idea from what I have said that there was bitter feeling toward the white people on the part of my race, because of the fact that most of the white population was away fighting in a war which would result in keeping the Negro in slavery if the South was successful. In the case of slaves on our place this was not true, and it was not true of any large portion of the slave population in the South where the Negro was treated with anything like decency. During the Civil War one of my young masters was killed, and two were severely wounded. I recall the feeling of sorrow which existed among the slaves when they heard of the death of 'Mars' Billy'. It was no sham sorrow, but real. Some of the slaves had nursed 'Mars' Billy'; others had played with him when he was a child. 'Mars' Billy' had begged for mercy in the case of others when the overseer or master was thrashing them. The sorrow in the slave quarter was only second to that in the 'big house'. When the two young masters were brought home wounded, the sympathy of the slaves was shown in many ways. They were just as anxious to assist in the nursing as the family relatives of the wounded. Some of the slaves would even beg for the privilege of sitting up at night to nurse their wounded masters. This tenderness and sympathy on the part of those held in bondage was a result of their kindly and generous nature. In order to defend and protect the women and children who were left on the plantations when the white males went to war, the slaves would have laid down their lives. The slave who was selected to sleep in the 'big house' during the absence of the males was considered to have the place of honour. Any one attempting to harm 'young Mistress' or 'old Mistress' during the night would have had to cross the dead body of the slave to do so. I do not know how many have noticed it, but I think that it will be found to be true that there are few instances, either in slavery or freedom, in which a member of my race has been known to betray a specific trust.

As a rule, not only did the members of my race entertain no feelings of bitterness against the whites before and during the war, but there are many instances of Negroes tenderly caring for their former masters and mistresses who for some reason have become poor and dependent since the war. I know of instances where the former masters of slaves have for years been supplied with money by their former slaves to keep them from suffering. I have known of still other cases in which the former slaves have assisted in the education of the descendants of their former owners. I know of a case on a large plantation in the South in which a young white man, the son of the former owner of the estate, has become so reduced in purse and self-control by reason of drink that he is a pitiable creature; and yet, notwithstanding the poverty of the coloured people themselves on this plantation, they have for years supplied this young white man with the necessities of life. One sends him a little coffee or sugar, another a little meat, and so on. Nothing that the coloured people possess is too good for the son of 'old Mars' Tom', who will perhaps never be permitted to suffer while any remain on the place who knew directly or indirectly of 'old Mars' Tom.'

I have said that there are few instances of a member of my race betraying a specific trust. One of the best illustrations of this which I know of is in the case of an ex-slave from Virginia whom I met not long ago in a little town in the state of Ohio. I found that this man had made a contract with his master, two or three years previous to the Emancipation Proclamation, to the effect that the slave was to be permitted to buy himself, by paying so much a year for his body; and while he was paying for himself, he was to be permitted to labour where and for whom he pleased. Finding that he could secure better wages in Ohio, he went there. When freedom came, he was still in debt to his master some three hundred dollars. Notwithstanding that the Emancipation Proclamation freed him from any obligation to his master, this black man walked the greater portion of the distance back to where his old master lived in Virginia, and placed the last dollar, with interest, in his hands. In talking to me about this, the man told me that he knew that he did not have to pay the debt, but that he had given his word to his master, and this word he had never broken. He felt that he could not enjoy his freedom till he had fulfilled that promise.

From some things that I have said one may get the idea that some of the slaves did not want freedom. This is not true. I have never seen one who did not want to be free, or one who would return to slavery.

I pity from the bottom of my heart any nation or body of people that is so unfortunate as to get entangled in the net of slavery. I have long since ceased to cherish any spirit of bitterness against the Southern white people on account of the enslavement of my race. No one section of our country was wholly responsible for its introduction, and, besides, it was recognized and protected for years by the General Government. Having once got its tentacles fastened to the economic and social life of the Republic, it was no easy matter for the country to relieve itself of the institution. Then, when we rid ourselves of prejudice, or racial feeling, and look facts in the face, we must acknowledge that, notwithstanding the cruelty and moral wrong of slavery, the ten million Negroes inhabiting this country, who themselves or whose ancestors went through the school of American slavery, are in a stronger and more hopeful condition, materially, intellectually, morally, and religiously, than is true of an equal number of black people in any other portion of the globe. This is so to such an extent that Negroes in this country, who themselves or whose forefathers went through the school of slavery, are constantly returning to Africa as missionaries to enlighten those who remained in the fatherland. This I say, not to justify slavery—on the other hand, I condemn it as an institution, as we all know that in America it was established for selfish and financial reasons, and not from a missionary motive—but to call attention to a fact, and to show how Providence so often uses men and institutions to accomplish a purpose. When persons ask me in these days how, in the midst of what sometimes seem hopelessly discouraging conditions, I can have such faith in the future of my race in this country, I remind them of the wilderness through which and out of which, a good Providence has already led us.

Ever since I have been old enough to think for myself, I have entertained the idea that, notwithstanding the cruel wrongs inflicted upon us, the black man got nearly as much out of slavery as the white man did. The hurtful influences of the institution were not by any means confined to the Negro. This was fully illustrated by the life upon our own plantation. The whole machinery of slavery was so constructed as to cause labour, as a rule, to be looked upon as a badge of degradation, of inferiority. Hence labour was something that both races on the slave plantation sought to escape. The slave system on our place, in a large measure, took the spirit of self-reliance and self-help out of the white people. My old master had many boys and girls, but not one, so far as I know, ever mastered a single trade or special line of productive industry. The girls were not taught to cook, sew, or to take care of the house. All this was left to the slaves. The slaves, of course, had little personal interest in the life of the plantation, and their ignorance prevented them from learning how to do things in the most improved and thorough manner. As a result of the system, fences were out of repair, gates were hanging half off the hinges, doors creaked, window-panes were out, plastering had fallen but was not replaced, weeds grew in the yard. As a rule, there was food for the whites and blacks, but inside the house, and on the dining-room table, there was wanting that delicacy and refinement of touch and finish which can make a home the most convenient, comfortable, and attractive place in the world. Withal there was a waste of food and other materials which was sad. When freedom came, the slaves were almost as well fitted to begin life anew as the master, except in the matter of book-learning and ownership of property. The slave owner and his sons had mastered no special industry. They unconsciously had imbibed the feeling that manual labour was not the proper thing for them. On the other hand, the slaves, in many cases, had mastered some handicraft, and none were ashamed, and few unwilling, to labour.

Finally the war closed, and the day of freedom came. It was a momentous and eventful day to all upon our plantation. We had been expecting it. Freedom was in the air, and had been for months. Deserting soldiers returning to their homes were to be seen every day. Others who had been discharged, or whose regiments had been paroled, were constantly passing near our place. The 'grape-vine telegraph' was kept busy night and day. The news and mutterings of great events were swiftly carried from one plantation to another. In the fear of 'Yankee' invasions, the silverware and other valuables were taken from the 'big house', buried in the woods, and guarded by trusted slaves. Woe be to any one who would have attempted to disturb the buried treasure. The slave would give the Yankee soldiers food, drink, clothing—anything but that which had been specifically entrusted to their care and honour. As the great day drew nearer, there was more singing in the slave quarters than usual. It was bolder, had more ring, and lasted later into the night. Most of the verses of the plantation songs had some reference to freedom. True, they had sung those same verses before, but they had been careful to explain that the 'freedom' in these songs referred to the next world, and had no connection with life in this world. Now they gradually threw off the mask, and were not afraid to let it be known that the 'freedom' in their songs meant freedom of the body in this world. The night before the eventful day, word was sent to the slave quarters to the effect that something unusual was going to take place at the 'big house' the next morning. There was little, if any, sleep that night. All was excitement and expectancy. Early the next morning word was sent to all the slaves, old and young, to gather at the house. In company with my mother, brother, and sister, and a large number of other slaves, I went to the master's house. All of our master's family were either standing or seated on the verandah of the house, where they could see what was to take place and hear what was said. There was a feeling of deep interest, or perhaps sadness on their faces, but not bitterness. As I now recall the impression they made upon me, they did not at the moment seem to be sad because of the loss of property, but rather because of parting with those whom they had reared and who were in many ways close to them. The most distinct thing that I now recall in connection with the scene was that some man who seemed to be a stranger (a United States officer, I presume) made a little speech and then read a rather long paper—the Emancipation Proclamation, I think. After the reading we were told that we were all free, and could go when and where we pleased. My mother, who was standing by my side, leaned over and kissed her children, while tears of joy ran down her cheeks. She explained to us what it all meant, that this was the day for which she had been so long praying, but fearing that she would never live to see.

For some minutes there was great rejoicing, and thanksgiving, and wild scenes of ecstasy. But there was no feeling of bitterness. In fact, there was pity among the slaves for our former owners. The wild rejoicing on the part of the emancipated coloured people lasted but for a brief period, for I noticed that by the time they returned to their cabins there was a change in their feelings. The great responsibility of being free, of having charge of themselves, of having to think and plan for themselves and their children, seemed to take possession of them. It was very much like suddenly turning a youth of ten or twelve years out into the world to provide for himself. In a few hours the great questions with which the Anglo-Saxon race had been grappling for centuries had been thrown upon these people to be solved. These were the questions of a home, a living, the rearing of children, education, citizenship, and the establishment and support of churches. Was it any wonder that within a few hours the wild rejoicing ceased and a feeling of deep gloom seemed to pervade the slave quarters? To some it seemed that, now that they were in actual possession of it, freedom was a more serious thing than they had expected to find it. Some of the slaves were seventy or eighty years old; their best days were gone. They had no strength with which to earn a living in a strange place and among strange people, even if they had been sure where to find a new place of abode. To this class the problem seemed especially hard. Besides, deep down in their hearts there was a strange and peculiar attachment to 'old Master' and 'old Missus', and to their children, which they found it hard to think of breaking off. With these they had spent in some cases nearly a half-century, and it was no light thing to think of parting. Gradually, one by one, stealthily at first, the older slaves began to wander from the slave quarters back to the 'big house' to have a whispered conversation with their former owners as to the future.

Theodore Roosevelt

1858–1919

*Born of a distinguished New York family, Theodore
Roosevelt was in turn an aspiring cowboy, a successful
author and a hero of the Spanish-American war before
becoming the twenty-sixth President of the United States.
The following extract from his lively autobiography harks
back to his early, rough-and-ready days out West.*

I FIRST REACHED the Little Missouri on a Northern Pacific train about
three in the morning of a cool September day in 1883. Aside from the
station, the only building was a ramshackle structure called the Pyramid
Park Hotel. I dragged my duffle-bag thither, and hammered at the door
until the frowsy proprietor appeared, muttering oaths. He ushered me

upstairs, where I was given one of the fourteen beds in the room which by itself constituted the entire upper floor. Next day I walked over the abandoned army post, and after some hours among the gray log shacks, a ranchman who had driven into the station agreed to take me out to his ranch, the Chimney Butte ranch, where he was living with his brother and their partner.

The ranch was a log structure with a dirt roof, a corral for the horses near by, and a chicken-house jabbed against the rear of the ranch house. Inside there was only one room, with a table, three or four chairs, a cooking-stove, and three bunks. The owners were Sylvane and Joe Ferris and William J Merrifield. Later all three of them held my commissions while I was President. Merrifield was Marshal of Montana, and as Presidential elector cast the vote of that State for me in 1904; Sylvane Ferris was Land Officer in North Dakota, and Joe Ferris Postmaster at Medora. There was a fourth man, George Meyer, who also worked for me later. That evening we all played old sledge round the period, and at one period the game was interrupted by a frightful squawking outside which told us that a bobcat had made a raid on the chicken-house.

After a buffalo hunt with my original friend, Joe Ferris, I entered into partnership with Merrifield and Sylvane Ferris, and we started a cow ranch, with the Maltese cross brand—always known as 'maltee cross' by the way, as the general impression along the Little Missouri was that 'maltese' must be a plural. Twenty-nine years later my four friends of that night were delegates to the First Progressive National Convention at Chicago. They were among my most constant companions for the few years next succeeding that evening when the bobcat interrupted the game of old sledge. I lived and worked with them on the ranch, and with them and many others like them on the round-up; and I brought out from Maine, in order to start the Elkhorn ranch lower down the river, my two backwoods friends Sewall and Dow. My brands for the lower ranch were the elkhorn and triangle.

I do not believe there ever was any life more attractive to a vigorous young fellow than life on a cattle ranch in those days. It was a fine, healthy life too; it taught a man self-reliance, hardihood, and the value of instant decision—in short, the virtues that ought to come from life in the open country. I enjoyed the life to the full. After the first year I built on the Elkhorn ranch a long, low ranch house of hewn logs, with a veranda, and with, in addition to the other rooms, a bedroom for myself, and a sitting-room with a big fire-place. I got out a rocking-chair—I am very fond of rocking chairs—and enough books to fill two or three shelves, and a rubber bathtub so that I could get a bath. And then I do not see how any one could have lived more comfortably. We had buffalo robes and bearskins of our own killing. We always kept the house clean—using the word in a rather large sense. There were at least two rooms that were always warm, even in the bitterest weather; and we had plenty to eat. Commonly the mainstay of every meal was game of our own killing, usually antelope or deer, sometimes grouse or ducks, and occasionally, in the earlier days, buffalo or elk. We also had flour and bacon, sugar, salt, and canned tomatoes. And later, when some of the men married and brought their wives, we had all kinds of good things, such as jams and jellies made from the wild plums and the buffalo berries, and potatoes from the forlorn little garden patch. Moreover, we had milk. Most ranchmen at that time never had milk. I knew more than one ranch with ten thousand head of cattle where there was not a cow that could be milked. We made up our minds that we would be more enterprising. Accordingly, we started to domesticate some of the cows. Our first effort was not successful, chiefly because we did not devote the needed time and patience to the matter. And we found that to race a cow two miles at full speed on horseback, then rope her, throw her, and turn her upside to milk her, while exhilarating as a pastime, was not productive of results. Gradually we accumulated tame cows, and after we had thinned out the bobcats and coyotes, more chickens.

The ranch house stood on the brink of a low bluff overlooking the broad, shallow bed of the Little Missouri, through which at most seasons there ran only a trickle of water, while in times of freshet it was filled brimful with the boiling, foaming muddy torrent. There was no neighbor for ten or fifteen miles on either side of me. The river twisted down in long curves between narrow bottoms bordered by sheer cliff walls, for the Bad Lands, a chaos of peaks, plateaus, and ridges, rose abruptly from the edges of the level, tree-clad, or grassy, alluvial meadows. In front of the ranch-house veranda was a row of cottonwood trees with gray-green leaves which quivered all day long if there was a breath of air. From these trees came the far-away, melancholy cooing of mourning doves, and little owls perched in them and called tremulously at night. In the long summer afternoons we would sometimes sit on the piazza, when there was no work to be done, for an hour or two at a time, watching the cattle on the sand-bars, and the sharply channeled

and strangely carved amphitheater of cliffs across the bottom opposite;
while thevultures wheeled overhead, their black shadows gliding across
the glaring white of the dry river-bed. Sometimes from the ranch we
saw deer, and once I stood on the piazza. In the winter, in the days
of iron cold, when everything was white under the snow, the river
lay in its bed fixed and immovable as a bar of bent steel, and then at
night wolves and lynxes traveled up and down it as if it had been a
highway passing in front of the ranch house. Often in the late fall or
early winter, after a hard day's hunting, or when returning from one
of the winter line camps, we did not reach the ranch until hours after
sunset; and after the weary tramping in the cold it was keen pleasure
to catch the first red gleam of the fire-lit windows across the snowy
wastes.

The Elkhorn ranch house was built mainly by Sewall and Dow, who,
like most men from the Maine woods, were mighty with the ax. I could
chop fairly well for an amateur, but I could not do one-third the work
they could. One day when we were cutting down the cottonwood trees,
to begin our building operations, I heard some one ask Dow what the
total cut had been, and Dow, not realizing that I was within hearing,
answered: 'Well, Bill cut down fifty-three, I cut forty-nine, and the boss
he beavered down seventeen.' Those who have seen the stump of a
tree which has been gnawed down by a beaver will understand the
exact force of the comparison.

In those days on a cow ranch the men were apt to be away on the
various round-ups at least half the time. It was interesting and exciting
work, and except for the lack of sleep on the spring and summer round-
ups it was not exhausting work; compared to lumbering or mining or
black-smithing, to sit in the saddle is an easy form of labor. The ponies
were of course grass-fed and unshod. Each man had his own string
of nine or ten. One pony would be used for the morning work, one
for the afternoon, and neither would again be used for the next three
days. A separate pony was kept for night riding.

The spring and early summer round-ups were especially for the brand-
ing of calves. There was much hard work and some risk on a round-up,
but also much fun. The meeting-place was appointed weeks beforehand,
and all the ranchmen of the territory to be covered by the round-up
seat their representatives. There were no fences in the West that I knew,
and their place was taken by the cowboy and the branding-iron. The
cattle wandered free. Each calf was branded with the brand of the cow

it was following. Sometimes in winter there was what we called line riding; that is, camps were established and the line riders traveled a definite beat across the desolate wastes of snow, to and fro from one camp to another, to prevent the cattle from drifting. But as a rule nothing was done to keep the cattle in any one place. In the spring there was general round-up in each locity. In the spring there was a general round-up in each locality. Each outfit took part in its own round-up, and all the outfits of a given region combined to send representatives to the two or three round-ups that covered the neighborhoods near by into which their cattle might drift. For example, our Little Missouri round-up generally worked down the river from a distance of some fifty or sixty miles above my ranch towards the Kildeer Mountains, about the same distance below. In addition we would usually send representatives to the Yellowstone round-up, and to the round-up along the upper Little Missouri; and, moreover, if we heard that cattle drifted, perhaps toward the Indian reservation southeast of us, we would send a wagon and rider after them.

At the meeting-point, which might be in the valley of a half-day stream, or in some broad bottom of the river itself, or perchance by a couple of ponds under some queerly shaped butte that was a landmark for the region round about, we would all gather on the appointed day. The chuck-wagons, containing the bedding and food, each drawn by four horses, and driven by the teamster cook, would come jolting and rattling over the uneven sward. Accompanying each wagon were eight or ten riders, the cow-punchers, while their horses, a band of a hundred or so, were driven by the two herders, one of whom was known as the day wrangler and one as the night wrangler. The men were lean, sinewy fellows, accustomed to riding half-broken horses at any speed over any country by day or by night. They wore flannel shirts, with loose handkerchiefs knotted round their necks, broad hats, high-heeled boots with jingling spurs, and sometimes leather shaps, although often they merely had their trousers tucked into the tops of their high boots. There was a good deal of rough horse-play, and, as with any other gathering of men or boys of high animal spirits, the horse-play sometimes became very rough indeed; and as the men usually carried revolvers, and as there were occasionally one or two noted gun-fighters among them, there was now and then a shooting affray. A man who was a coward or who shirked his work had a bad time, of course; a man could not afford to let himself be bullied or treated as a butt; and on the other hand, if he was 'looking for a fight' he was certain to find it. But my own experience was that if a man did not talk until his associates knew him well and liked him, and if he did his work, he never had any difficulty in getting on. In my own roundup district I speedily grew to be friends with most of the men. When I went among strangers I always had to spend twenty-four hours in living down the fact that I wore spectacles, remaining as long as I could judiciously deaf to any side remarks about 'four-eyes' unless it became evident that my being quiet was misconstrued and that it was better to bring matters to a head at once.

If, for instance, I was sent off to represent the Little Missouri brands on some neighboring round-up, such as the Yellowstone, I usually showed that kind of diplomacy which consisted in not uttering one word that can be avoided. I would probably have a couple of days' solitary ride, mounted on one horse and driving eight or ten others before me, one of them carrying my bedding. Loose horses drive best at a trot, or canter, and if a man is traveling alone in this fashion it is a good thing to have them reach the camp ground sufficiently late to make them desire to feed and sleep where they are until morning. In consequence I never spent more than two days on the journey from whatever the point was at which I left the Little Missouri, sleeping one night for as limited a number of hours as possible.

As soon as I reached the meeting-place I would find out the wagon to which I was assigned. Riding to it, I turned my horses into the saddle brand and reported to the wagon boss, or, in his absence, to the cook— always a privileged character, who was allowed and expected to order men around. He would usually grumble savagely and profanely about my having been put with his wagon, but this was merely conventional on his part; and if I sat down and said nothing he would probably soon ask me if I wanted anything to eat, to which the correct answer was that I was not hungry and would wait until meal-time. The bedding rolls of the riders would be strewn around the grass, and I would put mine down a little outside the ring, where I would not be in any one's way, with my six or eight branding-irons beside it. The men would ride in, laughing and talking with one another, and perhaps nodding to me. One of their number, usually the wagon foreman, might put some question to me as to what brands I represented, but no other word would be addressed to me, nor would I be expected to volunteer any conversation. Supper would consist of bacon, Dutch oven bread and possibly beef; once I won the good graces of my companions at the outset by appearing with two antelope which I had shot. After supper I would roll up my bedding as soon as possible, and the others would follow suit at their pleasure.

At three in the morning or thereabouts, at a yell from the cook, all hands would turn hurriedly out. Dressing was a simple affair. Then each man rolled and corded his bedding—if he did not the cook would leave it behind and he would go without any for the rest of the trip—and came to the fire, where he picked out a tin cup, tin plate, and knife and fork, helped himself to coffee and whatever food there was, and ate it standing or squatting as best suited him. Dawn was probably breaking by this time, and the trampling of unshod hoofs showed that the night wrangler was bringing in the pony herd. Two of the men would then run ropes from the wagon at right angles to one another, and into this as a corral the horses would be driven. Each man might rope one of his own horses, or more often point it out to the most skillful roper of the outfit, who would rope it for him—for if the man was an unskillful roper and roped the wrong horse or roped the horse in the wrong place there was a chance of the whole herd stampeding. Each man then saddled and bridled his horse. This was usually followed by some resolute bucking on the part of two or three of the horses, especially in the early days of each round-up. The bucking was always a source of amusement to all the men whose horses did not buck, and these fortunate ones would gather round giving ironical advice, and especially adjuring the rider not to 'go to leather'—that is not to steady himself in the saddle by catching hold of the saddle-horn.

As soon as the men had mounted, the whole outfit started on the long circle, the morning circle. Usually the ranch foreman who bossed a given wagon was put in charge of the men of one group by the round-up foreman; he might keep his men together until they had gone some ten or fifteen miles from camp, and then drop them in couples at different points. Each couple made its way toward the wagon, gathering all the cattle it could find. The morning's ride might last six or eight hours, and it was still longer before some of the men got in. Singly and in twos and threes they appeared from every quarter of the horizon, the dust rising from the hoofs of the steers and bulls, the cows and calves, they had collected. Two or three of the men were left to take care of the herd while the others changed horses, ate a hasty dinner, and then came out to the afternoon work. This consisted of each man in succession being sent into the herd, usually with a companion, to cut out the cows of his brand or brands which were followed by unbranded calves, and also to cut out any mavericks or unbranded yearlings. We worked each animal gently out to the end of the herd, and then with a sudden dash took it off at a run. It was always desperately anxious to break back and rejoin the herd. There was much breakneck galloping and twisting and turning before its desire was thwarted and it was driven to join the rest of the cut—that is, the other animals which had been cut out, and which were being held by one or two other men. Cattle hate being alone, and it was no easy matter to hold the first one or two that were cut out; but soon they got a little herd of their own, and then they were contented. When the cutting out had all been done, the calves were branded, and all misadventures of the 'calf wrestlers', the men who seized, threw, and held each calf when roped by the mounted roper, were hailed with yelling laughter. Then the animals which for one reason or another it was desired to drive along with the round-up were put into one herd and left in charge of a couple of night guards, and the rest of us would loaf back to the wagon for supper and bed.

By this time I would have been accepted as one of the rest of the outfit, and all strangeness would have passed off, the attitude of my fellow cow-punchers being one of friendly forgiveness even toward my spectacles. Night guards for the cattle herd were then assigned by the captain of the wagon, or perhaps by the round-up foreman, according to the needs of the case, the guards standing for two hours at a time from eight in the evening till four in the morning. The first and last watches were preferable, because sleep was not broken as in both of the other two. If things went well, the cattle would soon bed down and nothing further would occur until morning when there was a repetition of the work, the wagon moving each day eight or ten miles to some appointed camping-place.

Each man would picket his night horse near the wagon, usually choosing the quietest animal in his string for that purpose, because to saddle and mount a 'mean' horse at night is not pleasant. When utterly tired, it was hard to have to get up for one's trick at night herd. Nevertheless, on ordinary nights the two hours round the cattle in the still darkness were pleasant. The loneliness, under the vast empty sky, and the silence, in which the breathing of the cattle sounded loud, and the alert readiness to meet any emergency which might suddenly arise out of the formless night, all combined to give one a sense of subdued interest. Then, one soon got to know the cattle of marked individuality, the ones that led the others into mischief; and one also grew to recognize the traits they all possessed in common, and the impulses, which, for instance, made a whole herd get up towards midnight, each beast turning round and then lying down again. But by the end of the watch each rider had studied the cattle until it grew monotonous, and heartily welcomed his relief guard. A newcomer, of course, had any amount to learn, and sometimes the simplest things were those which brought him to grief.

One night early in my career I failed satisfactorily to identify the direction in which I was to go in order to reach the night-herd. It was a pitch-dark night. I managed to get started wrong, and I never found either the herd or the wagon again until sunrise, when I was greeted with withering scorn by the injured cow-puncher who had been obliged to stand double guard because I failed to relieve him.

There are other misadventures which I met with where the excuse was greater. The punchers on night guard usually rode round the cattle in reverse directions; calling and singing to them if the beasts seemed restless, to keep them quiet. On rare occasions something happened that made the cattle stampede, and then the duty of the riders was to keep with them as long as possible and try gradually to get control of them.

One night there was a heavy storm, and all of us who were at the wagons were obliged to turn out hastily to help the night herders. After a while there was a terrific peal of thunder, the lightning struck right by the herd, and away all the beasts went, heads and horns and tails in the air. For a minute or two I could make out nothing except the dark forms of the beasts running on every side of me, and I should have been very sorry if my horse had stumbled, for those behind would have trodden me down. Then the herd split, part going to one side, while the other part seemingly kept straight ahead, and I galloped as hard as ever beside them. I was trying to reach the point—the leading animals—in order to turn them, when suddenly there was a tremendous splashing in front. I could dimly make out that the cattle immediately ahead and to one side of me were disappearing, and the next moment the horse and I went off a cut bank into the Little Missouri. I bent away back in the saddle, and though the horse almost went down he just recovered himself, and plunging and struggling through water and quicksand we made the other side. Here I discovered that there was another cowboy with the same part of the herd that I was with; but almost immediately we separated. I galloped hard through a bottom covered with big cottonwood trees, and stopped the part of the herd that I was with, but very soon they broke on me again, and repeated this twice. Finally toward morning the few I had left came to a halt.

It had been raining hard for some time. I got off my horse and leaned against a tree, but before long the infernal cattle started on again, and I had to ride after them. Dawn came soon after this, and I was able to make out where I was and head the cattle back, collecting other little bunches as I went. After a while I came on a cowboy on foot carrying his saddle on his head. He was my companion of the previous night. His horse had gone full speed into a tree and killed itself, the man, however, not being hurt. I could not help him, as I had all I could do to handle the cattle. When I got them to the wagon, most of the other men had come in and the riders were just starting on the long circle. One of the men changed my horse for me while I ate a hearty breakfast, and then we were off for the day's work.

As only about half of the night herd had been brought back, the circle riding was particularly heavy, and it was ten hours before we were back at the wagon. We then changed horses again and worked the whole herd until after sunset, finishing just as it grew too dark to do anything more. By this time I had been nearly forty hours in the saddle, changing horses five times, and my clothes had thoroughly dried on me, and I feel asleep as soon as I touched the bedding. Fortunately some men who had gotten in late in the morning had had their sleep during the daytime, so that the rest of us escaped night guard and were not called until four next morning. Nobody ever gets enough sleep on a round-up.

The above was the longest number of consecutive hours I ever had to be in the saddle. But, as I have said, I changed horses five times, and it is a great lightening of labor for a rider to have a fresh horse. Once when with Sylvane Ferris I spent about sixteen hours on one horse, riding seventy or eighty miles. The round-up had reached a place called the ox-bow of the Little Missouri, and we had to ride there, do some work around the cattle, and ride back.

Another time I was twenty-four hours on horseback in company with Merrifield without changing horses. On this occasion we did not travel fast. We had been coming back with the wagon from a hunting trip in the Big Horn Mountains. The team was fagged out, and we were tired of walking at a snail's pace beside it. When we reached country that the driver thoroughly knew, we thought it safe to leave him, and we loped in one night across a distance which it took the wagon the three following days to cover. It was a beautiful moonlight night, and the ride was delightful. All day long we had plodded at a walk, weary and hot. At supper time we had rested two or three hours, and the tough little riding horses seemed as fresh as ever. It was in September. As we rode out of the circle of the firelight, the air was cool in our faces. Under the bright moonlight, and then under the starlight, we loped and cantered mile after mile over the high prairie. We passed bands of antelope and herds of long-horn Texas cattle, and at last, just as the first red beams of the sun flamed over the bluffs in front of us, we rode down into the valley of the Little Missouri, where our ranch house stood.

I never became a good roper, nor more than an average rider, according to ranch standards. Of course a man on a ranch has to ride a good many bad horses, and is bound to encounter a certain number of accidents, and of these I had my share, at one time cracking a rib, and on another occasion the point of my shoulder. We were hundreds of miles from a doctor, and each time, as I was on the round-up, I had to get through my work for the next few weeks as best I could, until the injury healed of itself. When I had the opportunity I broke my own horses, doing it gently and gradually and spending much time over it, and choosing the horses that seemed gentle to begin with. With these horses I never had any difficulty. But frequently there was neither time nor opportunity to handle our mounts so elaborately. We might get a band of horses, each having been bridled and saddled two or three times, but none of them having been broken beyond the extent implied in this bridling and saddling. Then each of us in succession would choose a horse (for his string), I as owner of the ranch being given the first choice on each round, so to speak. The first time I was ever on a round-up Sylvane Ferris, Merrifield, Meyer, and I each chose his string in this fashion. Three or four of the animals I got were not easy to ride. The effort both to ride them and to look as if I enjoyed doing so, on some cool morning, when my grinning cowboy friends had gathered round 'to see whether the high-headed bay could buck the boss off' doubtless was of benefit to me, but lacked much of being enjoyable. The time I smashed my rib I was bucked off on a stone. The time I hurt the point of my shoulder I was riding a big, sulky horse named Ben Butler, which went over backwards with me. When we got up it still refused to go anywhere; so, while I sat it, Sylvane Ferris and George Meyer got their ropes on its neck and dragged it a few hundred yards, choking but stubborn, all four feet firmly planted and plowing the ground. When they released the ropes it lay down and wouldn't get up. The round-up had started; so Sylvane gave me his horse, Baldy, which sometimes bucked but never went over backwards, and he got on the now rearisen Ben Butler. To my discomfiture Ben started quietly beside us, while Sylvane remarked, 'Why, there's nothing the matter with this horse; he's a plumb gentle horse.' Then Ben fell slightly behind and I heard Sylvane again, 'That's all right! Come along! Here, you! Go on, you! Hi, hi, fellows, help me out! he's lying on me!' Sure enough, he was; and when we dragged Sylvane from under him the first thing the rescued Sylvane did was to execute a war dance, spurs and all, on the iniquitous Ben. We could do nothing with him that day; subsequently we got him so that we could ride him; but he never became a nice saddle horse.

As with all other forms of work, so on the round-up, a man of ordinary power, who nevertheless does not shirk things merely because they are disagreeable or irksome, soon earns his place. There were crack riders and ropers who, just because they felt such overweening pride in their own prowess, were not really very valuable men. Continually on the circles a cow or a calf would get into some thick patch of bulberry bush and refuse to come out; or when it was getting late we would pass some bad lands that would probably not contain cattle, but might; or a steer would turn fighting mad, or a calf grow tired and want to lie down. If in such a case the man steadily persists in doing the unattractive thing, and after two hours of exasperation and harassment does finally get the cow out, and keep her out, of the bulberry bushes, and drives her to the wagon, or finds some animals that have been passed by in the fourth or fifth patch of bad lands he hunts through, or gets the calf up on his saddle and takes it in anyhow, the foreman soon grows to treat him as having his uses and as being an asset of worth in the round-up, even though neither a fancy roper nor a fancy rider.

When at the Progressive Convention last August, I met George Meyer for the first time in many years, and he recalled to me an incident on one round-up where we happened to be thrown together while driving some cows and calves to camp. When the camp was only just across the river, two of the calves positively refused to go any further. He took one of them in his arms, and after some hazardous maneuvering managed to get his horse, in spite of the objections of the latter, and rode into the river. My calf was too big for such treatment, so in despair I roped it, intending to drag it over. However, as soon as I roped it, the calf started bouncing and bleating, and owing to some lack of dexterity on my part, suddenly swung round the rear of the horse, bringing the rope under his tail. Down went the tail tight, and the horse 'went into figures', as the cow-puncher phrase of that day was. There was a cut bank about four feet high on the hither side of the river, and over this the horse bucked. We went into the water with a splash. With a 'pluck' the calf followed, described a parabola in the air, and landed beside us. Fortunately this took the rope out from under the horse's tail, but left him thoroughly frightened. He could not do much bucking in the stream, for there were one or two places where we had to swim, and the shallows were either sandy or muddy; but across we went, at speed, and the calf made a wake like Pharoah's army in the Red Sea.

On several occasions we had to fight fire. In the geography books of my youth prairie fires were always portrayed as taking place in long grass, and all living things ran before them. On the Northern cattle plains the grass was never long enough to be a source of danger to man or beast. The fires were nothing like the forest fires in the Northern woods. But they destroyed large quantities of feed, and we had to stop them where possible. The process we usually followed was to kill a steer, split it in two length-wise, and then have two riders draft each half-steer, the rope of one running from his saddle-horn to the front leg, and that of the other to the hind leg. One of the men would spur this horse over or through the line of fire, and the two would then ride forward, dragging the steer bloody side downward along the line of flame, men following on foot with slickers or wet horse-blankets to beat out any flickering blaze that was still left. It was exciting work, for the fire and the twitching and plucking of the ox carcass over the uneven ground maddened the fierce little horses so that it was necessary to do some riding in order to keep them to their work. After a while it also became very exhausting, the thirst and fatigue being great, as with parched lips and blackened from head to foot, we toiled at our task.

In those years the Stockman's Association of Montana was a powerful body. I was the delegate to it from the Little Missouri. The meetings that I attended were held in Miles City, at that time a typical cow town. Stockmen of all kinds attended, including the biggest men in the stock business, men like old Conrad Kohrs, who was and is the finest type of pioneer in all the Rocky Mountain country; and Granville Stewart, who was afterwards appointed Minister by Cleveland, I think to the Argentine; and 'Hashknife' Simpson, a Texan who had brought his cattle, the Hashknife brand, up the trail into our country. He and I grew to be great friends. I can see him now the first time we met, grinning at me as, none too comfortable, I sat a half-broken horse at the edge of a cattle herd we were working. His son Sloan Simpson went to Harvard, was one of the first-class men in my regiment, and afterwards held my commission as Postmaster at Dallas.

At the stockmen's meeting in Miles City, in addition to the big stockmen, there were always hundreds of cowboys galloping up and down the wide dusty streets at every hour of the day and night. It was a picturesque sight during the three days the meetings lasted. There was always at least one big dance at the hotel. There werc few dress suits, but there was perfect decorum at the dance, and in the square dances most of the men knew the figures far better than I did. With such a crowd in town, sleeping accommodations of any sort were at a premium, and in the hotel there were two men in every bed. On one occasion I had a roommate whom I never saw, because he always went to bed much later than I did and I always got up much earlier than he did. On the last day, however, he rose at the same time and I saw that he was a man I knew named Carter, and nicknamed 'Modesty' Carter. He was a stalwart, good-looking fellow, and I was sorry when later I heard that he had been killed in a shooting row.

When I went West, the last great Indian wars had just come to an end, but there were still sporadic outbreaks here and there, and occasionally bands of marauding young braves were a menace to outlying and lonely settlements. Many of the white men themselves were lawless and brutal, and prone to commit outrages on the Indians. Unfortunately, each race tended to hold all the members of the other race responsible for the misdeeds of a few, so that the crime of the miscreant, red or white, who committedthe original outrage too often invited retaliation upon entirely innocent people, and this action would in its turn arouse bitter feeling which found vent in still more indiscriminate retaliation. The first year I was on the Little Missouri some Sioux bucks ran off all the horses of a buffalo-hunter's outfit. One of the buffalo-hunters tried to get even by stealing the horses of a Cheyenne hunting party, and when pursued made for a cow camp, with, as a result, a long-range skirmish between the cowboys and the Cheyennes. One of the latter was wounded, but this particular wounded man seemed to have more sense than the other participants in the chain of wrong-doing, and discriminated among the whites. He came into our camp and had his wound dressed.

A year later I was at a desolate little mud road ranch on the Deadwood trail. It was kept by a very capable and very forceful woman, with sound ideas of justice and abundantly well able to hold her own. Her husband was a worthless devil, who finally got drunk on some whisky he obtained from an outfit of Missouri bull-whackers—that is, freighters, driving ox wagons. Under the stimulus of the whisky he picked a quarrel with his wife and attempted to beat her. She knocked him down with a stove-lid lifter, and the admiring bull-whackers bore him off, leaving the lady in full possession of the ranch. When I visited her she had a man named Crow Joe working for her, a slab-sided, shifty-eyed person who later, as I heard my foreman explain, 'skipped the country with a bunch of horses.' The mistress of the ranch made first-class buckskin shirts of great durability. The one she made for me, and which I used for years, was used by one of my sons in Arizona a couple of winters ago. I had ridden down into the country after some lost horses, and visited the ranch to get her to make me the buckskin shirt in question. There were, at the moment, three Indians there, Sioux, well behaved and self-respecting, and she explained to me that they had been resting there waiting for dinner, and that a white man had come along and tried to run off their horses. The Indians were on the lookout, however, and running out, they caught the man; but, after retaking their horses and depriving him of his gun, they let him go. 'I don't see why they let him go' exclaimed my hostess. 'I don't believe in stealing Indians' horses any more than white folks'; so I told 'em they could go along and hang him—I'd never cheep. Anyhow I won't charge them anything for their dinner' concluded my hostess. She was in advance of the usual morality of the time and place, which drew a sharp line between stealing citizens' horses and stealing horses from the Government or the Indians.

A fairly decent citizen, Jap Hunt, who long ago met a violent death, exemplified this attitude towards Indians in some remarks I once heard him make. He had started a horse ranch, and had quite honestly purchased a number of broken-down horses of different brands, with the view of doctoring them and selling them again. About this time there had been much horse-stealing and cattle-killing on our Territory and in Montana, and under the direction of some of the big cattle-growers a committee of vigilantes had been organized to take action against the rustlers, as the horse thieves and cattle thieves were called. The vigilantes, or stranglers, as they were locally known, did their work thoroughly; but, as always happens with bodies of that kind, toward the end they grew reckless in their actions, paid off private grudges, and hung men on slight provocation. Riding into Jap Hunt's ranch, they nearly hung him because he had so many horses of different brands. He was finally let off. He was much upset by the incident, and explained again and again, 'The idea of saying that I was a horse thief! Why, I never stole a horse in my life—leastways from a white man. I don't count Indians nor the Government, of course.' Jap had been reared among men still in the stage of tribal morality, and while they recognized their obligations to one another, both the Government and the Indians seemed alien bodies, in regard to which the laws of morality did not apply.

On the other hand, parties of savage young bucks would treat lonely settlers just as badly, and in addition sometimes murder them. Such a party was generally composed of young fellows burning to distinguish themselves. Some one of their number would have obtained a pass from the Indian Agent allowing him to travel off the reservation, which pass would be flourished whenever their action was questioned by bodies of whites of equal strength. I once had a trifling encounter with such a band. I was making my way along the edge of the bad lands, northward from my lower ranch, and was just crossing a plateau when five Indians rode up over the further rim. The instant they saw me they whipped out their guns and raced full speed at me, yelling and flogging their horses. I was on a favorite horse, Manitou, who was a wise old fellow, with nerves not to be shaken by anything. I at once leapt off him and stood with my rifle ready.

It was possible that the Indians were merely making a bluff and intended no mischief. But I did not like their actions, and I thought it likely that if I allowed them to get hold of me they would at least take my horse and rifle, and possible kill me. So I waited until they were a hundred yards off and then drew a bead on the first. Indians— and, for the matter of that, white men—do not like to ride in on a man who is cool and means shooting, and in a twinkling every man was lying over the side of his horse, and all five had turned and were galloping backwards, having altered their course as quickly as so many teal ducks.

After this one of them made the peace sign, with his blanket first, and then, as he rode toward me, with his open hand. I halted him at a fair distance and asked him what he wanted. He exclaimed, 'How! Me good Injun, me good Injun' and tried to show me the dirty piece of paper on which his agency pass was written. I told him with sincerity that I was glad that he was a good Indian, but that he must not come any closer. He then asked for sugar and tobacco. I told him I had none. Another Indian began slowly drifting toward me in spite of my calling out to keep back, so I once more aimed with my rifle, whereupon both Indians slipped to the other side of their horses and galloped off, with oaths that did credit to at least one side of their acquaintance with English. I now mounted and pushed over the plateau on to the open prairie. In those days an Indian, although not as good a shot as a white man, was infinitely better at crawling under and taking advantage of cover; and the worst thing a white man could do was to get into cover, whereas out in the open if he kept his head he had a good chance of standing off even half a dozen assailants. The Indians accompanied me for a couple of miles. Then I reached the open prairie, and resumed my northward ride, not being further molested.

Stephen Crane

1871–1900

When the great masterpiece of war The Red Badge of
Courage *was published, its author Stephen Crane had no
first hand experience of battle. Its success, however, led
him naturally into a career as a war reporter and the
following despatches were sent from The Spanish-American
War of 1898.*

STEPHEN CRANE'S VIVID STORY
OF THE BATTLE OF SAN JUAN

IN FRONT OF Santiago, July 4, via Old Point Comfort, Va., July 13. —
The action at San Juan on July 1 was, particularly speaking, a soldier's

battle. It was like Inkerman, where the English fought half leaderless all day in a fog. Only the Cuban forest was worse than any fog.

No doubt when history begins to grind out her story we will find that many a thundering, fine, grand order was given for that day's work; but after all there will be no harm in contending that the fighting line, the men and their regimental officers, took the hill chiefly because they knew they could take it, some having no orders and others disobeying whatever orders they had.

In civil life the newspapers would have called it a grand, popular movement. It will never be forgotten as long as America has a military history.

A line of intrenched hills held by men armed with a weapon like a Mauser is not to be taken by a front attack of infantry unless the trenches have first been heavily shaken by artillery fire. Any theorist will say that it is impossible, and prove it to be impossible. But it was done, and we owe the success to the splendid gallantry of the American private soldier.

As near as one can learn, headquarters expected little or no fighting on the 1st. Lawton's division was to go by the Caney road, chase the Spaniards out of that interesting village, and then, wheeling half to the left, march down to join the other divisions in some kind of attack on San Juan at daybreak on the 2d.

[MISINFORMED AS TO SPANISH STRENGTH]

But somebody had been entirely misinformed as to the strength and disposition of the Spanish forces at Caney, and instead of taking Lawton six minutes to capture the town it took him nearly all day, as well it might.

The other divisions lying under fire, waiting for Lawton, grew annoyed at a delay which was, of course not explained to them, and suddenly arose and took the formidable hills of San Juan. It was impatience suddenly exalted to one of the sublime passions.

Lawton was well out toward Caney soon after daybreak, and by 7 o'clock we could hear the boom of Capron's guns in support of the infantry. The remaining divisions—Kent's and Wheeler's—were trudging slowly along the muddy trail through the forest.

When the first gun was fired a grim murmur passed along the lean column. 'They're off!' somebody said.

The marching was of necessity very slow, and even then the narrow road was often blocked. The men, weighted with their packs, cartridge belts and rifles, forded many streams, climbed hills, slid down banks and forced their way through thickets.

Suddenly there was a roar of guns just ahead and a little to the left. This was Grimes's battery going into action on the hill which is called El Paso. Then, all in a moment, the quiet column moving forward was opposed by men carrying terrible burdens. Wounded Cubans were being carried to the rear. Most of them were horribly mangled.

The second brigade of dismounted American cavalry had been in support of the battery, its position being directly to the rear. Some Cubans had joined there. The Spanish shrapnel fired at the battery was often cut too long, and, passing over, burst amid the supports and the Cubans.

[SHORT LULL IN THE BATTLE.]

The loss of the battery, the cavalry and the Cubans from this fire was forty men killed and wounded, the First regular cavalry probably suffering most grievously. Presently there was a lull in the artillery fire, and down through spaces in the trees we could see the infantry still plodding on with its packs steadily toward the front.

The artillerymen were greatly excited. Some showed with glee fragments of Spanish shells which had come dangerously near their heads. They had gone through their ordeal and were talking over it lightly.

In the mean time Lawton's division, some three miles away, was making plenty of noise. Caney is just at the base of a high willow-green, crinkled mountain, and Lawton was making his way over little knolls which might be termed foothills. We could see the great white clouds of smoke from Capron's guns and hear their roar punctuating the incessant drumming of the infantry. It was plain even then that Lawton was having considerably more of a fete than anybody had supposed previously.

At about 2,500 yards in front of Grimes's position on El Paso arose the gentle green hills of San Juan, dotted not too plentifully with trees—hills that resembled the sloping orchards of Orange County in summer. Here and there were houses built evidently as summer villas, but not

loopholed and barricaded. They had heavy roofs of red tiles and were
shaped much like Japanese, or, better, Javanese houses. Here and there,
too, along the crests of these curving hillocks were ashen streaks, the
rifle-pits of the Spaniards.

At the principal position of the enemy were a flag, a redoubt, a block-
house and some sort of pagoda, in the shade of which Spanish officers
were wont to promenade during the lulls and negligently gossip about
the battle. There was one man in a summer-resort straw hat. He did
a deal of sauntering in the coolest manner possible, walking out in the
clear sunshine and gazing languidly in our direction. He seemed to be
carrying a little cane.

[GRIMES SMASHED THEM.]

At 11.25 our artillery reopened on the central block-house and intrenchments. The Spanish fire had been remarkably fine, but it was our turn
now. Grimes had his ranges to a nicety. After the great 'shout of the
gun' came the broad, windy, diminishing noise of the flung shell; then
a fainter boom and a cloud of red debris out of the block-house or up
from the ground near the trenches.

The Spanish infantry in the trenches fired a little volley immediately
after every one of the American shells. It puzzled many to decide at
what they could be firing, but it was finally resolved that they were
firing just to show us that they were still there and were not afraid.

It must have been about 2 o'clock when the enemy's battery again
retorted.

The cruel thing about this artillery duel was that our battery had
nothing but old-fashioned powder, and its position was always as clearly
defined as if it had been the Chicago fire. There is no secrecy about
a battery that uses that kind of powder. The great billowy white smoke
can be seen for miles. On the other hand, the Spaniards were using
the best smokeless. There is no use groaning over what was to be, but!—

However, fate elected that the Spanish shooting should be very bad.
Only two-thirds of their shells exploded in this second affair. They all
whistled high, and those that exploded raked the ground long since
evacuated by the supports and the timbers. No one was hurt.

[A MISPLACED BALLOON.]

From El Paso to San Juan there is a broad expanse of dense forest, spotted infrequently with vividly green fields. It is traversed by a single narrow road which leads straight between the two positions, fording two little streams. Along this road had gone our infantry and also the military balloon. Why it was ever taken to such a position nobody knows, but there it was—huge, fat, yellow, quivering—being dragged straight into a zone of fire that would surely ruin it.

There were two officers in the car for the greater part of the way, and there surely were never two men who valued their lives less. But they both escaped unhurt, while the balloon sank down, torn to death by the bullets that were volleyed at it by the nervous Spaniards who suspected dynamite. It was never brought out of the woods where it recklessly met its fate.

In these woods, unknown to some, including the Spaniards, was fulminated the gorgeous plan of taking an impregnable position.

One saw a thin line of black figures moving across a field. They disappeared in the forest. The enemy was keeping up a terrific fire. Then suddenly somebody yelled, 'By God, there go our boys up the hill!'

There is many a good American who would give an arm to get the thrill of patriotic insanity that coursed through us when we heard that yell.

Yes, they were going up the hill, up the hill. It was the best moment of anybody's life. An officer said to me afterwards: 'If we had been in that position and the Spaniards had come at us, we would have piled them up so high the last man couldn't have climbed over.' But up went the regiments with no music save that ceaseless, fierce crashing of rifles.

[FOREIGN ATTACHES SAID 'IMPOSSIBLE']

The foreign attaches were shocked. 'It is very gallant, but very foolish' said one sternly.

'Why, they can't take it, you know. Never in the world' cried another, much agitated. 'It is slaughter, absolute slaughter.'

The little Japanese shrugged his shoulders. He was the one who said nothing.

The road from El Paso to San Juan was now a terrible road. It should have a tragic fame like the sunken road at Waterloo. Why we did not later hang some of the gentry who contributed from the trees to the terror of this road is not known.

The wounded were stringing back from the front, hundreds of them. Some walked unaided, an arm or a shoulder having been dressed at a field station. They stopped often enough to answer the universal hail 'How is it going?' Others hobbled or clung to a friend's shoulders. Their slit trousers exposed red bandages. A few were shot horribly in the face and were led, bleeding and blind, by their mates.

And then there were the slow pacing stretcher-bearers with the dying, or the insensible, the badly wounded, still figures with blood often drying brick color on their hot bandages.

Prostrate at the roadside were many, others who had made their way thus far and were waiting for strength. Everywhere moved the sure-handed, invaluable Red Cross men.

Over this scene was a sort of haze of bullets. They were of two kinds. First, the Spanish lines were firing just a trifle high. Their bullets swept over our firing lines and poured into this devoted roadway, the single exit, even as it had been the single approach. The second fire was from guerillas concealed in the trees and in the thickets along the trail. They had come in under the very wings of our strong advance, taken good positions on either side of the road and were peppering our line of communication whenever they got a good target, no matter, apparently, what the target might be.

Red Cross men, wounded men, sick men, correspondents and attaches were all one to the guerilla. The move of sending an irregular force around the flanks of the enemy as he is making his front attack is so legitimate that some of us could not believe at first that the men hidden in the forest were really blazing away at the non-combatants or the wounded. Viewed simply as a bit of tactics, the scheme was admirable. But there is not doubt now that they intentionally fired at anybody they thought they could kill.

You can't mistake an ambulance driver when he is driving his ambulance. You can't mistake a wounded man when he is lying down and being bandaged. And when you see a field hospital you don't mistake it for a squadron of cavalry or a brigade of infantry.

As we went along the road we suddenly heard a cry behind us. 'Oh, come quick! Come quick!' We turned and saw a young soldier spinning around frantically and grabbing at his leg. Evidently he had been going to the stream to fill his canteen, but a guerilla had barred him from that drink. Two Red Cross men rushed for him.

At the last ford, in the shelter of a muddy bank, lay a dismal band, forty men on their backs with doctors working at them and bullets singing in flocks over their heads. They rolled their eyes quietly at us. There was no groaning. They exhibited that profound patience which has been the marvel of every one.

After the ford was passed the woods cleared. The road passed through lines of barbed wire. There were, in fact, barbed wire fences running in almost every direction.

The mule train, galloping like a troop of cavalry, dashed up with a reinforcement of ammunition, every mule on the jump, the cowboys swinging their whips. They were under a fairly strong fire, but up they went.

One does not expect gallantry in a pack train, but incidentally it may be said that this charge, led by the bell mare, was one of the sights of the day.

[BORROWE'S DYNAMITE GUN.]

At a place where the road cut through the crest of the ridge Burrowe and some of his men were working over his dynamite gun. After the fifth discharge something had got jammed. There was never such devotion to an inanimate thing as these men give to their dynamite gun. They will quarrel for her, starve for her, lose sleep for her and fight for her to the last ditch.

In the army there have always been two opinions of the dynamite gun. Some have said it was a most terrific engine of destruction, while others have called it a toy. With the bullets winging their long flights not very high overhead, Burrowe and his crowd, at sight of us, began their little hymn of praise, the chief note of which was one of almost pathetic insistence. If they ever get that gun into action again they will make her hum.

The discomfited Spaniards, recovering from their panic, opened from their second line a most furious fire. It was first directed against one part of our line and then against another, as if they were feeling for our weakest point, fumbling around after the throat of the army.

Somebody on the left caught it for a time, and then suddenly the enemy apparently devoted their entire attention to the position occupied by the Rough Riders. Some shrapnel, with fuses cut too long, passed over and burst from 100 to 200 yards to the rear. They acted precisely like things with strings to them. When the string was jerked, bang! went the hurtling explosive. But the infantry fire was very heavy, albeit high.

The American reply was in measured volleys. Part of a regiment would remain on the firing line while the other companies rested near by under the brow of the hill. Parties were sent after the packs. The commands knew with what other organizations they were in touch on the two flanks. Otherwise they knew nothing, save that they were going to hold their ground. They said so.

From our line could be seen a long, gray, Spanish intrenchment, from 400 to 1,000 yards away, according to what part of our line one measured from. From it floated no smoke and no men appeared there, but it was making a noise like a million champagne corks.

Back of their entrenchments, perhaps another thousand yards was a long building of masonry tinted pink. It flew many Red Cross flags and near it were other smaller structures also flying Red Cross flags. In fact, the enemy's third line of defense seemed to be composed of hospitals.

The city itself slanted down toward the bay, just a glimpse of silver. In the clear, white sunshine the houses of the suburbs, the hospitals and the long gray trenches were so vivid that they seemed far closer than they were.

To the rear, over the ground that the army had taken, a breeze was gently stirring the long grass and ruffling the surface of a pool that lay in a sort of meadow. The army took its glory calmly. Having nothing else to do, the army sat down and looked tranquilly at the scenery. There was not that exuberance of enthusiasm which surrounds the vicinity of a candidate for the Assembly.

The army was dusty, dishevelled, its hair matted to its forehead with sweat, its shirts glued to its back with the same, and indescribably dirty, thirsty, hungry, and a-weary from its bundles and its marches and its fights. It sat on the conquered crest and felt satisfied.

'Well, hell! here we are.'

[LAWTON'S HEAVY LOSSES.]

News began to pass along the line. Lawton had taken Caney after a long fight and had lost heavily. The siege pieces were being unloaded at Siboney. Pando had succeeded in reinforcing Santiago that very morning with 8,400 men, 6,000 men, 4,500 men. Pando had not succeeded. And so on.

At dusk a comparative stillness settled upon the ridge. The shooting subsided to little nervous outbursts. In the trenches taken by our troops lay dead Spaniards.

The road to the rear increased its terrors in the darkness. The wounded men, stumbling along in the mud, a miasmic mist from the swampish ground filling their nostrils, heard often in the air the whiplash sound of a bullet that was meant for them by the lurking guerillas. A mile, two miles, two miles and a half to the rear, great populous hospitals had been formed.

[CAMPING ON THE GROUND THEY WON.]

The long lines of the hill began to intrench under cover of night, each regiment for itself, still, however, keeping in touch on the flanks. Each regiment dug in the ground that it had taken by its own valor. Some commands had two or three shovels, an axe or two, maybe a pick. Other regiments dug with their bayonets and shovelled out the dirt with their meat ration cans.

Darkness swallowed Santiago and the new intrenchments. The large tropic stars illumined the sky. On the safe side of the ridge our men had built some little red fires, no larger than hats, at which they cooked what food they possessed. There was no sound save to the rear, where throughout the night our pickets could be faintly heard exchanging shots with the guerillas.

On the very moment, it seemed, of the break of day, bang! the fight was on again. The firing broke out from one end of the prodigious V-shaped formation to the other. Our artillery took new advanced positions, but they were driven away by the swirling Mauser fire.

When the day was in full bloom Lawton's division, having marched all night, appeared in the road. The long, long column wound around the base of the ridge and disappeared among the woods and knolls on the right of Wheeler's line. The army was now concentrated in a splendid position.

[CUBANS HELD IN CONTEMPT]

It becomes necessary to speak of the men's opinion of the Cubans. To put it shortly, both officers and privates have the most lively contempt for the Cubans. They despise them. They came down here expecting to fight side by side with an ally, but this ally has done little but stay in the rear and eat army rations, manifesting an indifference to the cause of Cuban liberty which could not be exceeded by some who had never heard of it.

In the great charge up the hills of San Juan the American soldiers who, for their part, sprinkled a thousand bodies in the grass, were not able to see a single Cuban assisting in what might easily turn out to be the decisive battle for Cuban freedom.

At Caney a company of Cubans came into action on the left flank of one of the American regiments just before the place was taken. Later they engaged a blockhouse of 2,000 yards and fired away all their ammunition. They sent back to the American commander for more, but they got only a snort of indignation.

As a matter of fact, the Cuban soldier, ignorant as only such isolation as has been his can make him, does not appreciate the ethics of the situation.

This great American army he views as he views the sky, the sea, the air; it is a natural and most happy phenomenon. He will go to sleep while this flood drowns the Spaniards.

The American soldier, however, thinks of himself often as a disinterested benefactor, and he would like the Cubans to play up to the ideal now and then. His attitude is mighty human. He does not really want to be thanked, and yet the total absence of anything like gratitude makes him furious. He is furious, too, because the Cubans apparently consider themselves under no obligation to take part in an engagement; because the Cubans will stay at the rear and collect haversacks, blankets, coats and shelter tents dropped by our troops.

The average Cuban here will not speak to an American unless to beg. He forgets his morning, afternoon or evening salutation unless he is reminded. If he takes a dislike to you he talks about you before your face, using a derisive undertone.

[DEMORALIZED BY AID.]

The truth probably is that the food, raiment and security furnished by the Americans have completely demoralized the insurgents. When the force under Gomez came to Guantanamo to assist the marines they were a most efficient body of men. They guided the marines to the enemy and fought with them shoulder to shoulder, not very skilfully in the matter of shooting, but still with courage and determination.

After this action there ensued at Guantanamo a long peace. The Cubans built themselves a permanent camp and they began to eat, eat much, and to sleep long, day and night, until now, behold, there is no more useless a body of men anywhere! A trifle less than half of them are on Dr Edgar's sick list, and the others are practically insubordinate. So much food seems to act upon them like a drug.

Here with the army the demoralization has occurred on a big scale. It is dangerous, too, for the Cuban. If he stupidly, drowsily remains out of these fights, what weight is his voice to have later in the final adjustments? The officers and men of the army, if their feeling remains the same, will not be happy to see him have any at all. The situation needs a Gomez. It is more serious than these bestarred machete bearers know how to appreciate, and it is the worst thing for the cause of an independent Cuba that could possibly exist.

[THE BATTLE OF JULY 2.]

At San Juan the 2d of July was a smaller edition of the 1st. The men deepened their intrenchments, shot, slept and ate. On the 1st every man had been into the fighting line. There was not a reserve as big as your hat. If the enemy broke through any part of the line there was nothing to stop them short of Siboney. On the 2d however, some time after the arrival of Lawton, the Ninth Massachusetts and the Thirty-fourth Michigan came up.

Along the road from El Paso they had to pass some pretty grim sights. And there were some pretty grim odors, but the men were steady enough. 'How far are they off?' they asked of a passing regular. 'Oh, not far; but it's all right. We think they may run out of ammunition in the course of a week or ten days.'

The volunteers laughed. But the pitiful thing about this advance was to see in the hands of the boys these terrible old rifles that smoke like brush fires and give the regimental line away to the enemy as plainly as an illuminated sign.

I remember that on the first day men of the Seventy-first who had lost their command would try to join one of the regular regiments, but the regulars would have none of them. 'Get out of here with that ---- gun!' the regulars would say. During the battle just one shot from a Spaniard would call a volley, for the Spaniards then knew just where to shoot. It was very hard on the Seventy-first New York and the Second Massachusetts.

At Caney about two hundred prisoners were taken. Two big squads of them were soldiers of the regular Spanish infantry in the usual blue and white pajamas. The others were the rummiest-looking set of men one could possibly imagine. They were native-born Cubans, reconcentrados, traitors, guerillas of the kind that bushwacked us so unmercifully. Some were doddering old men, shaking with the palsy of their many years. Some were slim, dirty, bad-eyed boys. They were all of a lower class than one could find in any United States jail.

At first they had expected to be butchered. In fact, to encourage them to fight, their officers had told them that if they gave in they need expect no mercy from the dreadful Americans.

Our great, good, motherly old country has nothing in her heart but mercy, and nothing in her pockets but beef, hard-tack and coffee for all of them—lemon-colored refugee from Santiago, wild-eyed prisoners from the trenches, Spanish guerilla from out the thickets, half-naked insurgent from the mountains—all of them.

Helen Keller

1880–1968

Blind and deaf from the age of two, Helen Keller yet overcame her handicap, graduated from Radcliffe with honors and became an author, lecturer and prominent worker for social reforms. She describes her first breakthrough from lonely darkness into a world of language, of communication and new hope in this extract from The Story of My Life.

THE MOST IMPORTANT day I remember in all my life is one on which my teacher, Anne Mansfield Sullivan came to me. I am filled with wonder when I consider the immeasurable contrast between the two lives which it connects. It was the third of March, 1887, three months before I was seven years old.

On the afternoon of that eventful day, I stood on the porch, dumb, expectant. I guessed vaguely from my mother's signs and from the hurrying to and fro in the house that something unusual was about to happen, so I went to the door and waited on the steps. The afternoon sun penetrated the mass of honeysuckle that covered the porch, and fell on my upturned face. My fingers lingered almost unconsciously on the familiar leaves and blossoms which had just come forth to greet the sweet southern spring. I did not know what the future held of marvel or surprise for me. Anger and bitterness had preyed upon me continually for weeks and a deep languor had succeeded this passionate struggle.

Have you ever been at sea in a dense fog, when it seemed as if a tangible white darkness shut you in, and the great ship, tense and anxious, groped her way toward the shore with plummet and soundingline, and you waited with beating heart for something to happen? I was like that ship before my education began, only I was without compass or sounding-line, and had no way of knowing how near the harbour was. 'Light! give me light!' was the wordless cry of my soul, and the light of love shone on me in that very hour.

I felt approaching footsteps. I stretched out my hand as I supposed to my mother. Some one took it, and I was caught up and held close in the arms of her who had come to reveal all things to me, and more than all things else, to love me.

The morning after my teacher came she led me into her room and gave me a doll. The little blind children at the Perkins Institution had sent it and Laura Bridgman had dressed it; but I did not know this until afterwards. When I had played with it a little while, Miss Sullivan slowly spelled into my hand the word 'd-o-l-l'. I was at once interested in this finger play and tried to imitate it. When I finally succeeded in making the letters correctly I was flushed with childish pleasure and pride. Running downstairs to my mother I held up her hand and made the letters for doll. I did not know that I was spelling a word or even that words existed; I was simply making my fingers go in monkey-like imitation. In the days that followed I learned to spell in this uncomprehending way a great many words, among them *pin, hat, cup* and a few verbs like *sit, stand* and *walk*. But my teacher had been with me several weeks before I understood that everything has a name.

One day while I was playing with my new doll, Miss Sullivan put my big rag doll into my lap also, spelled 'd-o-l-l' and tried to make me understand that 'd-o-l-l' applied to both. Earlier in the day we had had a tussle over the words 'm-u-g' and 'w-a-t-e-r'. Miss Sullivan had tried to impress it upon me that 'm-u-g' is *mug* and that 'w-a-t-e-r' is *water*, but I persisted in confounding the two. In despair she had dropped the subject for the time, only to renew it at the first opportunity. I became impatient at her repeated attempts and, seizing the new doll, I dashed it upon the floor. I was keenly delighted when I felt the fragments of the broken doll at my feet. Neither sorrow nor regret followed my passionate outburst. I had not loved the doll. In the still, dark world in which I lived there was no strong sentiment or tenderness. I felt my teacher sweep the fragments to one side of the hearth, and I had a sense of satisfaction that the cause of my discomfort was being removed. She brought me my hat, and I knew I was going out into the warm sunshine. This thought, if a wordless sensation may be called a thought, made me hop and skip with pleasure.

We walked down the path to the well-house, attracted by the fragrance of the honeysuckle with which it was covered. Some one was drawing water and my teacher placed my hand under the spout. As the cool stream gushed over one hand she spelled into the other the word *water*, first slowly, then rapidly. I stood still, my whole attention fixed upon the motions of her fingers. Suddenly I felt a misty consciousness as of something forgotten—a thrill of returning thought; and somehow the mystery of language was revealed to me. I knew then that 'w-a-t-e-r' meant the wonderful cool something that was flowing over my hand. That living word awakened my soul, gave it light, hope, joy, set it free! There were barriers still, it is true, but barriers that could in time be swept away.

I left the well-house eager to learn. Everything had a name, and each name gave birth to a new thought. As we returned to the house every object which I touched seemed to quiver with life. That was because I saw everything with the strange, new sight that had come to me. On entering the door I remembered the doll I had broken. I felt my way to the hearth and picked up the pieces. I tried vainly to put them together. Then my eyes filled with tears; for I realized what I had done, and for the first time I felt repentance and sorrow.

I learned a great many new words that day. I do not remember what they all were; but I do know that *mother, father, sister, teacher* were among them—words that were to make the world blossom for me, 'like Aaron's rod, with flowers.' It would have been difficult to find a happier child than I was as I lay in my crib at the close of that eventful day and lived over the joys it had brought me, and for the first time long for a new day to come.

I recall many incidents of the summer of 1887 that followed my soul's sudden awakening. I did nothing but explore with my hands and learn the name of every object that I touched; and the more I handled things and learned their names and uses, the more joyous and confident grew my kinship with the rest of the world.

When the time of daisies and buttercups came Miss Sullivan took me by the hand across the fields, where men were preparing the earth for the seed, to the banks of the Tennessee River, and there, sitting on the warm grass, I had my first lessons in the beneficence of nature. I learned how the sun and the rain make to grow out of the ground every tree that is pleasant to the sight and good for food, how birds build their nests and live and thrive from land to land, how the squirrel, the deer, the lion and every other creature finds food and shelter. As my knowledge of things grew I felt more and more the delight of the world I was in. Long before I learned to do a sum in arithmetic or describe the shape of the earth, Miss Sullivan taught me to find beauty in the fragrant woods, in every blade of grass, and in the curves and dimples of my baby sister's hand. She linked my earliest thoughts with nature, and made me feel that 'birds and flowers and I were happy peers.'

But about this time I had an experience which taught me that nature is not always kind. One day my teacher and I were returning from a long ramble. The morning had been fine, but it was growing warm and sultry when at last we turned our faces homeward. Two or three times we stopped to rest under a tree by the wayside. Our last halt was under a wild cherry tree a short distance from the house. The shade was grateful, and the tree so easy to climb that with my teacher's assistance I was able to scramble to a seat in the branches. It was so cool up in the tree that Miss Sullivan proposed that we have our luncheon there. I promised to keep still while she went to the house to fetch it.

Suddenly a change passed over the tree. All the sun's warmth left the air. I knew the sky was black, because all the heat, which meant light to me, had died out of the atmosphere. A strange odour came up from the earth. I knew it, it was the odour that always precedes a thunder storm, and a nameless fear clutched at my heart. I felt absolutely alone, cut off from my friends and the firm earth. The immense unknown, enfolded me. I remained still and expectant; a chilling terror crept over me. I longed for my teacher's return; but above all things I wanted to get down from that tree.

There was a moment of sinister silence, then a multitudinous stirring of the leaves. A shiver ran through the tree, and the wind sent forth a blast that would have knocked me off had I not clung to the branch with might and main. The tree swayed and strained. The small twigs snapped and fell about me in showers. A wild impulse to jump seized me, but terror held me fast. I crouched down in the fork of the tree. The branches lashed about me. I felt the intermittent jarring that came now and then as if something heavy had fallen and the shock had traveled up the till it reached the limb I sat on. It worked my suspense up to the highest point, and just as I was thinking the tree and I should fall together, my teacher seized my hand and helped me down. I clung to her, trembling with joy to feel the earth under my feet once more. I had learned a new lesson—that nature 'wages open war against her children, and under softest touch hides treacherous claws.'

After this experience it was a long time before I climbed another tree. The mere thought filled me with terror. It was the sweet allurement of the mimosa tree in full bloom that finally overcame my fears. One beautiful spring morning when I was alone in the summer-house reading, I became aware of a wonderful subtle fragrance in the air. I started up and instinctively stretched out my hands. It seemed as if the spirit of spring had passed through the summer-house. 'What is it?' I asked, and the next minute I recognized the odour of the mimosa blossoms. I felt my way to the end of the garden, knowing that the mimosa tree was near the fence, at the turn of the path. Yes, there it was, all quivering in the warm sunshine, its blossom-laden branches almost touching the long grass. Was there ever anything so exquisitely beautiful in the world before! Its delicate blossoms shrank from the slightest earthly touch; it seemed as if a tree of paradise had been transplanted to earth. I made my way through a shower of petals to the great trunk and for one minute stood irresolute; then, putting my foot in the broad space between the forked branches, I pulled myself up into the tree. I had some difficulty in holding on, for the branches were very large and the bark hurt my hands. But I had a delicious sense that I was doing something unusual and wonderful, so I kept on climbing higher and higher, until I reached a little seat which somebody had built there so long ago that it had grown part of the tree itself. I sat there for a long, long time, feeling like a fairy on a rosy cloud. After that I spent many happy hours in my tree of paradise, thinking fair thoughts and dreaming bright dreams.

I had now the key to all language, and I was eager to learn to use it. Children who hear acquire language without any particular effort; the words that fall from others' lips they catch on the wing, as it were, delightedly, while the little deaf child must trap them by a slow and often painful process. But whatever the process, the result is wonderful. Gradually from naming an object we advance step by step until we have traversed the vast distance between our first stammered syllable and the sweep of thought in a line of Shakespeare.

At first when my teacher told me about a new thing I asked very few questions. My ideas were vague, and my vocabulary inadequate; but as my knowledge of things grew, and I learned more and more words, my field of inquiry broadened, and I would return again and again to the same subject, eager for further information. Sometimes a new word revived an image that some earlier experience had engraved on my brain.

I remember the morning that I first asked the meaning of the word 'love'. This was before I knew many words. I had found a few early violets in the garden and brought them to my teacher. She tried to kiss me; but at that time I did not like to have any one kiss me except my mother. Miss Sullivan put her arm gently round me and spelled into my hand, 'I love Helen'.

'What is love?' I asked.

She drew me closer to her and said, 'It is here' pointing to my heart, whose beats I was conscious of for the first time. Her words puzzled me very much because I did not then understand anything unless I touched it.

I smelt the violets in her hand and asked, half in words, half in signs, a question which meant, 'Is love the sweetness of flowers?'

'No,' said my teacher.

Again I thought. The warm sun was shining on us.

'Is this not love?' I asked, pointing in the direction from which the heat came, 'Is this not love?'

It seemed to me that there could be nothing more beautiful than the sun, whose warmth makes all things grow. But Miss Sullivan shook her head, and I was greatly puzzled and disappointed. I thought it strange that my teacher could not show me love.

A day or two afterward I was stringing beads of different sizes in symmetrical groups—two large beads, three small ones, and so on. Miss Sullivan had pointed them out again and again with gentle patience. Finally I noticed a very obvious error in the sequence and for an instant I concentrated my attention on the lesson and tried to think how I should have arranged the beads. Miss Sullivan touched my forehead and spelled with decided emphasis, 'Think.'

In a flash I knew that the word was the name of the process that was going on in my head. This was my first conscious perception of an abstract idea.

For a long time I was still—I was not thinking of the beads in my lap, but trying to find a meaning for 'love' in the light of this new idea. The sun had been under a cloud all day, and there had been brief showers; but suddenly the sun broke forth in all its southern splendour.

Again I asked my teacher, 'Is this not love?'

'Love is something like the clouds that were in the sky before the sun came out' she replied. Then in simpler words than these, which at that time I could not have understood, she explained: 'You cannot touch the clouds, you know; but you feel the rain and know how glad the flowers and the thirsty earth are to have it after a hot day. You cannot touch love either; but you feel the sweetness that it pours into everything. Without love you would not be happy or want to play.'

The beautiful truth burst upon mind—I felt that there were invisible lines stretched between my spirit and the spirits of others.

From the beginning of my education Miss Sullivan made it a practice to speak to me as she would speak to any hearing child; the only difference was that she spelled the sentences into my hand instead of speaking them. If I did not know the words and idioms necessary to express my thoughts she supplied them, even suggesting conversation when I was unable to keep up my end of the dialogue.

This process was continued for several years; for the deaf child does not learn in a month, or even in two or three years, the numberless idioms and expressions used in the simplest daily intercourse. The little hearing child learns these from constant repetition and imitation. The conversation he hears in his home stimulates his mind and suggests topics and calls forth the spontaneous expression of his own thoughts. This natural exchange of ideas is denied to the deaf child. My teacher, realizing this, determined to supply the kinds of stimulus I lacked. This she did by repeating to me as far as possible, verbatim, what she heard, and by showing me how I could take part in the conversation. But it was a long time before I ventured to take the initiative, and still longer before I could find something appropriate to say at the right time.

The deaf and the blind find it very difficult to acquire the amenities of conversation. How much more this difficulty must be augmented in the case of those who are both deaf and blind! They cannot distinguish the tone of the voice or, without assistance, go up and down the gamut of tones that give significance to words; nor can they watch the expression of the speaker's face, and a look is often the very soul of what one says.

The next important step in my education was learning to read.

As soon as I could spell a few words my teacher gave me slips of cardboard on which were printed words in raised letters. I quickly learned that each printed word stood for an object, an act, or a quality. I had a frame in which I could arrange the words in little sentences; but before I ever put sentences in the frame I used to make them in objects. I found the slips of paper which represented for example, 'doll', 'is', 'on', 'bed' and placed each name on its object; then I put my doll on the bed with the words *is, on, bed* arranged beside the doll, thus making a sentence of the words, and at the same time carrying out the idea of the sentence with the things themselves.

One day, Miss Sullivan tells me, I pinned the word *girl* on my pinafore and stood in the wardrobe. On the shelf I arranged the words, *is, in, wardrobe.* Nothing delighted me so much as this game. My teacher and I played it for hours at a time. Often everything in the room was arranged in object sentences.

From the printed slip it was but a step to the printed book. I took my 'Reader for Beginners' and hunted for the words I knew; when I found them my joy was like that of a game of hide-and-seek. Thus I began to read. Of the time when I began to read connected stories I shall speak later.

For a long time I had no regular lessons. Even when I studied most earnestly it seemed more like play than work. Everything Miss Sullivan taught me she illustrated by a beautiful story or a poem. Whenever anything delighted or interested me she talked it over with me just as if she were a little girl herself. What many children think of with dread, as a painful plodding through grammar, hard sums and harder definitions, is to-day one of my most precious memories.

I cannot explain the peculiar sympathy Miss Sullivan had with my pleasures and desires. Perhaps it was the result of long association with the blind. Added to this she had a wonderful faculty for description. She went quickly over uninteresting details, and never nagged me with questions to see if I remembered the day-before-yesterday's lesson. She introduced dry technicalities of science little by little, making every subject so real that I could not help remembering what she taught.

We read and studied out of doors, preferring the sunlit woods to the house. All my early lessons have in them the breath of the woods—the fine resinous odour of pine needles, blended with the perfume of wild grapes. Seated in the gracious shade of a wild tulip tree, I learned to think that everything has a lesson and a suggestion. 'The loveliness of things taught me all their use.' Indeed, everything that could hum, or buzz, or sing, or bloom, had a part in my education—noisy-throated frogs, katydids and crickets held in my hand until, forgetting their embarrassment, they trilled their reedy note, little downy chickens and wild flowers, the dogwood blossoms, meadow-violets and budding fruit trees. I felt the bursting cotton-bolls and fingered their soft fiber and fuzzy seeds; I felt the low soughing of the wind through the cornstalks, the silky rustling of the long leaves, and the indignant snort of my pony, as we caught him in the pasture and put the bit in his mouth—ah me! how well I remember the spicy, clovery smell of his breath!

Sometimes I rose at dawn and stole into the garden while the heavy dew lay on the grass and flowers. Few know what joy it is to feel the roses pressing softly into the hand, or the beautiful motion of the lilies as they sway in the morning breeze. Sometimes I caught an insect in the flower I was plucking, and I felt a faint noise of a pair of wings rubbed together in a sudden terror as the little creature became aware of the pressure from without.

Another favourite haunt of mine was the orchard, where the fruit ripened early in July. The large, downy peaches would reach themselves into my hand, and as the joyous breezes flew about the trees the apples tumbled at my feet. Oh, the delight with which I gathered up the fruit in my pinafore, pressed my face against the smooth cheeks of the apples, still warm from the sun, and skipped back to the house!

Our favourite walk was to Keller's Landing, an old tumble-down lumber-wharf on the Tennessee River, used during the Civil War to land soldiers. There we spent many happy hours and played at learning geography. I built dams of pebbles, made islands and lakes, and dug river-beds, all for fun, and never dreamed that I was learning a lesson. I listened with increased wonder to Miss Sullivan's descriptions of the great round world with its burning mountains, buried cities, moving rivers of ice, and many other things as strange. She made raised maps in clay, so that I could feel the mountain ridges and valleys. I liked this, too, but the division of the earth into zones and poles confused and teased my mind. The illustrative strings and the orange stick representing the poles seemed so real that even to this day the mere mention of a temperate zone suggests a series of twine circles; and I believe that if any one should set about it he could convince me that white bears actually climb the North Pole.